NETWORKS OF OUTRAGE
AND HOPE

Pour Alain Touraine
My intellectual father,
theorist of social movements

NETWORKS OF
OUTRAGE AND HOPE
SOCIAL MOVEMENTS IN
THE INTERNET AGE

MANUEL CASTELLS

polity

First published in 2012 by Polity Press

Polity Press
65 Bridge Street
Cambridge CB2 1UR, UK

Polity Press
350 Main Street
Malden, MA 02148, USA

ISBN-13: 978-0-7456-6284-8
ISBN-13: 978-0-7456-6285-5(pb)

A catalogue record for this book is available from the British Library.

Typeset in 10.75 on 14 pt Janson Text
by Servis Filmsetting Ltd, Stockport, Cheshire SK2 5AJ
Printed and bound in Great Britain by MPG Books Group Limited, Bodmin, Cornwall

The publisher has used its best endeavours to ensure that the URLs for external websites referred to in this book are correct and active at the time of going to press. However, the publisher has no responsibility for the websites and can make no guarantee that a site will remain live or that the content is or will remain appropriate.

Every effort has been made to trace all copyright holders, but if any have been inadvertently overlooked the publisher will be pleased to include any necessary credits in any subsequent reprint or edition.

For further information on Polity, visit our website: www.politybooks.com

CONTENTS

ACKNOWLEDGMENTS

November 2011 was a good month for me. I had been invited to Cambridge by my friend John Thompson, one of the most distinguished sociologists in media politics, to give a series of lectures in the University of Cambridge's CRASSH program. I was housed in the magnificent medieval quarters of St. John's College, where the monastic atmosphere and collegial interaction provided a serene space/time to reflect on my ideas, after an intense year of being immersed in the theory and practice of social movements. Like many people around the world, I had been struck first, and then mobilized, by the uprisings that started in Tunisia in December 2010 and diffused virally throughout the Arab world. During the previous years, I had followed the emergence of social movements that were powered by the use of the Internet and wireless communication networks, in Madrid in 2004, in Iran in 2009, in Iceland in 2009, and in a number of countries around the world. I had spent most of the last decade studying the transformation of power relationships in interaction with the transformation of communication, and I detected the development of a new pattern of social movements, perhaps the new forms of social change in the twenty-first century. This phenomenon resonated with my personal experience, as a veteran of the May 1968 movement in Paris. I felt the same kind of exhilaration I felt at that time: suddenly, everything appeared to be possible; the world was not necessarily doomed to political cynicism and bureaucratic enforcement of absurd ways of life. The symptoms of a new revolutionary era, an age of revolutions aimed at exploring the meaning of life rather than seizing the state, were apparent everywhere, from Iceland to Tunisia, from WikiLeaks to Anonymous, and, soon, from Athens to Madrid to New York. The crisis of global financial capitalism was not necessarily a dead end – it could even signal a new beginning in unexpected ways.

Throughout 2011 I began to collect information on these new social movements, discussed my findings with my students at the University of Southern California, and then gave some lectures to communicate my preliminary thoughts at Northwestern University, at the College d'Etudes Mondiales in Paris, at the Oxford Internet Institute, at Barcelona's Seminar on Communication and Civil Society in the Internet Interdisciplinary Institute of the Universitat Oberta de Catalunya, and at the London School of Economics. I became increasingly convinced that something truly meaningful was taking place around the world. Then two days before returning to Barcelona from Los Angeles, on 19 May, I received an email from a young woman from Madrid whom I had never met before, letting me know that they were occupying the squares of Spanish cities, and wouldn't it be nice if I joined in some way, given my writings on the subject? My heart accelerated. Could it be possible? Hope again? As soon as I landed in Barcelona I headed to Plaza Catalunya.

There they were, by the hundreds, peacefully and seriously debating under the sun. I met the *indignadas*. It turned out that my two main research collaborators in Barcelona, Joana and Amalia, were already a part of the movement. But not with the intention of conducting research. They were just *indignadas* like all the others, and had decided to act. I did not camp myself; my old bones would not take easily to sleeping on the pavement. But since then I have followed daily the activities of the movement, visiting the camps at times, in Barcelona and Madrid; occasionally talking, at the request of someone, in Acampada Barcelona or Occupy London; and helping to elaborate some of the proposals that emerged from the movement. I connected spontaneously with the values and style of the movement, largely free of obsolete ideologies and manipulative politics. There began a journey of trying to support these movements while exploring their meaning. With no specific purpose, and certainly no intention of writing a book – not in the short term anyway. Living it was much more fascinating than writing about it, particularly after having already written 25 books.

So, there I was in Cambridge, with the opportunity to lecture/debate with a fantastic group of smart students who were also committed citizens. I decided to focus my lecture series on "Social Movements in the Internet Age," to put my ideas in order for myself, with the hope of better understanding the meaning of these variegated movements in my interaction with students and colleagues. It went very well. It was intense, rigorous, truthful and absent of academic pomp. At the end of the month, while saying farewell, my colleagues John Thompson and Isidora Chacon insisted that I should write a book on the basis of these lectures. A short, quick book, and less academic than usual. Short? Quick? I have never done that. My books are usually over five years in the making and over 400 pages when published. Yes, they said, you may do another one in five years, but what is needed now is a simple book that organizes the debate and contributes to the reflection of the movement and to the broader understanding of these new movements by people at large. They succeeded in making me feel guilty for not doing it, since my only potential useful contribution to a better world comes from my lifelong experience as a social researcher, writer and lecturer, not from my often confused activism. I yielded to their request, and here I am, four months later. It was quick, and exhausting. It is short by my standards. As for its relevance, that is for you to judge. So, my first acknowledgement goes to John and Isidora, the initiators of this enterprise. They backed up their interest by following and commenting on my draft chapters during the elaboration of this project. Thus, I am deeply indebted to them for their generosity and intellectual contribution.

Yet, for all the impulse I received in and from Cambridge, I would not have been able to keep my promise without the help of an extraordinary group of young researchers with whom I worked regularly in Barcelona and in Los Angeles. As soon as I returned from England, I realized that I was in big trouble, and called my friends and co-investigators to the rescue. Joana Conill, Amalia Cardenas, and I had created a small research team at the Open University of Barcelona (UOC) to study the rise of alternative economic cultures in Barcelona. Many of the groups and individuals we observed became in fact participants in the *indignadas* movement. Since Joana and Amalia were already within the movement, they agreed to help with information and analysis, on the condition of not being involved in the final writing of the research, for their own personal reasons. Amalia also collected and analyzed information on Iceland and on Occupy Wall Street, while I used my networks of colleagues and former students around the world to retrieve information, check facts, and listen to ideas, particularly about the Arab countries. Other persons in the movement also agreed to discuss with me or with my collaborators some of the issues and history of the movement. I want to thank particularly Javier Toret and Arnau Monterde, both in Barcelona.

Then, in Los Angeles, my research collaborator Lana Swartz, an outstanding doctoral student at the Annenberg School of Communication at USC, was also involved in Occupy Los Angeles, and also accepted with incredible generosity, intelligence, and rigor to help me in the data collection and analysis of the Occupy movement in the United States. Joan Donovan, an active participant in Occupy Los Angeles and Inter-Occupy, a veteran of many battles for social justice, and a doctoral student at UC San Diego, gave me some key ideas that helped my understanding. Dorian Bon, a student at Columbia University, conveyed to me his experience in the student movement connected to Occupy Wall Street. My friend and colleague Sasha Costanza-Chock, a professor at MIT, shared with me his unpublished survey data on the Occupy movement in the US. Maytha Alhassen, an Arab-American journalist and doctoral student in American Studies and Ethnicity at the University of Southern California in Los Angeles, who had traveled in the Arab countries during the time of the uprisings, worked closely with me, reporting on key events that she witnessed first-hand, allowing me access to Arabic sources, and most importantly educating me about what had really happened everywhere. Of course, I am the only one responsible for the many mistakes I have probably made in my interpretation. But without her invaluable help there would have been many more mistakes. It is because of the quality of her contribution that I dared to go into the analysis of specific processes in the Arab uprisings.

Thus my gratitude and recognition goes to this very

diverse group of exceptional individuals who agreed to collaborate in the project of this book, which became a truly collective endeavor, although the end result was elaborated in the solitude of authorship.

As for my previous books, Melody Lutz, a professional writer and my personal editor, was the key link between me, the author, and you, the reader, making our communication possible. My heartfelt recognition goes to Melody.

The complexity of the process of work that I just outlined, which led to this book, required exceptional management and organizational skills, and a great deal of patience. Thus, my deepest thanks go to Clelia Azucena Garciasalas, my personal assistant at the Annenberg School of Communication, who directed the entire project, coordinated research and editing, filled in the gaps, collected information, corrected mistakes, and made sure that you would have in your hands this volume with full assurance of her quality control. I also want to thank the contribution of Noelia Diaz Lopez, my personal assistant at the Open University of Catalonia, for her ongoing outstanding support of all my research activities.

Finally, as with my previous research and writing, none of this would have been possible without the supportive family environment that this author enjoys. For this, my love and my gratitude go to my wife Emma Kiselyova, my daughter Nuria, my stepdaughter Lena, my grandchildren Clara, Gabriel, and Sasha, my sister Irene, and my brother-in-law Jose.

Thus, it is in the crossroads between emotion and cognition, work and experience, personal history and hope for the future that this book was born. For you.

Barcelona and Santa Monica, December 2011–April 2012

OPENING:

NETWORKING MINDS, CREATING

MEANING, CONTESTING POWER

No one expected it. In a world darkened by economic distress, political cynicism, cultural emptiness and personal hopelessness, it just happened. Suddenly dictatorships could be overthrown with the bare hands of the people, even if their hands had been bloodied by the sacrifice of the fallen. Financial magicians went from being the objects of public envy to the targets of universal contempt. Politicians became exposed as corrupt and as liars. Governments were denounced. Media were suspected. Trust vanished. And trust is what glues together society, the market, the institutions. Without trust, nothing works. Without trust, the social contract dissolves and people disappear as they transform into defensive individuals fighting for survival. Yet, at the fringe of a world that had come to the brink of its capacity for humans to live together and to share life with nature, individuals did come together again to find new forms of being us, the people. There were first a few, who were joined by hundreds, then networked by thousands, then supported by millions with their voices and their internal quest for hope, as muddled as it was, that cut across ideology and hype, to connect with the real concerns of real people in the real human experience that had been reclaimed. It began on the Internet social networks, as these are spaces of autonomy, largely beyond the control of governments and corporations that had monopolized the channels of communication as the foundation of their power, throughout history. By sharing sorrow and hope in the free public space of the Internet, by connecting to each other, and by envisioning projects from multiple sources of being, individuals formed networks, regardless of their personal views or organizational attachments. They came together. And their togetherness helped them to overcome fear, this paralyzing emotion on which the powers that be rely in order to prosper and reproduce, by intimidation or discouragement, and when necessary by sheer violence, be it naked or institutionally enforced. From the safety of cyberspace, people from all ages and conditions moved towards occupying urban space, on a blind date with each other and with the destiny they wanted to forge, as they claimed their right to make history – their history – in a display of the self-awareness that has always characterized major social movements.[1]

The movements spread by contagion in a world networked by the wireless Internet and marked by fast, viral diffusion of images and ideas. They started in the South and in the North, in Tunisia and in Iceland, and from there the spark lit fire in a diverse social landscape devastated by greed and manipulation in all quarters of the blue planet. It was not just poverty, or the economic crisis, or the lack of democracy that caused the multifaceted rebellion. Of course, all these poignant manifestations of an unjust society and of an undemocratic polity were present in the protests. But it was primarily the humiliation provoked by the cynicism and arrogance of those in power, be it financial, political or cultural, that brought together those who turned fear into outrage, and outrage into hope for a better humanity. A humanity that had to be reconstructed from scratch, escaping the multiple ideological and institutional traps that had led to dead ends again and again, forging a new path by treading it. It was the search for dignity amid the suffering of humiliation – recurrent themes in most of the movements.

Networked social movements first spread in the Arab world and were confronted with murderous violence by Arab dictatorships. They experienced diverse fates, from victory to concessions to repeated massacres to civil wars. Other movements arose against the mishandled management of the economic crisis in Europe and in the United States by governments who sided with the financial elites responsible for the crisis at the expense of their citizens: in Spain, in Greece, in Portugal, in Italy (where women's mobilizations contributed to finishing off the buffoon-esque *commedia dell'arte* of Berlusconi), in Britain (where occupations of squares and the defense of the public sector by trade unions and students joined hands) and with less intensity but similar symbolism in most other European countries. In Israel, a spontaneous movement with multiple demands became the largest grassroots mobilization in Israeli history, obtaining the satisfaction of many of its requests. In the United States, the Occupy Wall Street movement, as spontaneous as all the others, and as networked in cyberspace and urban space as the others, became the event of the year, and affected most of the country, so much so that *Time* magazine named "The Protester" the person of the year. And the motto of the 99 percent, whose well-being had been sacrificed to the interests of the 1 percent, who control 23 percent of the country's wealth, became a mainstream topic in American political life. On October 15, 2011, a global network of occupying movements under the banner of "United for Global Change" mobilized hundreds of thousands in 951 cities in 82 countries around the world, claiming social justice and true democracy. In all cases the movements ignored political parties, distrusted the media, did not recognize any leadership and rejected all formal organization, relying on the Internet and local assemblies for collective debate and decision-making.

This book attempts to shed light on these movements: on their formation, their dynamics, their values and their prospects for social transformation. This is an inquiry into the social movements of the network society, the movements that will ultimately make societies in the twenty-first century by engaging in conflictive practices rooted in the fundamental contradictions of our world. The analysis presented here is based on observation of the movements, but it will not try to describe them, nor will it be able to provide definitive proof for the arguments conveyed in this text. There is already available a wealth of information, articles, books, media reports, and blog archives that can be easily consulted by browsing the Internet. And it is too early to construct a systematic, scholarly interpretation of the movements. Thus, my purpose is more limited: to suggest some hypotheses, grounded on observation, on the nature and perspectives of networked social movements, with the hope of identifying the new paths of social change in our time, and to stimulate a debate on the practical (and ultimately political) implications of these hypotheses.

This analysis is based on a grounded theory of power that I presented in my book *Communication Power* (2009), a theory that provides the background for the understanding of the movements studied here.

I start from the premise that power relationships are constitutive of society because those who have power construct the institutions of society according to their values and interests. Power is exercised by means of coercion (the monopoly of violence, legitimate or not, by the control of the state) and/or by the construction of meaning in people's minds, through mechanisms of symbolic manipulation. Power relations are embedded in the institutions of society, and particularly in the state. However, since societies are contradictory and conflictive, wherever there is power there is also counterpower, which I understand to be the capacity of social actors to challenge the power embedded in the institutions of society for the purpose of claiming representation for their own values and interests. All institutional systems reflect power relations, as well as the limits to these power relations as negotiated by an endless historical process of conflict and bargaining. The actual configuration of the state and other institutions that regulate people's lives depends on this constant interaction between power and counterpower.

Coercion and intimidation, based on the state's monopoly of the capacity to exercise violence, are essential mechanisms for imposing the will of those in control of the institutions of society. However, the construction of meaning in people's minds is a more decisive and more stable source of power. The way people think determines the fate of the institutions, norms and values on which societies are organized. Few institutional systems can last long if they are based just on coercion. Torturing bodies is less effective than shaping minds. If a majority of people think in ways that are contradictory to the values and norms institutionalized in the laws and regulations enforced by the state, the system will change, although not necessarily to fulfill the hopes of the agents of social change. This is why the fundamental power struggle is the battle for the construction of meaning in the minds of the people.

Humans create meaning by interacting with their natural and social environment, by networking their neural networks with the networks of nature and with social networks. This networking is operated by the act of communication. Communication is the process of sharing meaning through the exchange of information. For society at large, the key source of the social production of meaning is the process of socialized communication. Socialized communication exists in the public realm beyond interpersonal communication. The ongoing transformation of communication technology in the digital age extends the reach of communication media to all domains of social life in a network that is at the same time global and local, generic and customized in an ever-changing pattern. The process of constructing meaning is characterized by a great deal of diversity. There is, however, one feature common to all processes of symbolic construction: they are largely dependent on the messages and frames created, formatted and diffused in multimedia communication networks. Although each individual human mind constructs its own meaning by interpreting the communicated materials on its own terms, this mental processing is conditioned by the communication environment. Thus, the transformation of the communication environment directly affects the forms of meaning construction, and therefore the production of power relationships. In recent years, the fundamental change in the realm of communication has been the rise of what I have called mass self-communication – the use of the Internet and wireless networks as platforms of digital communication. It is mass communication because it processes messages from many to many, with the potential of reaching a multiplicity of receivers, and of connecting to endless networks that transmit digitized information around the neighborhood or around the world. It is self-communication because the production of the message is autonomously decided by the sender, the designation of the receiver is self-directed and the retrieval of messages from the networks of communication is self-selected. Mass self-communication is based on horizontal networks of interactive communication that, by and large, are difficult to control by governments or corporations. Furthermore, digital communication is multimodal and allows constant reference to a global hypertext of information whose components can be remixed by the communicative actor according to specific projects of communication. Mass self-communication provides the technological platform for the construction of the autonomy of the social actor, be it individual or collective, vis-à-vis the institutions of society. This is why governments are afraid of the Internet, and this is why corporations have a love-hate relationship with it and are trying to extract profits while limiting its potential for freedom (for instance, by controlling file sharing or open source networks).

In our society, which I have conceptualized as a network society, power is multidimensional and is organized around networks programmed in each domain of human activity according to the interests and values of empowered actors.[2] Networks of power exercise their power by influencing the human mind predominantly (but not solely) through multimedia networks of mass communication. Thus, communication networks are decisive sources of power-making.

Networks of power in various domains of human activity are networked among themselves. Global financial networks and global multimedia networks are intimately linked, and this particular meta-network holds extraordinary power. But not all power, because this meta-network of finance and media is itself dependent on other major networks, such as the political network, the cultural production network (which encompasses all kinds of cultural artefacts, not just communication products), the military/security network, the global criminal network and the decisive global network of production and application of science, technology and knowledge management. These networks do not merge. Instead, they engage in strategies of partnership and competition by forming ad hoc networks around specific projects. But they all share a common interest: to control the capacity of defining the rules and norms of society through a political system that primarily responds to their interests and values. This is why the network of power constructed around the state and the political system does play a fundamental role in the overall networking of power. This is, first, because the stable operation of the system, and the reproduction of power relationships in every network, ultimately depend on the coordinating and regulatory functions of the state, as was witnessed in the collapse of financial markets in 2008 when governments were called to the rescue around the world. Furthermore, it is via the state that different forms of exercising power in distinct social spheres relate to the monopoly of violence as the capacity to enforce power in the last resort. So, while communication networks process the construction of meaning on which power relies, the state constitutes the default network for the proper functioning of all other power networks.

And so, how do power networks connect with one another while preserving their sphere of action? I propose that they do so through a fundamental mechanism of power-making in the network society: switching power. This is the capacity to connect two or more different networks in the process of making power for each one of them in their respective fields.

Thus, who holds power in the network society? The *programmers* with the capacity to program each one of the main networks on which people's lives depend (government, parliament, the military and security establishment, finance, media, science and technology institutions, etc.). And the *switchers* who operate the connections between different networks (media moguls introduced in the political class, financial elites bankrolling political elites, political elites bailing out financial institutions, media corporations intertwined with financial corporations, academic institutions financed by big business, etc.).

If power is exercised by programming and switching networks, then counterpower, the deliberate attempt to change power relationships, is enacted by reprogramming networks around alternative interests and values, and/or disrupting the dominant switches while switching networks of resistance and social change. Actors of social change are able to exert decisive influence by using mechanisms of power-making that correspond to the forms and processes of power in the network society. By engaging in the production of mass media messages, and by developing autonomous networks of horizontal communication, citizens of the Information Age become able to invent new programs for their lives with the materials of their suffering, fears, dreams and hopes. They build their projects by sharing their experience. They subvert the practice of communication as usual by occupying the medium and creating the message. They overcome the powerlessness of their solitary despair by networking their desire. They fight the powers that be by identifying the networks that are.

Social movements, throughout history, are the producers of new values and goals around which the institutions of society are transformed to represent these values by creating new norms to organize social life. Social movements exercise counterpower by constructing themselves in the first place through a process of autonomous communication, free from the control of those holding institutional power. Because mass media are largely controlled by governments and media corporations, in the network society communicative autonomy is primarily constructed in the Internet networks and in the platforms of wireless communication. Digital social

networks offer the possibility for largely unfettered deliberation and coordination of action. However, this is only one
component of the communicative processes through which
social movements relate to society at large. They also need
to build public space by creating free communities in the
urban space. Since the institutional public space, the consti-
tutionally designated space for deliberation, is occupied by
the interests of the dominant elites and their networks, social
movements need to carve out a new public space that is not
limited to the Internet, but makes itself visible in the places
of social life. This is why they occupy urban space and symbolic buildings. Occupied spaces have played a major role
in the history of social change, as well as in contemporary
practice, for three basic reasons:

1. They create community, and community is based on
   togetherness. Togetherness is a fundamental psychologi-
   cal mechanism to overcome fear. And overcoming fear
   is the fundamental threshold for individuals to cross in
   order to engage in a social movement, since they are well
   aware that in the last resort, they will have to confront
   violence if they trespass the boundaries set up by the
   dominant elites to preserve their domination. In the history of social movements, the barricades erected in the
   streets had very little defensive value; in fact, they became
   easy targets either for the artillery or for the riot squads,
   depending on the context. But they always defined an "in
   and out," an "us versus them," so that by joining an occupied site, and defying the bureaucratic norms of the use
   of space, other citizens could be part of the movement
   without adhering to any ideology or organization, just by
   being there for their own reasons.
2. Occupied spaces are not meaningless: they are usually
   charged with the symbolic power of invading sites of state

power, or financial institutions. Or else, by relating to history, they evoke memories of popular uprisings that had expressed the will of citizens when other avenues of representation were closed. Often, buildings are occupied either for their symbolism or to affirm the right of public use of idle, speculative property. By taking and holding urban space, citizens reclaim their own city, a city from where they were evicted by real estate speculation and municipal bureaucracy. Some major social movements in history, such as the 1871 Paris commune or the Glasgow strikes of 1915 (at the origin of public housing in Britain), started as rent strikes against housing speculation.[3] The control of space symbolizes the control over people's lives.

3. By constructing a free community in a symbolic place, social movements create a public space, a space for deliberation, which ultimately becomes a political space, a space for sovereign assemblies to meet and to recover their rights of representation, which have been captured in political institutions predominantly tailored for the convenience of the dominant interests and values. In our society, the public space of the social movements is constructed as a hybrid space between the Internet social networks and the occupied urban space: connecting cyberspace and urban space in relentless interaction, constituting, technologically and culturally, instant communities of transformative practice.

The critical matter is that this new public space, the networked space between the digital space and the urban space, is a space of autonomous communication. The autonomy of communication is the essence of social movements because it is what allows the movement to be formed, and what enables the movement to relate to society at large beyond the control of the power holders over communication power.

Where do social movements come from? And how are they formed? Their roots are in the fundamental injustice of all societies, relentlessly confronted by human aspirations of justice. In each specific context, the usual horses of humanity's apocalypses ride together under a variety of their hideous shapes: economic exploitation, hopeless poverty, unfair inequality, undemocratic polity, repressive states, unjust judiciary, racism, xenophobia, cultural negation, censorship, police brutality, warmongering, religious fanaticism (often against others' religious beliefs), carelessness towards the blue planet (our only home), disregard of personal liberty, violation of privacy, gerontocracy, bigotry, sexism, homophobia and other atrocities in the long gallery of portraits featuring the monsters we are. And of course, always, in every instance and in every context, sheer domination of males over females and their children, as the primary foundation of a/n (unjust) social order. Thus, social movements always have an array of structural causes and individual reasons to rise up against one or many of the dimensions of social domination. Yet, to know their roots does not answer the question of their birth. And since, in my view, social movements are the sources of social change, and therefore of the constitution of society, the question is a fundamental one. So fundamental that entire libraries are dedicated to a tentative approach to the answer, and so, consequently, I will not deal with it here, since this book is not intended to be another treatise on social movements but a small window on a nascent world. But I will say this: social movements, certainly now, and probably in history (beyond the realm of my competence), are made of individuals. I say it in plural, because in most of what I have read of analyses of social movements in any time and society, I find few individuals, sometimes only the one hero, accompanied by an undifferentiated crowd, called social class, or ethnia, or gender, or

nation, or believers, or any of the other collective denomina-
tions of the subsets of human diversity. Yet, while grouping
people's living experience in convenient analytical categories
of social structure is a useful method, the actual practices
that allow social movements to rise and change institutions
and, ultimately, social structure, are enacted by individuals: persons in their material flesh and minds. And so the
key question to understand is when and how and why one
person or one thousand persons decide, individually, to do
something that they are repeatedly warned not to do because
they will be punished. There are usually a handful of persons, sometimes just one, at the start of a movement. Social
theorists usually call these people agency. I call them individuals. And then we have to understand the motivation of
each individual: how these individuals network by connecting mentally to other individuals, and why they are able to
do so, in a process of communication that ultimately leads to
collective action; how these networks negotiate the diversity
of interests and values present in the network to focus on a
common set of goals; how these networks relate to the society at large, and to many other individuals; and how and why
this connection works in a large number of cases, activating
individuals to broaden the networks formed in the resistance
to domination, and to engage in a multimodal assault against
an unjust order.

At the individual level, social movements are emotional
movements. Insurgency does not start with a program or
political strategy. This may come later, as leadership emerges,
from inside or from outside the movement, to foster political, ideological and personal agendas that may or may not
relate to the origins and motivations of participants in the
movement. But the big bang of a social movement starts
with the transformation of emotion into action. According
to the theory of affective intelligence,[4] the emotions that

are most relevant to social mobilization and political behavior are fear (a negative affect) and enthusiasm (a positive affect).[5] Positive and negative affects are linked to two basic motivational systems that result from human evolution: approach and avoidance. The approach system is linked to goal-seeking behavior that directs the individual to rewarding experiences. Individuals are enthusiastic when they are mobilized towards a goal that they cherish. This is why enthusiasm is directly related to another positive emotion: hope. Hope projects behavior into the future. Since a distinctive feature of the human mind is the ability to imagine the future, hope is a fundamental ingredient in supporting goal-seeking action. However, for enthusiasm to emerge and for hope to rise, individuals have to overcome the negative emotion resulting from the avoidance motivational system: anxiety. Anxiety is a response to an external threat over which the threatened person has no control. Thus, anxiety leads to fear, and has a paralyzing effect on action. The overcoming of anxiety in socio-political behavior often results from another negative emotion: anger. Anger increases with the perception of an unjust action and with the identification of the agent responsible for the action. Neurological research shows that anger is associated with risk-taking behavior. Once the individual overcomes fear, positive emotions take over, as enthusiasm activates action and hope anticipates the rewards for the risky action. However, for a social movement to form, the emotional activation of individuals must connect to other individuals. This requires a communication process from one individual experience to others. For the communication process to operate, there are two requirements: cognitive consonance between senders and receivers of the message, and an effective communication channel. The empathy in the communication process is determined by experiences similar to those that motivated the original emotional outburst. Concretely speaking: if many individuals feel humiliated, exploited, ignored or misrepresented, they are ready to transform their anger into action, as soon as they overcome their fear. And they overcome their fear by the extreme expression of anger, in the form of outrage, when learning of an unbearable event suffered by someone with whom they identify. This identification is better achieved by sharing feelings in some form of togetherness created in the process of communication. Thus, the second condition for individual experiences to link up and form a movement is the existence of a communication process that propagates the events and the emotions attached to it. The faster and more interactive the process of communication is, the more likely the formation of a process of collective action becomes, rooted in outrage, propelled by enthusiasm and motivated by hope.

Historically, social movements have been dependent on the existence of specific communication mechanisms: rumors, sermons, pamphlets and manifestos, spread from person to person, from the pulpit, from the press, or by whatever means of communication were available. In our time, multimodal, digital networks of horizontal communication are the fastest and most autonomous, interactive, reprogrammable and self-expanding means of communication in history. The characteristics of communication processes between individuals engaged in the social movement determine the organizational characteristics of the social movement itself: the more interactive and self-configurable communication is, the less hierarchical is the organization and the more participatory is the movement. This is why the networked social movements of the digital age represent a new species of social movement.[6]

If the origins of social movements are to be found in the emotions of individuals and in their networking on the basis of cognitive empathy, what is the role of the ideas, ideologies and programmatic proposals traditionally considered to be the stuff of which social change is made? They are in fact the indispensable materials for the passage from emotion-driven action to deliberation and project construction. Their embedding in the practice of the movement is also a communication process, and how this process is constructed determines the role of these ideational materials in the meaning, evolution and impact of the social movement. The more the ideas are generated from within the movement, on the basis of the experience of their participants, the more representative, enthusiastic and hopeful the movement will be, and vice versa. It is too often the case that movements become raw materials for ideological experimentation or political instrumentation by defining goals and representations of the movement that have little to do with their reality. Sometimes even in its historical legacy, the human experience of the movement tends to be replaced by a reconstructed image for the legitimization of political leaders or for the vindication of the theories of organic intellectuals. A case in point is how the Commune of Paris came to be in its ideological reconstruction, in spite of the historians' efforts to restore its reality, a proto-proletarian revolution in a city that at the time counted few industrial workers among its dwellers. Why a municipal revolution, sparked by a rent strike and partly led by women, came to be misrepresented has to do with the inaccuracy of Karl Marx's sources in his writings about the Commune, mainly based on his correspondence with Elizabeth Dmitrieva, president of the Women's Union, a committed socialist Communard who saw just what she and her mentor wanted to see.[7] The misrepresentation of the movements by their leaders, ideologues or chroniclers does have considerable consequences, as it introduces an irreversible cleavage between the actors of the movement and the projects constructed on their behalf, often without their knowledge and consent.

The next question for the understanding of social movements has to do with the evaluation of the actual impact of the joint action of these networks of individuals on the institutions of society, as well as on themselves. This will require a different set of data and analytical instruments, as the characteristics of institutions and of the networks of domination will have to be brought into confrontation with the characteristics of the networks of social change. In a nutshell, for the networks of counterpower to prevail over the networks of power embedded in the organization of society, they will have to reprogram the polity, the economy, the culture or whatever dimension they aim to change by introducing in the institutions' programs, as well as in their own lives, other instructions, including, in some utopian versions, the rule of not ruling anything. Furthermore, they will have to switch on the connection between different networks of social change, e.g. between pro-democracy networks and economic justice networks, women's rights networks, environmental conservation networks, peace networks, freedom networks, and so on. To understand under which conditions these processes take place and which are the social outcomes that result from each specific process cannot be a matter of formal theory. It requires one to ground the analysis on observation.

The theoretical tools I have proposed here are simply so, tools, whose usefulness or futility can only be evaluated by using them to examine the practices of networked social movements this book intends to analyze. However, I will not code the observation of these movements in abstract terms to fit into the conceptual approach presented here. Rather, my theory will be embedded in a selective observation of the movements, to bring together at the end of my intellectual journey the most salient findings of this study in an analytical framework. This is what I intend to be my contribution to the understanding of networked social movements as harbingers of social change in the twenty-first century.

One last word about the origins and conditions of the reflections I am presenting here. I have been a marginal participant in the Barcelona *indignadas* movement, and a supporter and sympathizer of movements in other countries. But I have kept, as is usual in my case, as much distance as I could between my personal beliefs and my analysis. Without pretending to achieve objectivity, I have tried to present the movements in their own words and by their own actions, using some direct observation and a considerable amount of information: some from individual interviews and some from secondary sources that are detailed in the references to each chapter and in the appendices to this book. In fact, I am in full accordance with the basic principle of this leaderless movement of multiple faces: I only represent myself, and this is simply my reflection on what I have seen, heard or read. I am an individual, doing what I learned to do throughout my life: investigate processes of social transformation, with the hope that this investigation could be helpful to the endeavors of those fighting, at great risk, for a world we would like to live in.

NOTES

1 For an excellent, analytical and informed overview of the social movements that sprung up everywhere in 2011, see Paul Mason, *Why It's Kicking Off Everywhere: The New Global Revolutions* (2012, Verso, London).

2 For my characterization of the network society, see my book, *The Rise of the Network Society* (1996; 2010, 2nd edn. Blackwell, Oxford). For a succinct presentation of my network theory of power, see my 2011 article, "A Network

Theory of Power," *International Journal of Communication* 5, 773–87.

3 For a presentation of a historical analysis of urban social movements, see my book, *The City and the Grassroots* (1983, University of California Press, Berkeley), pp. 15–48.

4 W. Russell Neuman, G. E. Marcus, A. N. Crigler and M. MacKuen (eds.), *The Affect Effect: Dynamics of emotions in political thinking and behavior* (2007, University of Chicago Press, Chicago, IL).

5 I have discussed the contributions of the theory of affective intelligence to the study of socio-political mobilization in my book, *Communication Power* (2009, Oxford University Press, Oxford), pp. 146–55.

6 A pioneer analysis of the rise of contemporary networked social movements is Jeff Juris's *Networked Futures* (2008, Duke University Press, Durham, NC).

7 I discuss the historical record of the Commune of Paris in my book, *The City and the Grassroots* (1983): 15–26.

PRELUDE TO REVOLUTION:

WHERE IT ALL STARTED

What do Tunisia and Iceland have in common? Nothing at all. And yet, the political insurgencies that transformed the institutions of governance in both countries in 2009–11 have become the point of reference for the social movements that shook up the political order in the Arab world and challenged the political institutions in Europe, and in the United States. In the first mass demonstration in Cairo's Tahrir Square on January 25, 2011, thousands shouted "Tunisia is the solution," purposely modifying the slogan "Islam is the solution" that had dominated social mobilizations in the Arab world in recent years. They were referring to the toppling of the dictatorship of Ben Ali, who fled his country on January 14 after weeks of grassroots protests that overcame the bloody repression of the regime. When Spain's *indignadas* started camping in the main squares of cities around the country in May 2011, they proclaimed that "Iceland is the solution." And when New Yorkers occupied public spaces around Wall Street on September 17, 2011,

they named their first encampment Tahrir Square, as did
the occupiers of Catalunya Square in Barcelona. What could
be the common thread that united in people's minds their
experiences of revolt in spite of the vastly diverse cultural,
economic and institutional contexts? In a nutshell: their
feeling of empowerment. It was born from their disgust
with their governments and the political class, be it dictatorial or, in their view, pseudo-democratic. It was prompted
by their outrage towards the perceived complicity between
the financial elite and the political elite. It was triggered by
the emotional upheaval that resulted from some unbearable
event. And it was made possible by overcoming fear through
togetherness built in the networks of cyberspace and in the
communities of urban space. Moreover, both in Tunisia and
in Iceland, there were tangible political transformations, as
well as new civic cultures emerging from the movements in
a very short span of time. They materialized the possibility of fulfilling some of the key demands of the protesters.
Thus, it is analytically meaningful to focus briefly on these
two processes to identify the seeds of social change that
were spread by the wind of hope to other contexts; at times
to germinate in new social forms and values, and in other
instances to be suffocated by machines of repression put on
alert by the powers that be who were at first surprised, then
afraid, and ultimately called into preventive action all over
the world. New avenues of political change, through autonomous capacity to communicate and organize, have been
discovered by a young generation of activists, beyond the
reach of the usual methods of corporate and political control. And, while there were already a number of precedents
of such new social movements in the last decade (particularly in Spain in 2004 and in Iran in 2009), we may say that
in its full-fledged manifestation it all started in Tunisia and
in Iceland.

TUNISIA: "THE REVOLUTION OF
LIBERTY AND DIGNITY"[1]

It began in a most unlikely site: Sidi Bouzid, a small town
of 40,000 residents in an impoverished central region of
Tunisia, south of Tunis. The name of Mohamed Bouazizi,
a 26-year-old street vendor, has now been engraved in history as the one who changed the destiny of the Arab world.
His self-immolation by fire at half past eleven on the morning of December 17, 2010 in front of a government building
was his ultimate cry of protest against the humiliation of
repeated confiscation of his fruit and vegetable stand by the
local police after he refused to pay a bribe. The last confiscation took place one hour earlier that day. He died on January
3, 2011 in the Tunis hospital where the dictator had trans-
ported him to placate the wrath of the population. Indeed,
only a few hours after he set himself on fire, hundreds of
youth, sharing similar experiences of humiliation by the
authorities, staged a protest in front of the same building.
Mohamed's cousin, Ali, recorded the protest and distributed the video over the Internet. There were other symbolic
suicides and attempted suicides that fed the anger and stimulated the courage of youth. In a few days, demonstrations
started spontaneously around the country, beginning in the
provinces and then spreading to the capital in early January,
in spite of savage repression by the police, who killed at least
147 persons and injured hundreds. But on January 12, 2011,
General Rachid Ammar, the Chief of Staff of the Tunisian
Armed Forces, refused to open fire on the protesters. He was
immediately dismissed, but on January 14, 2011, the dictator
Ben Ali and his family left Tunisia to find refuge in Saudi
Arabia when confronted with the withdrawal of support
from the French Government, Ben Ali's closest ally since
his coming to power in 1987. He had become an embarrass-

ment to his international sponsors, and a replacement had to be found within the political elite of the regime itself. Yet, the demonstrators were not appeased by this victory. In fact they were encouraged to pressure for the removal of all commanding personnel of the regime, demanding political freedom and freedom of the press, and calling for truly democratic elections under a new electoral law. They kept shouting "*Degage! Degage!* (Get out of here!)" vis-à-vis all powers that be: corrupt politicians, financial speculators, brutal police and subservient media. The diffusion of videos of protests and police violence over the Internet was accompanied by calls to action in the streets and squares of cities around the country, starting in the Central Western provinces and then moving to Tunis itself. The connection between free communication on Facebook, YouTube and Twitter and the occupation of urban space created a hybrid public space of freedom that became a major feature of the Tunisian rebellion, foreshadowing the movements to come in other countries. Convoys of solidarity were formed by hundreds of cars converging in the capital. On January 22, 2011, the Convoy of Liberty (*Qâfilat al-hurriyya*), beginning in Sidi Bouzid and Menzel Bouzaiane, reached the Kasbah in the Tunis Medina, calling for the resignation of the provisional government of Mohamed Ghannouchi, an obvious continuation of the regime in personnel and policies. Asserting symbolically the people's power, that day the protesters occupied the Place du Gouvernement, at the heart of the Kasbah, the site of most government ministries. They set up tents and organized a permanent forum that engaged in animated debates lasting well into the night. Discussions would go on in some cases for two weeks in a row. They filmed themselves and diffused the video of the debates on the Internet. But their language was not only digital. The walls of the square were covered with slogans in Arabic,

French and English, since the movement wanted to relate
to the outside world to claim their rights and aspirations.
They sang rhythmic slogans and protest songs. Most frequently they chanted the most popular line of the national
anthem: "If the people one day wish to live, destiny will
have to respond" (*Idhâ I-sha 'bu yawman arâda I-hayât, fa-lâ
budda an yastadjiba al-qadar*). Although there were no leaders, some informal organization emerged to take care of the
logistics and to enforce rules of engagement in the debates
in the square: discussions should be polite and respectful and
free from shouting, with everybody entitled to express an
opinion, and devoid of endless tirades so that there would be
enough time for everyone to exercise the newly found freedom of speech. A soft surveillance network, organized by the
protesters themselves, made sure the rules were respected.
The same informal organization protected the encampment
against violence and provocation, either from the outside or
from within. There was indeed police violence, and the occupiers were evicted from the square several times, but they
came back on February 20, 2011 to re-occupy the square,
and then again on April 1, 2011. They debated everything
– rejecting a rotten government, calling for true democracy,
asking for a new electoral regime, defending the rights of
the regions against centralism – but also asked for jobs, as
a large proportion of the young demonstrators were unemployed and requesting better education. They were outraged
by the control of both politics and the economy by the clan
of the Trabelsi, the family of the second wife of Ben Ali,
whose crooked deals had been exposed in the diplomatic
cables revealed by WikiLeaks. They also discussed the role
of Islam in providing a moral guide against corruption and
abuse. Yet, this was not an Islamic movement, in spite of the
presence of a strong Islamist current among the protesters,
for the simple reason that there is widespread influence of

political Islamism in the Tunisian society. But secularism and Islamism coexisted in the movement without major tensions. Indeed, in terms of the community of reference, this was a national Tunisian movement that used the national flag and sang the national anthem as a rallying cry, claiming the legitimacy of the nation against the appropriation of the nation by an illegitimate political regime backed by the former colonial powers, particularly France and the United States. This was neither an Islamic revolution nor a Jasmine revolution (the poetic name given by the Western media for no clear reason, which in fact was the original name for the coup of Ben Ali in 1987!). In the words of the protesters themselves, this was a "Revolution for liberty and dignity" (*Thawrat al-hurriya wa-l Karâma*). The search for dignity in response to institutionally-backed humiliation was an essential emotional driver of the protests.

Who were these protesters? After a few weeks of demonstrations we can say that a cross-section of the Tunisian society was in the streets, with a strong presence of the professional class. Moreover, the large majority of the population supported the demand to end the dictatorial regime. Yet, in the view of most observers, those who started the movement and those who played the most active role in the protest were mainly unemployed educated youth. Indeed, while the unemployment rate in Tunisia was 13.3 percent, it had risen to 21.1 percent among young college graduates. This mixture of education and lack of opportunities was a breeding ground for revolt in Tunisia, as in all other Arab countries. It was also significant that unionized workers were important participants once the movement had reached a critical mass. While the leadership of the Union Generale des Travailleurs Tunisiens (UGTT) was delegitimized by its deep connection with the regime (particularly its secretary general, Abdeslem Jrad), the rank and file and the middle level cadres used the opportunity to voice their demands and launched a number of strikes that contributed to bringing the country out of control of the authorities. Instead, the opposing political parties were ignored by the activists and had no organized presence in the revolt. The protesters generated spontaneously their own ad hoc leadership in specific times and places. Most of these self-appointed leaders were in their twenties and early thirties. Although the movement was intergenerational, the trust was created among the youth. A post on Facebook expressed clearly a certain state of mind: "Most politicians have white hair and a black heart. We want people who have black hair and a white heart."

Why did this movement succeed so quickly in subverting a stable dictatorship with a façade of institutional democracy, a huge surveillance system of the entire society (as many as one percent of Tunisians worked in one way or another for the Minister of Interior) and strong support from the major Western powers? After all, social struggles and gestures of opposition have been swiftly repressed by the regime with relative ease on prior occasions. Intense working class struggles had taken place in Ben Guerdane (2009) and in the phosphate mines of Gafsa (2010), but they were violently repressed with scores of people killed, injured and arrested, and ultimately contained. Dissidents were tortured and jailed. Street demonstrations were rare. We know that the spark of the revolt came from the sacrifice of Mohamed Bouazizi. But how did the spark set fire to the prairie and how and why did it spread?

New, distinctive factors made possible the success of the Tunisian popular revolts in 2011 over a sustained period of time. Among these factors appears prominently the role played by the Internet and Al Jazeera in triggering, amplifying and coordinating spontaneous revolts as an expression of outrage, particularly among the youth. Granted, any social uprising – and Tunisia was no exception – takes place as an expression of protest against dire economic, social and political conditions, such as unemployment, high prices, inequality, poverty, police brutality, lack of democracy, censorship, and corruption as a way of life throughout the state. But from these objective conditions emerged emotions and feelings – feelings of outrage often induced by humiliation – and these feelings prompted spontaneous protests initiated by individuals: by young people using their networks; the networks where they live and express themselves. Certainly, this includes the Internet's social networks as well as mobile phone networks. But this also means their social networks: their friends, their families and, in some cases, their soccer clubs, most of them offline. It was in the connection between social networks on the Internet and social networks in people's lives where the protest was forged. Thus, the precondition for the revolts was the existence of an Internet culture, made up of bloggers, social networks and cyberactivism. For instance, blogger journalist Zouhair Yahiaoui was imprisoned in 2001 and died in prison. Other critical bloggers, such as Mohamed Abbou (2005) and Slim Boukdir (2008), were jailed for their exposure of government's wrongdoings.

These growing free voices that spread on the Internet in spite of censorship and repression found a powerful ally in satellite television beyond government control, particularly Al Jazeera. There was a symbiotic relationship between mobile phone citizen journalists uploading images and information to YouTube and Al Jazeera using feeds from citizen journalism and then broadcasting them to the population at large (40 percent of Tunisians in urban centers watched Al Jazeera, since official television had been reduced to a primitive propaganda tool). This Al Jazeera–Internet link was essential during the weeks of the revolts, both in Tunisia and in relation to the Arab world. Al Jazeera went so far as to develop a communication program to allow mobile phones to connect directly to its satellite without requiring sophisticated equipment. Twitter also played a major role in discussing the events and coordinating actions. Demonstrators used the hashtag #sidibouzid on Twitter to debate and communicate, thus indexing the Tunisian revolution. According to the study on information flows in the Arab revolutions conducted by Lotan et al. (2011), "bloggers played an important role in surfacing and disseminating news from Tunisia, as they had a substantially higher likelihood to engage their audience to participate, compared with any other actor type" (1389).

Given the role of the Internet in spreading and coordinating the revolt, it is significant to point out that Tunisia has one of the highest rates of Internet and mobile phone penetration in the Arab world. In November 2010, 67 percent of the urban population had access to a mobile phone, and 37 percent were connected to the Internet. In early 2011, 20 percent of Internet users were on Facebook, a percentage that is two times higher than in Morocco, three times higher than in Egypt, five times higher than in Algeria or Libya, and twenty times higher than in Yemen. Furthermore, the proportion of Internet users among the urban population and particularly among the urban youth was much higher. Since there is a direct connection between young age, higher education and the use of the Internet, the unemployed college graduates who were the key actors in the revolution were also frequent Internet users, and some were sophisticated users who utilized the communicative potential of the Internet to build and expand their movement. The communicative autonomy provided by the Internet made possible the viral diffusion of videos, messages and songs that incited rage and gave hope. For instance, the song "Rais Lebled" by a famous rapper from Sfax, El General, denouncing the dictatorship became a hit on the social networks. Of course, El General was arrested, but this incensed the protesters even further and strengthened their determination in the struggle for "complete transition," as they put it.

Thus, it seems that in Tunisia we find a significant convergence of three distinctive features:

1. The existence of an active group of unemployed college graduates, who led the revolt, bypassing any formal, traditional leadership;
2. The presence of a strong cyberactivism culture that had engaged in the open critique of the regime for over one decade;
3. A relatively high rate of diffusion of Internet use, including household connections, schools and cybercafés.

The combination of these three elements, which fed into each other, provides a clue to understanding why Tunisia was the harbinger of a new form of networked social movement in the Arab world.

The Tunisian protesters kept up their demands for full democratization of the country throughout 2011 in spite of persistent police repression and continuing presence of politicians from the old regime in the provisional government and in the high levels of administration. The army, however, was generally supportive of the democratization process, trying to find new legitimacy from its refusal to engage in further bloody repression during the revolution. With the support of a newly independent media, particularly in the case of the print press, the democratic movement opened a new political space and reached the milestone of clean, open elections on October 23, 2011. Ennahad, a moderate Islamist coalition, became the leading political force in the country, receiving 40 percent of the votes and obtaining 89 of the 217 seats of the Constitutional Assembly. Its leader, the veteran Islamist political intellectual Rached Gannouchi, became prime minister. He represents the brand of Islamism that would have come to power through free elections in most Arab countries, if the will of the people would have been respected. He does not represent a return to tradition or to the imposition of Sharia. In an often quoted interview given in his London exile in 1990, Rached Gannouchi put his political vision of Islamism in simple terms: "The only way to accede to modernity is by our own path, that which has been traced for us by our religion, our history and our civilization" (*Jeune Afrique*, July 1990, my translation). So, there is no rejection of modernity, but defence of a project of self-determined modernity. His most explicit contemporary reference is the Freedom and Development Party led by Erdogan in Turkey, but this has been consistent with his own position over the years. There are no indications that an Islamic fundamentalist regime will be the outcome of the Tunisian Revolution. The president, Moncef Marzuki, is a secular personality, and the draft of the new Constitution is no more reliant on God's will than is the Constitution of the United States. Indeed, the acceptance of a modern Islamist party at the forefront of the political system has marginalized, without excluding, the radical Islamic forces. However, this may change if the new democratic governments are not able to tackle the dramatic issues of mass unemployment, extreme poverty, widespread corruption and bureaucratic arrogance that have not been dissolved by the atmosphere of freedom. Tunisia will confront major challenges in the coming years. But it will do so with a reasonably democratic polity in place and, more importantly, with a conscious and active civil society, still occupying cyberspace and ready to come back into the urban space if and when necessary. Whatever the future will be, the hope for a humane and democratic Tunisian society will be the direct result of the sacrifice of Mohamed Bouazizi and of the struggle for the dignity he defended for himself, which had been taken up by his compatriots.

ICELAND'S KITCHENWARE REVOLUTION: FROM FINANCIAL COLLAPSE TO CROWDSOURCING A NEW CONSTITUTION[2]

The opening scenes of what is perhaps the best documentary film on the global financial crisis of 2008, Charles Ferguson's *Inside Job*, showcase Iceland. Indeed, the rise and fall of the Icelandic economy epitomizes the flawed model of speculative wealth creation that characterized financial capitalism in the last decade. In 2007, Iceland's average income was the fifth highest in the world. Icelanders earned 160 percent more than Americans. Its economy had been historically based in the fishing industry, representing 12 percent of GDP and 40 percent of exports. Yet, even adding tourism, software and aluminum as dynamic economic activities, and as profitable as fishing had been, the sources of the sudden Icelandic wealth were elsewhere. It resulted from the fast growth of the financial sector in the wake of the global expansion of speculative financial capitalism. The fast integration of Iceland in international finance was led by three Icelandic banks: Kaupthing, Landsbanki and Glitnir, which grew from local service banks in the late 1980s to major financial institutions by the mid-2000s. The three banks increased the value of their assets from 100 percent of GDP in 2000 to almost 800 percent of GDP by the year 2007. The strategy they followed for their outstanding growth was similar to that of many financial entities in the United States and the UK. They used their shares as collateral to borrow extensively from each other and then used these loans to finance the purchase of additional shares from the three banks, thus increasing the price of their shares and boosting their balance sheets. Furthermore, they plotted together to broaden the scope of their speculative operations on a global scale. Their fraudulent schemes were disguised through a web of jointly-owned firms headquartered in offshore banking locations, such as the Isle of Man, the Virgin Islands, Cuba and Luxembourg. Bank customers were persuaded to increase their debt, converting it into lower interest Swiss francs or Japanese yen. Unlimited credit permitted people to engage in unlimited consumption, artificially stimulating domestic demand and propelling economic growth. Furthermore, to cover their operations, the banks made favorable loans to selected politicians, as well as generous financial contributions to political parties for their election campaigns.

In February of 2006, Fitch downgraded the outlook of Iceland's economy to negative, triggering what was labeled a "mini crisis." To stop the main banks from losing credit, Iceland's Central Bank borrowed extensively to increase their foreign exchange reserves. The Chamber of Commerce, dominated by representatives of the large banks, hired as consultants two prominent academics: Frederic Mishkin, from the Columbia Business School, and Richards Portes, from the London Business School, both of whom certified the solvency of the Icelandic banks. However, by 2007, the government could no longer ignore the suspicious balance sheets of the banks, and realized that if one of the major banks failed, the whole financial system would follow. A special commission was appointed to assess the problem. The commission did very little, and did not even contemplate regulating the banking sector. Soon thereafter, the three banks, Landsbanki, Kaupthing and Glitnir, faced the urgency of repaying their short-term debt, as most of their assets were fictitious and long-term. Having more imagination than scruples, they designed new schemes to solve their insolvency. Landsbanki set up Internet-based financial accounts under the name of Icesave, offering high returns on short-term deposits. They offered this service through new branches in the UK and the Netherlands. It was a success: millions of pounds were deposited in the Icesave accounts. In the UK alone, 300,000 Icesave accounts were opened. The deposits appeared to be safe as Iceland was a member of the EEA (European Economic Area), and therefore was covered by the EEA's deposit insurance system, meaning that they were guaranteed by the Icelandic Government, as well as by the governments of the countries where the branches of the banks were located. A second strategy used by the three big banks to raise money in a hurry to pay their short-term debt was what became known as "love letters." The banks swapped debt securities with each other to use the others' debt as collateral to borrow more money from the Central Bank of Iceland. Furthermore, the Central Bank of Luxembourg lent the three banks €2.5 billion, with most of the collateral in the form of "love letters." Political support from the government for the big banks continued in spite of their obvious insolvency. In April 2008, the IMF sent a confidential memo to the Haarde government requesting the control of the banks and offering help, to no avail. The only reaction from the government was to instruct the Central Bank to take more loans in foreign exchange reserves. On September 29, Glitnir bank asked the Governor of the Central Bank for immediate help, as it could not cover its financial obligations. In response, the Central Bank bought 75 percent of Glitnir's shares. Yet, this action had the opposite effect: instead of reassuring the financial markets, the move prompted the free fall of Iceland's credit rating. In a few days, the stock market, bank bonds and real estate prices plummeted. The three banks collapsed, leaving US$25 billion in debt. The financial crisis caused losses, in Iceland and abroad, equivalent to seven times the GDP of Iceland. In proportion to the size of the economy, it was the largest destruction of financial value in history. The personal income of Icelanders was substantially reduced and their assets were sharply devalued. Iceland's GDP fell by 6.8 percent in 2009, and by an additional 3.4 percent in 2010. As its financial house of cards collapsed, Iceland's economic crisis became the catalyst of the Kitchenware Revolution.

Every revolution has its date of birth and its rebel hero. On October 11, 2008, singer Hordur Torfason sat in front of the building of the Althing (the Icelandic Parliament) in Reykjavik with his guitar, and sang his anger against the "banksters" and their subservient politicians. A few people joined him. Then someone recorded the scene and uploaded it to the Internet. Within days, hundreds and then thousands were staging their protest in the historic Austurvollur square. A group known as the Raddir fólksins vowed to protest every Saturday to obtain the resignation of the government. The protests intensified in January, both on the Internet and in the square, braving the Icelandic winter. According to observers in this process of social mobilization, the role of the Internet and social networks was absolutely critical, partly because 94 percent of Icelanders are connected to the Internet, and two-thirds are users of Facebook.

On January 20, 2009, the day the Parliament reconvened after a month-long holiday, thousands of people of all ages and conditions gathered in front of the Parliament to blame the government for the mishandling of the economy and for its inability to cope with the crisis. They beat on drums, pots and pans, thus earning the nickname "the kitchenware revolution" or "the pots-and-pans revolution." Protesters were calling for the government to resign and for new elections to

be held. Furthermore, they were also pushing for a re-foun-
dation of the republic, which had become corrupted, in their
view, by the subordination of politicians and political parties
to the financial elite. And so, they asked for the drafting of
a new Constitution, to replace the provisional Constitution
of 1944, a temporary charter at the time of the declaration
of independence from occupied Denmark, that was kept in
place because it favored the interests of the political class
(giving disproportionate weight to the conservative, rural
provinces). The social democrats and greens responded posi-
tively to this request while the conservative coalition led by
the Independence Party rejected it. As the pressure from the
social networks and from the streets intensified, on January
23, 2009, early parliamentary elections were announced, and
the conservative Prime Minister Geir Haarde declared that
due to his poor health he would not be running for reelec-
tion. The elections resulted in a resounding defeat of the
two major parties (both conservative) that, alone or in coalition, had been governing Iceland since 1927. A new coalition
formed by social democrats and "red-greens" came into
power on February 1, 2009. It was led by the social democratic leader Johanna Sigurdardottir, the first openly gay
prime minister. Half of her cabinet members are women.

The new government went to work on three fronts: to
clean up the financial mess and exact responsibilities for the
fraudulent management of the economy; to restore economic growth by transforming the economic model, setting
up strict financial regulations and strengthening the over-
seeing institutions; and to respond to the popular demand
by engaging in a process of constitutional reform with full
citizen participation.

The three major banks were nationalized and two of
them returned to the private sector to be owned by a pool of
the banks' foreign creditors, with participation of the state.

Icelanders were compensated by the government for the loss of their savings. However, at the initiative of the President of the Republic, Olafur Grimson, a referendum was held to decide on the payment of the loan guarantees owed by the extinct banks to the British and Dutch depositors and their governments. Ninety-three percent of Icelanders voted not to pay the $US5.9 billion debt owed to the UK and the Netherlands. Of course, this prompted a series of lawsuits still being sorted out in the courts. Iceland is facing a long legal battle to settle the foreign debt. The banks tried to avoid litigation by offering to pay with the sale of their assets, but the outcome of the negotiation is still pending at the time of this writing.

The new government proceeded with legal action against those responsible for the crisis. Speaking at the convention of the social democratic party on May 30, 2011, Prime Minister Johanna Sigurdardottir stated, in the clearest possible terms, that:

> The overpaid crowd, the "banksters," and the big property elites will not be allowed to gobble up the coming economic growth ... Their debauched party was held under the Independence party's neoconservative fanfare. The quality of life Icelanders have in the future, will, on the other hand, be built on equality.

Accordingly, leading figures of the banking sector were arrested in Reykjavik and London to respond to the charges against their unlawful financial management. And former Prime Minister Haarde was brought to trial under the accusation of mismanagement of public funds and yielding to the influence of pressure groups.

As expected, economic experts warned against the dire consequences of nationalizing the banks, controlling capital flows and refusing to pay foreign debt. However, after Iceland reversed its economic policies, asserting government control, the economy bounced back in 2011 and 2012, outperforming most economies of the European Union. After experiencing negative growth in 2009 and 2010, GDP increased by 2.6 percent in 2011 and was projected to increase by 4 percent in 2012. Unemployment dropped from 10 percent in 2009 to 5.9 percent in 2012, inflation was reduced from 18 percent to 4 percent and Iceland's financial standing improved in CDS ratings from 1,000 points to 200 points. Although the economy is still subject to the possibility of future crises, as is the whole of the European economy, its outlook was upgraded by Standard & Poor's in late 2011 from negative to stable. Government bond issues in 2011 were oversubscribed by international investors. In fact, according to Bloomberg in 2011, it cost less to insure Icelandic debt than sovereign debt in the eurozone. The attitudes of Icelanders towards the future became more positive by mid-2011, particularly among the most educated segments of society.

How was the new democratic government able to rescue the country from a major economic disaster in such a short span of time?

First, it did not promote the kind of drastic austerity measures that were implemented in other European countries. Iceland signed a "social stability" pact to protect citizens from the effects of the crisis. Thus public employment was not significantly reduced, and public spending kept domestic demand at a reasonable level. The government had sufficient revenue to keep spending and to buy back internal financial assets because it did not have to repay the banks' foreign debt, as mandated by the referendum. Furthermore, while compensating the bank customers for their losses, priority was given to deposit holders over bond holders. This contributed to keep liquidity in the economy, facilitating the recovery.

Second, the devaluation of the Króna, which fell by 40 percent, had a very positive impact on fish sales, aluminum exports and tourism. Furthermore, as imports became more expensive, local businesses picked up some of the consumer demand, facilitating the creation of an unprecedented number of start-up firms, which more than compensated for the disappearance of companies in financial services, construction and real estate.

Third, the government established control of capital flows and foreign currency, preventing the flight of capital from the country.

However, the Icelandic revolution, while provoked by the economic crisis, was not only about restoring the economy. It was primarily about a fundamental transformation of the political system that was blamed for its incapacity to manage the crisis, and its subordination to the banks. This is in spite of, or perhaps because of, the fact that Iceland is one of the oldest democracies in the world. The Althing (its representative assembly still in place nowadays under a different form) was established before the year 1000. And yet, after experiencing the cronyism and aloofness of the political class, Iceland plunged into the same crisis of legitimacy as most countries in the world. Only 11 percent of citizens trusted the Parliament, and obviously only 6 percent trusted the banks. Trying to win back people's trust, the government called for an election that was held by popular demand, honoring its promise of engaging in a constitutional reform with the broadest feasible citizen participation. A unique constitutional process was put in place, and actually implemented. The Parliament appointed a constitutional committee that convened a national assembly of 1,000 randomly selected citizens. After two days of deliberation, the assembly concluded

that a new constitution should be drafted and suggested
some of the principles that should be paramount in the constitutional text. Following action, in spite of the criticism
from the conservative opposition parties, the Parliament
then organized a popular election to designate a 25 member
Constitutional Assembly Council (CAC). All citizens were
entitled to candidacy, and 522 of them contested the 25 seats.
The election was held in November 2010 with the participation of 37 percent of the electorate. However, the Supreme
Court voided the election for technical legal reasons. To
circumvent the obstruction, the Parliament exercised its
right to appoint the 25 citizens elected in this process to the
constitutional council in charge of drafting the new constitution. The CAC sought the participation of all citizens via
the Internet. Facebook was the primary platform for debate.
Twitter was the channel to report on the work in progress
and to respond to queries from citizens. YouTube and Flickr
were used to set up direct communication between citizens
and the council members, as well as to participate in debates
taking place throughout Iceland.

The CAC received online and offline 16,000 suggestions
and comments that were debated on the social networks. It
wrote 15 different versions of the text, to take into consideration the results of this widespread deliberation. Thus,
the final constitutional bill was literally produced through
crowdsourcing. Some observers have labeled it a wiki-
constitution   (www.wired.co.uk./news/archive/2011-08/01/
iceland-constitution).

After months of deliberation online and among its members, the council approved a draft of the constitutional bill
by a vote of 25 to 0. On July 29, 2011, the CAC delivered
to the Parliament a bill containing 114 articles in 9 chapters. While the Parliament debated some minor points and
changed some language of the text, the left wing majority

overran the objections of the conservative opposition, and the bill was only slightly amended. The government decided that it should be submitted to a vote of citizens at large, and vowed to respect the popular decision in the final approval that is the prerogative of the Parliament. A vote on the Constitutional bill was scheduled for the same day as the presidential election, June 30, 2012.

If approved, the new Icelandic Constitution would enshrine philosophical principles, social values and political forms of representation that are prominent in the demands and the vision of the social movements that surged around the world in 2011. It is worthwhile to highlight some elements of this text (to see a draft of the Constitution in its English translation, visit http://www.politics.ie/forum/political-ref orm/173176-proposed-new-icelandic-constitution.html).

The preamble of the Constitution proclaims the fundamental principle of equality:

> We, the people of Iceland, wish to create a just society with equal opportunities for everyone.

The representative political principle of "one person, one vote" is emphasized, as this is the key in Iceland, as in many other countries, to avoiding the confiscation of popular will by political engineering. The text states that:

> The votes of voters everywhere in the country shall have equal weight.

To break the monopoly of political parties, it is established that voters will be free to vote for parties or for individual candidates on different slates.

The principle of free access to information is strongly affirmed:

The law shall ensure public access to all documents collected or processed by public entities.

This effectively would end government secrecy and make more difficult hidden political maneuvering, as all government and parliamentary meetings should have records and these records could be accessed by anyone. Furthermore:

All persons shall be free to collect and disseminate information.

There is a limitation of the number of terms politicians, and particularly the President, can serve. The right for citizens to initiate legislation and to call for referendums on specific issues is recognized.

The public interest in the management of the economy is asserted:

Iceland's natural resources that are not in private ownership are the common and perpetual property of the nation . . . The utilization of the resources shall be guided by sustainable development and the public interest.

And the respect of nature is paramount:

Iceland's nature is the foundation of life in the country . . . The use of natural resources shall be managed to minimize their depletion in the long term with respect for the rights of nature and future generations.

That the Constitution of a country could explicitly reflect principles that, in the context of global capitalism, are revolutionary shows the direct link between a process of genuinely popular crowdsourcing and the content resulting from such a participatory process. It should be remembered that the consultation and elaboration took place in four months as requested by the Parliament, belying the notion of the ineffectiveness of participatory democracy. Granted, Iceland has only 320,000 citizens. But the defenders of the experience argue that with the Internet and with full Internet literacy and unrestricted access, this model of political participation and crowdsourcing of the legislative process is scalable. If so, the cultural and technological bases for the deepening of representative democracy would have been laid out in a small country made of ice and fire on a North Atlantic island.

The reference that the Icelandic revolution came to be for European social movements battling the consequences of a devastating financial crisis is explained by its direct connection to the main issues that induced the protests.

Icelanders insurged, as did people in all other countries, against a brand of speculative financial capitalism that destroyed people's livelihood. But their outrage came from the realization that the democratic institutions did not represent the interests of citizens because the political class had become a self-reproducing cast that was catering to the interests of the financial elite, and to the preservation of their monopoly over the state.

This is why the primary target of the movement was the government in place, and the political class at large, although they offered a chance for the new government to legitimize its actions by following the people's will, as expressed in the public space offered by the Internet. The government responded by enacting effective economic policies leading to economic recovery in sharp contrast to many European economies that were burdened by misplaced austerity policies that aggravated the recession in the continent. The key differentiating factor between Iceland and the rest of Europe is that the Icelandic government made the bankers pay for the costs of the crisis, while relieving people from its hardship as much as possible. This is in fact one of the key demands from protesters throughout Europe. The results of this approach were positive both in economic terms and in terms of social and political stability.

Furthermore, Icelandic citizens fully realized their project of transformation of the political system by elaborating a new Constitution whose principles, if enacted, would ensure the practice of true democracy and the preservation of fundamental human values. In this particular sense it was indeed a true revolutionary experiment whose example, with all its limitations, has inspired a new generation of pragmatic idealists at the forefront of the social movements against the crisis. Indeed, in some posts on the Internet reflecting on Iceland's constitutional experience, there is reference to the Corsican Constitution of 1755 that is considered to be one of the sources of inspiration for the Constitution of the United States (www.nakedcapitalism.com/2011/10).

The first draft of the Constitution of Corsica was written by Jean Jacques Rousseau, at the request of the founders of the short-lived republic. While seeking to establish the principles on which the Constitution should be based, he wrote:

> The power derived from population is more real than derived from finance, and is more certain in its effects. Since the use of manpower cannot be concealed from view, it always reaches its public objective. It is not thus with the use of money, which flows off and is lost in private destinations; it is collected for one purpose and spent for another; the people pay for protection, and their payments are used to oppress them. That is why a state rich in money is always weak, and a state rich in men is always strong (Rousseau, J.J., "Constitutional Project for Corsica," drafted 1765,

Edinburgh, Thomas Nelson and Sons, retrieved from Liberty Library, www.constitution.org/jjr/corsica.htm).

The echo of this contrast between the poverty of finance and the richness of people reaches across history to the many squares where citizens envision new constitutional projects. In this sense, the making of the new Icelandic Constitution could well play the inspiring role for twenty-first century democracy that Corsica played for the proclamation of liberty in the United States.

SOUTHERN WIND, NORTHERN WIND: CROSS-CULTURAL LEVERS OF SOCIAL CHANGE

The precursors of networked social movements present, after close examination, striking similarities in spite of their sharply contrasted cultural and institutional contexts.

Both revolts insurged against the consequences of a dramatic economic crisis, although in Tunisia this was not as much due to a financial collapse as to the plundering of the country's economy by a clique rooted in the predatory state. Moreover, people felt powerless because of the obvious intertwining of the business oligarchs and the political class, be it democratically elected or dictatorially imposed. I am certainly not assimilating the Icelandic democracy, fully respectful of liberty and civil rights, to the torturing dictatorship of Ben Ali and his thugs. But from the perspective of citizens in both countries, the governments in place, and even politicians at large, did not represent their will because they had merged with the interests of the financial elite, and they had put their own interests above the interests of the people. The democratic deficit, although in vastly different proportions, was present in both countries, and it was a major source of discontent at the roots of the protests.

The crisis of political legitimacy combined with the crisis of speculative capitalism.

There is also an interesting common feature in these two countries. They are both highly homogeneous in ethnicity and in religion. Indeed, Iceland, because of its historical isolation, is used as a laboratory by genetic researchers looking for a homogeneous genetic heritage. As for Tunisia, it is the most ethnically homogeneous country of the Arab world, and Sunni Muslims represent the overwhelming proportion of the population. Thus, it will be significant to assess the impact of cultural and ethnic heterogeneity in other countries over the characteristics of social movements by comparing them to the baseline represented by these two countries.

Similarities extend to the practices of the movements themselves. Both were triggered by a dramatic event (financial collapse in Iceland, the self-immolation of Mohamed Bouazizi in Tunisia). In both cases, mobile phones and social networks on the Internet played a major role in spreading images and messages that mobilized people in providing a platform for debate, in calling for action, in coordinating and organizing the protests, and in relaying information and debate to the population at large. Television also played a role, but always used Internet and mobile phones to feed its images and information.

In both cases, the movement went from cyberspace to urban space, with the occupation of the symbolic public square as material support for both debates and protests, from chanting slogans in Tunis, to banging pans and pots in Reykjavik. A hybrid public space made of digital social networks and of a newly created urban community was at the heart of the movement, both as a tool for self-reflection and as a statement of people's power. Powerlessness was turned into empowerment.

From this empowerment came the strongest similarity between the movements in Tunisia and Iceland: their meaningful success in achieving institutional change. Democracy was established in Tunisia. A new constitutional order, enlarging the boundaries of representative democracy, was achieved in Iceland, and a new set of economic policies was implemented. The process of mobilization leading to successful political change transformed civic consciousness and made difficult any future attempt to return to political manipulation as a way of life. This is the reason why both movements became role models for the social movements that, inspired by them, emerged thereafter in the landscape of a world in crisis searching for new forms of living together.

It is the purpose of this book to investigate the extent to which the key features identified in these two movements are equally present as critical factors in movements arising in other social contexts. Because if they are, we may be observing the rise of new forms of social transformation. And if they are modified in their practice because of differences in context, we may suggest some hypotheses on the interaction between culture, institutions and movements, the key question for a theory of social change. And, for its practice.

NOTES

1 The best analysis I know of the Tunisian revolution is by Choukri Hmed (2011). Some key elements of my own analysis are based on his. A detailed account is the one by Viviane Bettaieb (2011). On the role of Internet social networks, television and mobile phones in the Tunisian protests, see Wagner (2011) and Lotan et al. (2011).

2 An insightful and well-documented analysis of the Icelandic revolution can be found in Gylfason et al. (2010)

and Gunnarson (2009). On the importance of the role of social networks on the Internet in the dynamics of the social movement, see Bennett (2011) and Garcia Lamarca (2011). On the financial crisis and economic policies in Iceland, see references.

REFERENCES AND SOURCES

On the Tunisian revolution

Beau, N. and Tuquoi, J. P. (2002) *Notre ami Ben Ali: l'envers du miracle tunisien.* La Decouverte, Paris.

Bettaieb, V. (2011) *Degage-La revolution tunisienne. 17 december 2010–14 Janvier 2011.* Editions du Layeur, Paris.

Cherni, A. (2011) *La revolution tunisienne: s'emparer de l'histoire.* Al Bouraq, Paris.

De Leon, J. C. and Jones, C. R. (eds.) (2011) *Tunisia and Egypt: Unrest and Revolution.* Global Political Studies, Novinka, New York.

Elseewi, T. A. (2011) A revolution of the imagination. *International Journal of Communication.* [Online] Vol. 5, 1197–206. Available at: <http://ijoc.org/ojs/index.php/ijoc/article/view/1237/596>.

Haloui, Y. (2011) *Life in Revolution: Resistance and everyday life in the Tunisian revolution.* Lambert Academic Publishers, Saarbrücken.

Hatzenberger, A. (2011) L'hiver à Tunis et le printemps. *Les Temps Modernes,* May–July: 21–25.

Hmed, C. (2011) "Si le peuple un jour aspire à vivre, le destin se doit de répondre": Apprender à devenir révolutionnaire en Tunisie. *Les Temps Modernes,* May–July: 4–20.

Laurent, J. (2011) Points d'inflexion des revoltes arabes. *Les Temps Modernes,* May–July: 63–84.

Lotan, G., Graeff, E., Ananny, M., Gaffney, D., Pearce, I. &

boyd, d. (2011) The revolutions were tweeted: Information flows during the 2011 Tunisian and Egyptian revolutions. *International Journal of Communication*, [Online] Vol. 5, 1375–405. Available at: <http://ijoc.org/ojs/index.php/ijoc/article/view/1246>.

Newsom, V.A., Lengel, L. & Cassara, C. (2011) Local knowledge and the revolutions: A framework for social media information flow. *International Journal of Communication*, [Online] Vol. 5, 1303–12. Available at: <http://ijoc.org/ojs/index.php/ijoc/article/view/1245/607>.

Piot, O. (2011) *Dix jours qui ebranlerent le monde arabe*. Les Petits Matins, Paris.

Wagner, B. (2011) "I have understood you": The co-evolution of expression and control on the internet, television and mobile phones during the Jasmine Revolution in Tunisia. *International Journal of Communication*, [Online] Vol. 5, 1295–303. Available at: <http://ijoc.org/ojs/index.php/ijoc/article/view/1174/606>.

On the Icelandic revolution

Web resources

Bennett, N. (2011) Iceland's crowdsourced constitution – a lesson in open source marketing. [online] Available at: <http://socialmediatoday.com/nick-bennett/305690/icelands-crowdsourced-constitution-lesson-opensource-marketing> [Accessed on January 9, 2012].

Boyes, R. (2009) Age of Testosterone comes to end in Iceland. *The Times.co.uk*, [online] February 7. Available at: <http://www.timesonline.co.uk/tol/news/world/europe/article5679378.ece> [Accessed on January 9, 2012].

Brown, M. (2011) Icelanders turn in first draft of crowdsourced constitution. *Wired News* [online] August 1. Available at: <http://www.wired.co.uk/news/archive/2011

-08/01/iceland-constitution> [Accessed on January 9, 2012].

Constitution Society. (1994) *Constitutional Project for Corsica*. [online] Available at: <http://www.constitution.org/jjr/corsica.htm> [Accessed on January 9, 2012].

Crawford, S. (2011) Digital Governance: from Iceland to New York City. *Center for Democracy and Technology*, [blog] August 1. Available at <www.cdt.org/blogs/018digital-governance> [Accessed on January 9, 2012].

DryIslandia. (2011) *El impulsor de la revolución islandesa, manda un mensaje de apoyo a los españoles*. [video online] Available at: http://www.youtube.com/watch?v=cBAgEU CCdq8&feature=player_embedded [Accessed on January 9, 2012].

Finbar10. (2011) Proposed New Icelandic Constitution. Politics.ie, [forum] October 16. Available at: <http://www.politics.ie/forum/political-reform/173176-proposed-new-icelandic-constitution.html> [Accessed on January 9, 2012].

Fontaine, P. (2011) Occupy Reykjavík begins, police clear out protesters camping in front of Parliament. *The Reykjavík Grapevine*, [online] October 31. Available at: <http://www.grapevine.is/Home/ReadArticle/Occupy-Reykjavik-Begins> [Accessed on January 9, 2012].

Garcia Lamarca, M. (2011) Learning from Iceland's "Kitchenware Revolution." *The Polis Blog* [blog] June 22. Available at: <http://www.thepolisblog.org/2011/06/learning-from-icelands-kitchenware.html> [Accessed on January 9, 2012].

Gunnarson, V. (2009) Iceland's Rainbow Revolution. *The Reykjavík Grapevine*, [online] February 2. Available at: <http://www.grapevine.is/Features/ReadArticle/icelands-rainbow-revolution> [Accessed on January 9, 2012].

Gylfason, T. (2010) Iceland's special investigation: The plot thickens. [online] Available at: <http://www.voxeu.org/index.php?q=node/4965> [Accessed on January 9, 2012].

Gylfason, T. (2011a) Crowds and constitutions. [online] Available at: <http://voxeu.org/index.php?q=node/7090> [Accessed on January 9, 2012].

Gylfason, T. (2011b) From crisis to constitution. [online] Available at: <http://www.VoxEU.org/index.php?q=node/7077> [Accessed on January 9, 2012].

Siddique, H. (2011) Mob rule: Iceland crowdsources its next constitution. *The Guardian*, [online] June 9. Available at: <http://www.guardian.co.uk/world/2011/jun/09/iceland-crowdsourcing-constitution-facebook/print> [Accessed on January 9, 2012].

On Iceland's financial crisis

Journal articles
Wade, R. & Sigurgeirsdottir, S. (2010) Lessons from Iceland. *New Left Review*, 65, 5–29.

Reports
Hreinsson, P., Tryggvi, G. & Sigríður, B. (2009) *Causes of the Collapse of the Icelandic Banks – Responsibility, Mistakes and Negligence* (Special Investigation Commission Report) (Act No. 142/2008) Althingi: Icelandic Parliament.

Web references
Barley, R. (2011) Investors reward Iceland's steady progress. *The Wall Street Journal*, [online] June 10. Available at: <http://online.wsj.com/article/SB10001424052702304259304576375340039763606.html> [Accessed on January 9, 2012].

Central Intelligence Agency. (2011) *The World Fact Book: Iceland*. [online] Available at: <https://www.cia.gov/library/

publications/the-world-factbook/geos/ic.html> [Accessed on January 9, 2012].

IceNews. (2011) Spain adopts Iceland's Kitchenware Revolution idea. *IceNews*, [online] May 21. Available at: <http://www.icenews.is/index.php/2011/05/21/spain-adop ts-icelands-kitchenware-revolution-idea/> [Accessed on January 9, 2012].

Jiménez, D. (2011) Islandia se mueve ante la crisis. *Noticias Positivas*, [online] March 21. Available at: <http://www. noticiaspositivas.net/2011/03/21/islandia-se-mueve-ante-la-crisis/> [Accessed on January 9, 2012].

Lamant, L. (2011) A gentle cure for the crisis. *Presseurop.eu*, [online] April 8. Available at: http://www.presseurop.eu/ en/content/article/590821-gentle-cure-crisis [Accessed on January 9, 2012].

Neate, R. (2011) Iceland's former premier denies criminal negligence over banking crisis. *The Guardian*, [online] June 7. Available at: <http://www.guardian.co.uk/bus iness/2011/jun/07/iceland-former-premier-trial-banking-crisis> [Accessed on January 9, 2012].

Roos, J. (2011) Democracy 2.0: Iceland crowdsources new constitution. *Roarmag.org*, [online]. Available at: <http:// roarmag.org/2011/06/iceland-crowdsources-constitution-investors-spain-greece/> [Accessed on January 9, 2012].

Sibert, A. (2010) Love letters from Iceland: Accountability of the Eurosystem. [online] Available at: <http://voxeu. org/index.php?q=node/5059> [Accessed on January 9, 2012].

Valdimarsson, O.R. (2011) Icelanders reject foreign deposi-tor claims, forcing year-long court battle. *Bloomberg*, [online] April 11. Available at: <http://www.bloomberg. com/news/2011-04-07/icelanders-may-reject-icesave-accord-in-april-9-referendum.html> [Accessed on January 9, 2012].

Wienberg, C. and Valdimarsson, O.R. (2011) Iceland

president defends pre-crisis tours promoting bank model. *Bloomberg*, [online] April 14. Available at: <http://www.bloomberg.com/news/2011-04-14/iceland-president-defends-pre-crisis-tours-promoting-bank-model.html> [Accessed on January 9, 2012].

THE EGYPTIAN
REVOLUTION

The 25 January Revolution (*Thawrat 25 Yanayir*), which in 18 days dethroned the last Pharaoh, arose from the depth of oppression, injustice, poverty, unemployment, sexism, mockery of democracy, and police brutality.[1]

It had been preceded by political protests (after the rigged elections of 2005 and 2010), women's rights struggles (harshly suppressed as in the Black Wednesday of 2005) and workers' struggles, such as the strike in the textile mills of Mahalla-al-Kubra on April 6, 2008, followed by riots and occupation of the city in response to the bloody repression against the striking workers. From that struggle was born the 6 April Youth Movement,[2] which created a Facebook group attracting 70,000 followers. Waleed Rashed, Asmaa Mahfouz, Ahmed Maher, Mohammed Adel[3] and many other activists of this movement played a significant role in the demonstrations that led to the occupation of Tahrir Square on January 25. They did it together with many other groups that were formed in back-room conspiracies, while reaching out on the Internet. Most prominent among these initiatives was the network created around the Facebook group "We are all Khaled Said," named in the memory of the young activist beaten to death by the police in June 2010 in an Alexandria cybercafé after he distributed a video exposing police corruption.[4] The group, set up by Wael Ghonim, a young Google executive, and AbdulRahman Mansour, was joined by tens of thousands in Egypt and around the world (Ghonim 2012). These groups, and others, called for supporters on Facebook to demonstrate in front of the Ministry of Interior to protest against the police brutality that had terrorized Egyptians for three decades. They chose January 25 because it was National Police Day.

However, the actual spark that ignited the Egyptian revolution, prompting protests on an unprecedented scale, was inspired by the Tunisian revolution, which added the hope of change to the outrage against unbearable brutality. The Egyptian revolution was dramatized, in the wake of the Tunisian example, by a series of self-immolations (six in total) to protest the rise of food prices that left many hungry. And it was conveyed to the Egyptian youth by one of the founders of the 6 April Youth Movement, Asmaa Mafhouz, a 26-year-old business student from the University of Cairo.

On January 18 she posted a vlog on her Facebook page, showed her veiled face, and identified herself by name before stating:

> Four Egyptians set themselves on fire . . . People, have some shame! I, a girl, posted that I will go down to Tahrir Square to stand alone and I'll hold the banner . . . I am making this video to give you a simple message: we are going to Tahrir on January 25th . . . If you stay home, you deserve all that's being done to you, and you will be guilty before

your nation and your people. Go down to the street, send SMSs, post it on the Net, make people aware.

Someone uploaded the vlog to YouTube, and it was virally diffused by thousands. It came to be known throughout the Middle East as "The Vlog that Helped Spark the Revolution" (Wall and El Zahed 2011). From Internet networks, the call to action spread through the social networks of friends, family and associations of all kinds. The networks connected not only to individuals but to each individual's networks. Particularly important were the fan networks of soccer teams, mainly al-Ahly as well as its rival Zamolek Sporting, who had a long history of battling the police.[5] Thus, on January 25, tens of thousands converged in Cairo's symbolic central square of Tahrir (Liberation) and, resisting the attacks of the police, occupied the square and transformed it into the visible public space of the revolution. In the following days, people from all conditions, including the urban poor, religious minorities (Copt Christians were highly present in the movement, alongside Islamists and secular protesters) and a large proportion of women, some with their children, used the safe space of the liberated square to stage their demonstrations by the hundreds of thousands, calling for the resignation of Mubarak and the end of the regime. It is estimated that over two million people demonstrated in Tahrir at different points in time.[6] Friday, January 28 came to be known as the Friday of Rage, when a violent effort by the central security police to put down the demonstrations was met with determination by the protesters who seized control of areas of the city and occupied government buildings and police stations, at the price of hundreds of lives and thousands of wounded people. Similar events took place in Egypt at large, as many other cities, particularly Alexandria, joined the protest. Fridays – this one and many others – have a special meaning in the

Egyptian revolution as well as in other uprisings around the Arab world because it is the day of congregational prayer (also known as *Jummah*), and it is a holiday, and people congregate in the mosques, or outside the mosques. This does not necessarily mean that these were religious movements inspired by the Friday sermons. In Egypt, this was not the case, but it was an appropriate time/space to meet other people, to feel the strength and the courage of being together, and so Fridays became the weekly moment to rekindle the revolution. Throughout the year of continuing struggle with the successors of Mubarak, the new rulers of the Supreme Council of the Armed Forces (SCAF), Fridays, with their symbolic tags, became the lightning moments of mass protests usually leading to violent repression by the military police: Friday of Anger (January 28), Friday of Cleaning (April 8), Second Friday of Anger (March 27), Friday of Retribution (July 1), Friday of Determination (July 7), the march of hundreds of thousands against SCAF (July 15), etc.

Thus, Internet networks, mobile networks, pre-existing social networks, street demonstrations, occupations of public squares and Friday gatherings around the mosques all contributed to the spontaneous, largely leaderless, multimodal networks that enacted the Egyptian revolution. In the assessment of Allagui and Kuebler: "If we learned political leadership and coalition building from the Russian Revolution, and popular initiative from the French Revolution, the Arab Revolutions in Tunisia and Egypt demonstrated the power of networks" (2011: 1435).

SPACE OF FLOWS AND SPACE OF PLACES IN THE EGYPTIAN REVOLUTION

There is no question that the original spaces of resistance were formed on the Internet, as traditional forms of protest were met with utmost ferocity by a police that had been torturing with impunity (occasionally subcontracted by the CIA for anti-terrorist operations) for as long as the thugs could remember. It is also clear that the calls to demonstrate on January 25, and then on successive dates, were sent via Facebook, to be received by an active following made up of youth for whom social networks and mobile phones were a central part of their way of life.

At the end of 2010, an estimated 80 percent of Egyptians had a cell phone, according to research firm Ovum. About a quarter of households had access to the Internet as of 2009, according to the International Telecommunications Union. But the proportion was much higher among the 20- to 35-year-old demographic group of Cairo, Alexandria and other major urban centers, who, in their majority, be it from home, school or cybercafés, are able to access the Internet. In less than two years after Facebook launched its Arabic version in 2009, the number of users tripled, reaching 5 million users by February 2011, of which 600,000 were added in January and February, the months leading up to the start of the revolution. Once the message sent over the Internet reached an active, technology savvy, large group of young Egyptians, mobile phone networks expanded the message to a broader segment of the population.

Thus, social media networks played an important role in the Egyptian revolution. Demonstrators recorded the events with their mobile phones, and shared their videos with people in the country at large and around the world via YouTube and Facebook, often with live streaming. They deliberated on Facebook, coordinated through Twitter, and used blogs extensively to convey their opinion and engage in debates.

An analysis of the Google trends in Egypt during the days of the revolution shows the growing intensity of searches related to the events, peaking on the day of the first demonstration, January 25, and the following days.

Aouragh and Alexander emphasize the relevance of Internet spaces as spheres of dissidence, alongside other spheres of dissidence, such as those formed in the "new quarters" of the urban poor. Noha Atef, an activist interviewed during the revolution, points to the specific role of online-based mobilization:

> To have a space, an on-line space, to write and talk to people, to give them messages which will increase their anger, this is my favorite way of on-line activism . . . When you ask people to go and to demonstrate against the police, they were ready because you had already provided them with materials which made them angry (Aouragh and Alexander 2011: 1348).

An analysis of a large data set of public tweets in Tahrir Square during the period of January 24–29 shows the intensity of Twitter traffic and provides evidence that individuals, including activists and journalists, were the most influential tweet originators, rather than the organizations present at the scene. In other words, Twitter provided the technological platform for multiple individuals to rise as trendsetters in the movement. On the basis of their observation, Lotan et al. concluded that "the revolutions were indeed tweeted" (2011: 1401).

Thus the activists, as some put it, planned the protests on Facebook, coordinated them through Twitter, spread them by SMSs and webcast them to the world on YouTube. Indeed, videos of security forces treating the protesters brutally were shared via the Internet, exposing the violence of the regime in unedited form. The viral nature of these videos and the volume and speed with which news on the events in Egypt became available to the wider public in the country and in the world was key to the process of mobilization against Mubarak.

The role of pre-existing offline social networks was also important, as they helped facilitate the canvassing of pamphlets in the digitally excluded slums, and the traditional forms of social and political gatherings in the mosques after the Friday prayers. It was this multimodality of autonomous communication that broke the barriers of isolation and made it possible to overcome fear by the act of joining and sharing.

Yet, the fundamental social form of the movement was the occupation of public space. All of the other processes of network formation were ways to converge on the liberation of a given territory that escaped the authority of the state and experimented with forms of self-management and solidarity. This is why Tahrir Square was attacked repeatedly to evict the occupiers, and why it was re-occupied again and again, at the cost of pitched battles with the security forces, every time the movement felt the need to step up the pressure, first against the dictatorship, and then against the military government that appeared determined to stay in power for as long as it would need to protect its business bounty.

This communal solidarity created in Tahrir Square became a role model for the Occupy movements that would spring up in the world in the following months. This solidarity was expressed in a variety of social practices, from the self-management of the logistics of daily life during the occupation (sanitation, food and water supply, medical care, legal assistance, communication) to gestures such as the protection of the square by Christian Copts during the siege of November 21 while Muslims were in their Friday prayers.

Moreover, by creating a public space where the movement could openly exist in its diverse reality, the mainstream media could report on the protests, give a face to their protagonists and broadcast to the world what the revolution was about. As in all Arab uprisings, Al Jazeera played a major role in communicating in Arabic to the Egyptian population and to the Arab audiences at large that the unthinkable was actually happening. It contributed to a powerful demonstration effect that fed the unfolding of the uprisings in the Arab countries. While Western mainstream media lost interest in daily reporting on Egypt once Mubarak was removed from power, Al Jazeera continued to connect the Egyptian protesters to the Egyptian and Arab public opinion. The quality of Al Jazeera reporting, conducted at great risk by its journalists, was supported by the station's openness to citizen journalism. Many of the feeds and information that it broadcast came from activists on the ground and from ordinary citizens that were recording history-making with their cell phones. By broadcasting live, and by keeping a permanent focus on developments in the public space, professional mainstream media created a certain mantle of protection for the movement against violent repression, as the international supporters of Mubarak first, and of SCAF later tried to avoid embarrassment vis-à-vis global public opinion because of unjustified repressive actions of their protégés. The connection between Internet's social media, people's social networks, and mainstream media was made possible because of the existence of an occupied territory that anchored the new public space in the dynamic interaction between cyberspace and urban space. Indeed, activists created a "media camp" in Tahrir, to gather videos and pictures produced by the protesters. In one instance, they collected in a few hours 75 gigabytes of images from people in the streets. The centrality of this hybrid public space was not limited to Cairo's Tahrir Square. It was replicated in all major urban centers in which hundreds of thousands of demonstrators mobilized at different points in time during the year: Alexandria,

Mansoura, Suez, Ismailia, Tanta, Beni Suez, Dairut, Shebin-el-Kan, Luxor, Minya, Zagagig and even the Sinai peninsula where reports indicate that Bedouins battled the police for weeks, and then by themselves secured the borders of the country. The Internet revolution does not negate the territorial character of revolutions throughout history. Instead, it extends it from the space of places to the space of flows.

STATE'S RESPONSE TO AN INTERNET-FACILITATED REVOLUTION: THE GREAT DISCONNECTION

No challenge to the state's authority is left unanswered. Thus, in the case of the Arab revolutions, and in Egypt, there was outright repression, media censorship and shutdown of the Internet.

Repression cannot be sustained against a massive movement supported by communication networks under global media attention unless the government is fully unified and can operate in cooperation with influential foreign powers. Because these conditions were not met in Egypt, the regime tried both violent repression and suppression of the Internet. So doing, it attempted to do what no regime had dared before: the great disconnection, switching off Internet access in the whole country as well as mobile phone networks.[7] Because of the significance of this event for the future of Internet-based movements, and because it actually echoes the implicit or explicit wishes of most governments around the world, I will dwell with some detail on what happened, how it happened, and, most importantly, why it failed.

Beginning on the first day of protests, the Egyptian government censored the media inside Egypt and took measures to block social media websites, which had helped to call for the protest and spread news about the events on the ground.

On January 27, it blocked text messaging and BlackBerry messaging services. On the nights of January 27 and 28, the Egyptian government blocked Internet access almost entirely. There was not a central switch button to be activated. The government used a much older and more efficient technology. It placed successive telephone calls to the four biggest Internet service providers – Link Egypt, Vodafone/Raya, Telecom Egypt and Etisalat Misr – and ordered them to turn off the connections. ISP's employees accessed each one of the ISP's routers, which contained lists of all the IP addresses connected through that provider, and deleted most or all of those IP addresses, thus cutting off anyone who wanted to access them from within or outside of the country. So, each ISP did not have to physically turn off their computers; they simply had to change the code. Some 3,500 individual BGP routes were withdrawn.[8] For two more days, Noor Data Networks, connecting Cairo's stock exchange, was still functioning. When it went offline, 93 percent of the Internet traffic in or from Egypt was eliminated. The shutdown was not total because some small ISPs, particularly in academic institutions, kept working. Web connections used by the government and military were also working, using their own private ISPs. A few Egyptian users were still able to access the Internet through old dial-up connections. The European-Asia fiber optic routes through Egypt were operational, but they could not be accessed from Egypt.

However, the most important obstacle governments face when trying to shut off the Internet comes from the vigilance of the global Internet community, which includes hackers, techies, companies, defenders of civil liberties, activist networks such as Anonymous and people from around the world for whom the Internet has become a fundamental right and a way of life. This community came to the rescue of Egypt as it did with Tunisia in 2010 and Iran in 2009. Furthermore, the ingenuity of Egyptian protesters made reconnection possible within the movement, and between the movement and Egypt and the world at large.

In fact, the revolution was never incommunicable because its communication platforms were multimodal. Al-Jazeera was crucial in its continuing reporting on the uprising against the regime. The movement was kept informed by images and news received from Al Jazeera, fed from reports by telephone on the ground. When the government closed its satellite connection, other Arab satellite television networks offered Al Jazeera the use of their own frequencies. Furthermore, other traditional communication channels like fax machines, ham radio and dial-up modems helped to overcome the blocking of the Internet. Protesters distributed information about how to avoid communication controls inside Egypt. Activists provided instructions for using dial-up modems and ham radios. ISPs in France, Sweden, Spain, the US and other countries set up pools of modems that accepted international calls to channel information to and from the protesters. Companies waived fees for people to connect free of charge. The Manalaa blog gave advice to Egyptians about how to use dial-up by using a mobile phone, Bluetooth and a laptop. The advice was posted to many blogs and diffused virally.

The most important means of circumventing the blackout was the use of telephone landlines. They were not cut because countries nowadays cannot function without telephony of some kind. Using landlines, activists in Egypt reached telephone numbers abroad that would automatically forward the messages to computer networks provided by volunteers, such as those of TOR (The Onion Router network), which forwarded the messages back to Egypt by a variety of means. Using networks such as HotSpot Shield, Egyptian internauts could access proxies (alternative Internet addresses beyond the control of the government). Companies such as the French NDF offered free connection to the global Internet via a telephone call to a number in Paris. Engineers from Google and Twitter designed a speak-to-tweet program that automatically converted a voicemail message left into an answering machine accessed by a landline into a tweet. The message was then sent out as a tweet with the hashtag of the state from where the call came. Since Twitter accounts in Egypt were blocked, Twitter created a new account – @twitterglobalpr – dedicated to the speak-to-tweet system in Egypt. An international hacker organization, Telecomix, developed a program that automatically retrieved messages by phone from Egypt and forwarded them to every fax machine in the country. Many fax machines were managed from the universities that were often used as communication centers. From the universities' faxes, messages were distributed to the occupied sites. Telecomix worked on receiving and decoding amateur radio messages, sent on frequencies recommended by the group of activists. Thus an old-fashioned technology became instrumental in overcoming government censorship. Altogether, these different means added to the formation of a dense, multimodal network of communication that kept the movement connected within Egypt and with the world at large. Activists published a manual of instructions on communicating by different channels, and any information that would be forwarded by any of the multiple channels still available would be distributed by leaflets printed and handed out by people gathered in the occupied squares and demonstrations.

On February 1, Internet access in Egypt was restored. Egyptian Internet service providers (ISPs) reconfigured their core routers, letting upstream providers and other networks reestablish data pathways. The speed with which the networks reconnected (in about half an hour, Internet in

Egypt was up and running) shows that rather than physically plugging in cables, Egypt's ISPs simply let other networks' routers know about their availability using BGP or "border gateway protocol." Thus, neither the disconnection nor the reconnection was physical. There was simply a matter of re-writing the code for the routers, once the government authorized the ISPs to operate again.

But why did the government restore the Internet while the movement was still in full swing? The first reason was to contribute, under some pressure from the United States, to a "return to normal," following Mubarak's announcement that he would not seek re-election in September. An army spokesman appeared on television to ask protesters to return home and help "bring stability back to the country." There were also economic reasons. According to the Organisation for Economic Co-operation and Development (OECD), the five-day shutdown of Internet access in Egypt resulted in a loss of about US$90 million in revenue due to blocked telecommunications and Internet services, which account for around US$18 million per day; about 3 or 4 percent of Egypt's annual GDP. But this estimate did not include loss of business in other sectors affected by the shutdown such as e-commerce, tourism and call centre services. Indeed, IT outsourcing firms in Egypt account for revenues of 3 million dollars a day, and this activity had to be interrupted during the Internet disconnection. Tourism, a fundamental sector in the Egyptian economy, was severely affected by the shutdown. Furthermore, foreign direct investors would be unable to operate in a country that would cut off the Internet for a prolonged period. In short, the Internet is the lifeline of the interconnected global economy, and so its disconnection can only be exceptional and for a limited period of time.

But the fundamental reason for the restoration of the Internet is that its shutdown was ineffective in stopping the movement. On the one hand, as argued above, the black-out was circumvented in many ways with the help of the world's Internet community. On the other hand, it was too late to have a paralyzing effect on the protest movement. Urban networks had taken over the role that Internet networks had played in the origins of the protest. People were in the streets, media were reporting, and the whole world had become aware of a revolution in the making. Indeed, the revolutionary potential of the Internet can only be tamed by permanent control and surveillance, as China attempts to do on a daily basis. Once a social movement has reached a certain threshold of size and impact, closing the Internet is neither possible nor effective. In the Internet Age, tyrants will have to reckon with people's autonomous communication capacity. Unless the Internet is constantly blocked or ad hoc mechanisms are ready to operate, as in China; once the movement has extended its reach from the space of flows to the space of places, it is too late to stop it, as many other networks of communication are set up in multimodal forms.

WHO WERE THE PROTESTERS, AND WHAT WAS THE PROTEST?

Bread, Freedom, and Social Justice were the main themes of the revolution, in the words of the demonstrators that took to the streets in January 2011. They wanted to bring down Mubarak and his regime, called for democratic elections and asked for justice and redistribution of wealth. Most protesters were young, and many were college students. But this is not a biased representation of the urban population, as two-thirds of Egyptians are under the age of 30, and as the rate of unemployment among college graduates is 10 times higher than among the less-educated. Indeed, the majority of the labor force takes part in informal activities as a means of survival, so that to be truly unemployed is a luxury few can afford. The poor, who account for at least 40 percent of the population, must participate in some income-generating activity, however meager the income may be, or they would starve. But while the movement was largely enacted by an impoverished middle class longing for freedom and human rights, segments of the urban poor, desperate as a result of rising food prices, joined in. And industrial workers, with or without union support, staged a number of powerful strikes, particularly intense in Suez, leading to the occupation of the city for a few days. Some reports indicate that fear of the movement extending to the industrial labor force was a factor in influencing the business-wary Army generals to sacrifice the dictator on the altar of their own profits. The so-called pro-Mubarak masses, epitomized in the picturesque and ruthless charge of the camels on Tahrir occupiers on February 1, were in most cases connected to the *balgatiya* (gangs of thugs paid by the police) (Elmeshad and Sarant 2011). The real support for the regime was to be found among the hundreds of thousands of bureaucrats, Central security forces, policemen, informers, thugs and thieves, whose livelihood depended on the patronage networks of the dictator, his sons and their cronies. However, all of these beautiful people had to share power with the Egyptian Army, which still held some prestige among the population, as it had incarnated the nationalist movement that established modern Egypt and led the Arab world in the wars against Israel.

It was precisely the economic power struggle between the Army and Gamal's boys (the businessmen protected by Mubarak's son and heir apparent) that created the conditions for a decisive split within the ruling elites and prompted the downfall of Mubarak, his family and their clique. The Army is at the heart of a vast business empire that anchors the wealth and growth potential of the old, national Egyptian capital. The internationalization of business promoted by Gamal Mubarak since 2000, with the full support of American, British and French political leaders, threatened directly its control of the economy. Thus, when the moment came, they were not ready to sacrifice their national legitimacy and their profitable business to support an aged dictator and a potentially dangerous successor. So, they refused to open fire against the demonstrators and, in due course, arrested the Mubaraks and their accomplices. By assuming full power, the Supreme Council of the Armed Forces (SCAF) tried to appease and deactivate the revolutionary movement, draping itself in the mantle of revolution to make sure that as everything changed, everything would remain the same. However, this revolution was not a military coup. It originated from a popular uprising. And so, the more SCAF wanted to limit its measures to cosmetic changes, the more the movement pressured the new authorities, demanding retribution and prosecution of those responsible for the killings of protesters and of those who had robbed the national wealth. They stepped up demands for political freedom, democratic elections and a new Constitution. The whole of 2011 witnessed a relentless confrontation between the SCAF and the movement, while old and new political parties positioned themselves for the elections. Elections for the Constituent Parliament did take place, starting on November 28 and going on for several weeks. But it was finally accepted by SCAF only after a series of bloody confrontations between the movement and the military throughout the year, with 12,000 civilians sentenced in military courts, about 1,000 protesters killed and tens of thousands injured. But even during and after the elections, repression continued, people were imprisoned, the independent media were attacked, dissidents were tried and sentenced by military courts, Egyptian and foreign NGOs were harassed or prohibited, and dozens of demonstrators were killed in Tahrir and elsewhere. And yet, the movement did not budge in their determination to achieve full democratization of the country. The defence of the occupation of Tahrir Square, of free communication on the Internet, and of media independence, continued to be the ramparts for the conquest of freedom in a country suffering from dramatic economic and social problems.

The future of democracy is not clear, as the victory of moderate Islamists of the Muslim Brotherhood (reborn as the Freedom and Justice Party, with 45 percent of the vote), together with the 25 percent of the vote obtained for the more strictly Islamic coalition of Nour,[9] raised doubts among the Western powers about the support to be given to a democracy that could slip away from their control. With the Egyptian army receiving US$1.3 billion annually in discretionary income from the United States, the Egyptian revolution may have to confront a military counter-revolution if the movement oversteps the geopolitical limits that it has been prescribed. However, the paths of revolution are always surprising, and some of the key struggles taking place in post-Mubarak Egypt have to do less with geopolitical strategies and class interests than with the cultural transformation of the society, starting with the conquest of new autonomy by women.

WOMEN IN REVOLUTION

Women played a major role in the Egyptian revolution. The vlogs (there were four in total) that Asmaa Mahfouz posted on Facebook in January and February 2011 were influential in sparking the movement and meaningful in terms of their content and style. She was a young woman addressing, in her own name, and with her own face, the people of Egypt, and particularly men; playing the card of patriarchalism with skillful irony in asking men to join her, a girl!:

> Whoever says women shouldn't go to the protests because they will get beaten, let him have some honor and manhood, and come with me on January 25th . . . If you have honor and dignity as a man, come and protect me, and other girls in the protest.

In short, you are not a man if you do not act as men are supposed to be: courageous, protective and willing to confront the security forces to defend freedom, dignity and honor. Because:

> . . . I am going down to Tahrir Square and I will stand alone and I will hold up a banner . . . I even wrote my number so maybe people will come down with me. No one came except three guys! Three guys. Three guys, three armored cars of riot police and tens of balgatiya . . . I am making this video to give you a simple message: we are going to Tahrir on 25 January.

People ultimately did come. And on January 26 she posted a new vlog:

> The people want to bring down the regime! . . . The most beautiful thing about [the protests] is those who worked on this were not politicians at all. It was all of us, all Egyptians.

Later, she invoked God, for Muslims or Christians, and cited chapter 13, verse 11 (Surat Ar-Ra'd) of the Quran: God says he will "not change the condition of a people until they change what is in themselves."

Her influence and moral authority were precursors of

what many women bloggers would do during the revolution and what many women would suffer during the demonstrations and the attacks on Tahrir. Blogger Nawara Nagu posted on January 21 a video of a young activist saying, "Do you see this girl? She is going to demonstrate." And she did, as did thousands of others.

Many women, young and old, many with headscarves and others dressed in Western-style clothing, were present in Tahrir and other occupied spaces, some of them with their children. In many cases they led the demonstrations. They participated in the security committees and managed the field hospitals. On March 8, International Women's Day, women's rights activists marched in Tahrir asking for the end of discrimination by the state and the end of violence against women (Elwakil 2011). Some of the marchers were attacked by a large group of men.

Women were also active participants in the public debate, and there were numerous women bloggers reporting from the ground. It did not go unnoticed by the military regime. Leil Zahura Mortada, a blogger reporting from Tahrir, was abused because of her denunciations. On August 14, Asmaa Mahfouz was arrested and ordered to face a military trial, although she was released after widespread public protests against her indictment. Women were targeted, beaten and often killed during the demonstrations and assaults on Tahrir. Sally Zahran was beaten to death in one of the protests. During January and February, at least 15 women were killed. Many women arrested in the square were subjected to virginity tests, which members of the military government openly acknowledged and justified in a CNN interview, on the grounds that these women were whores. Samira Ibrahim, a 25-year-old, filed a lawsuit against the military and obtained a court ruling making the virginity tests equivalent to sexual assault.[10] On December 19, 2011, during a new assault on

Tahrir, a young woman was beaten, stripped and left unconscious, wearing only a blue bra. Women who tried to help her were attacked by the police. The video of this barbaric act of sexist violence was diffused throughout the world and prompted universal outrage, particularly among women. It came to be known as the video of the "blue bra girl." The following day, tens of thousands of women demonstrated in Tahrir, Alexandria and around Egyptian university campuses against the military violations of women's rights. From balconies, office workers clapped and cheered. Referring to the head of SCAF, they displayed a banner that read "Tantawi is the supreme commander of harassment and violation of honor." After this march, SCAF was compelled to release a hypocritical "apology to the women of Egypt."

The awakening of Egyptian women during the revolution is one of the main fears of a deeply patriarchal society, and is triggering a wave of violence against women that may increase over time. Furthermore, while women have participated side by side with men in the revolution, even calling for their protection, many of the male protesters feel uncomfortable with the agency of women, and have not helped to defend them against the targeted sadistic violence of the military police.

Indeed, in spite of their prominent role in the revolution, throughout 2011 women were all but excluded from government positions, and were confined to the last positions in the political party candidacies, so that there were only eight women among the 498 elected members of the new parliament.[11] The program of the main political force resulting from the elections, the Freedom and Justice Party, bans women from being elected president of the country.[12]

It is no wonder that a report of the Egyptian Center for Women's Rights could write at the end of 2011: "Is El-Tharir Square will remain synonym to 'the freedom, justice, and equality'?! Or the revolution will eat/sacrifice its children and the forefront of them the women?!" (Komsan 2011: 2).[13]

It appears that there is a revolution within the revolution brewing in the Egyptian uprising, as a generation of educated women (who represent the majority of college graduates) confront the ancestral limits of men's definition of what a revolution should be.

THE ISLAMIC QUESTION

The parliamentary elections of 2011 confirmed the resilience of Islamic political forces in Egypt. The old Muslim Brotherhood survived decades of repression from nationalist, military regimes and, renamed as the Freedom and Justice Party, obtained a majority of seats in the Parliament. It benefitted from strong organization, political experience and a certain aura of resistance against the regime in large segments of the population. The more strictly Islamist coalition of Noor, dominated by the Salafists, secured 25 percent of the vote. This is a clear indication of the widespread sympathy for Islamism among the population at large. Indeed, in practically all Arab countries, there is a potential Islamic political majority that was held in check by force from nationalist authoritarian leaders backed by the army and the Western powers. Arab nationalism, invoking the anti-colonial nation-state, in spite of rhetorical religious references when the need arose, and Islamism, invoking the *ummah* (universal community of believers beyond the nation) and the *Sharia* (law inspired by God, not by the state), have been locked in a confrontation that evolved towards the defeat of nationalism in people's minds when it became subordinated to foreign powers and when corruption and brutality became the distinctive features of these regimes.

Islamism was widely seen by many in Egypt and elsewhere as a force of regeneration of politics, of hope for social justice, and of restoration of moral values. The unconditional support of foreign powers for Arab military regimes was precisely predicated on their fear of Islamism as a threat to oil supply and Israel's security. Thus, as expected, processes of democratization in the Arab world usually result in the hegemony of Islamism in the political system, as secular, progressive political forces have limited appeal beyond the small segments of Westernized elites. Yet, for Islamists to come to power, with the consent of the Army and without the opposition of the secular segments of the revolutionary movement, they had to moderate their religious standing. And they have done so. The program of the Freedom and Justice Party, and the public statements of its leaders, accept the principles of democracy, and focus on addressing the immense social and economic problems of the country. They do not oppose the notion of a secular state. At the same time, it is the stated goal of the party to govern, if they ever come to power, according to the Sharia law, but they emphasize that the meaning of this orientation is misunderstood in the West. It does not mean, in their view, to impose a theocracy, and they explicitly reject the Iranian model (Adib and Waziri 2011).[14] It simply means that they will find inspiration for their policies in the Quran, in the same way, they argue, European Christian Democrats try to follow Christian principles in the conduct of public affairs. This has serious implications for women and Copts, as the Freedom and Justice Party will not accept either as president of the country. However, even in this matter, they would still accept women or Copts in the government cabinet, a policy that is a long way from strict Muslim orthodoxy.[15] Furthermore, in foreign policy the Brothers have stated their commitment to respecting the existing treaties between Egypt and Israel, a "must" condition from the perspective of the United States, the supervisory power in the country, via the Egyptian army on its payroll (Adib and Waziri 2011).[16]

In sum, for the Muslim Brotherhood, Islam and democracy are fully compatible, as shown in the example of Turkey, albeit they concede that contexts are different, and they do not identify with Erdogan. While the Muslim Brotherhood has been often accused of being opportunistic, in reality they have had no other choice. Neither the army nor its Western sponsors will accept a radical Islamic state in Egypt. Thus, any consolidation of a democratic regime in Egypt will imply a moderate Islamic government at the helm. A different matter is the significant groundswell of support for the Salafists, whose uncompromising stand on the primacy of Sharia over civilian power could evolve into a full-scale confrontation against both the army and the secular wing of the revolutionary movement. If the economic situation continues to deteriorate, the religious fundamentalist way out of a Westernized regime could open a new chapter in the process of political change in Egypt.

However, while trying to understand the Egyptian revolution, it should be clear that neither in the origin nor in the process of transformation of the 2011 revolution was there any dominance of Islamism or Islamic themes. To be sure, Islamists from all tendencies, and particularly young Islamists, actively participated in the demonstrations, in the occupation of Tahrir and other public places, and in the deliberation over the Internet. But there were no direct religious confrontations (the attack on the Copts was a police provocation), and there was respectful sharing of the goals and practice of the revolution. During the 18 days that launched the revolution, the Muslim Brotherhood called for the departure of Mubarak, but always referred to the movement as the source of legitimacy of the protest. It was of course an intelligent tactic, as the call for democracy and parliamentary elections could well position the Brothers to access power on the grounds of popular support. Yet, it remains that neither the Brotherhood nor the Salafists were successful in controlling or leading the movement. They were a part of the movement, but they were not the movement. The Egyptian revolution was not and is not an Islamic revolution, even if it may have created the conditions for a democratic way towards an Islamic-dominated polity in the country. The networks formed around Islamism networked with networks constituted around the goals of political freedom and social justice, all converging towards the struggle for democracy, first against Mubarak and then against the SCAF, whose bloody repression to the movement could not stifle a revolution spoken in multiple voices.

"THE REVOLUTION WILL CONTINUE"

The Supreme Council of the Armed Forces attempted to capture the revolution for its own benefit by using even harsher repression than the Mubarak regime, once it become clear that the movement that toppled the dictatorship, in its multifaceted composition, would not accept a change of rulers without a change of rules. The military even tried to impose a document (known as the Selmi document from the name of the Deputy Prime Minister) as a guideline for the Constitution to be elaborated in 2012 by the new Parliament, before the Parliament was elected. It basically gave full control of the state and limitless autonomy to the Armed Forces. The uproar against this blatant attack on future democratic institutions unified all components of the movement in their opposition, including the Muslim Brotherhood, which for the first time had broken up openly with the generals. On November 18, a massive protest against SCAF took place in

Tahrir. On November 19, Central Security forces, the elite of former Mubarak's police, attacked Tahrir Square, occupied only by a small group of people. Media and the Internet came to the rescue and thousands rushed to defend the liberated public space. It followed a five day pitched battle in the streets of Cairo that left at least 42 people killed and 3,000 wounded. The prime minister resigned, but he was replaced by a former Mubarak minister. It became clear that the military council incarnated a new form of dictatorship, and the movement switched from the old unifying slogan of "Down with the Mubarak regime" to "Down with military rule." Women marched under a banner proclaiming "You Won't Intimidate Us." Fear had been overcome forever. Networks of outrage had multiplied with the savage repression against all forms of criticism of the new powers: in the media, in the streets and in the military courts, with women being particularly targeted. On January 20, 2012, Joda Elsadda, from the Women's Media Center, wrote:

> The current slogan is "the revolution will continue" because the job is not done. We may have deposed Mubarak, but the regime, led by the SCAF, is still intact. In the early days of the revolution, the military appeared to side with the people; today the people are against the SCAF and military rule. Why? Because the SCAF is trying to reinstate the old regime and people have lost faith in its ability to transition Egypt to a democratic future (2012: 1).

While the army was a far more formidable adversary than Mubarak himself, the strength of the movement was much greater than one year earlier, because the networks of solidarity and mobilization were now in place, and active, on the Internet, in the squares, in the streets, in a blossoming civil society, and in a diverse, and vital, new political sphere, with multiple parties. One year of deception and repression had not weakened the determination of a movement that had begun to envision a revolution capable of ushering in real democracy.

UNDERSTANDING THE EGYPTIAN REVOLUTION

The Egyptian revolution of 2011 altered power relationships in the country, brought down the Mubarak dictatorship and continued to fight with determination the reincarnation of oppression in the form of a military regime. To understand how it could happen after decades of ruthless domination and the repeated crushing of the resistance that took place in many instances, we have to go back to the theory of power and counterpower presented at the onset of this book.

Power is exercised by a combination of coercion and intimidation with persuasion and consensus building. The monopoly of violence is a necessary condition for holding power, but not a sufficient one in the long run. It requires the construction of legitimacy, or of acceptance and resignation, in people's minds. In modern Egypt the power of the state (the decisive agency in the country) was originally based on selective legitimacy and targeted repression. The rise of Nasserism, as the harbinger of Arab nationalism, provided a mantle of legitimacy to a populist regime, and to an army geared for the decisive battle with Zionism. Yet, at the same time nationalism was determined to suppress the main alternative source of legitimacy: Islamic influence, politically represented by the Muslim Brotherhood, and a few influential Islamic intellectuals, some of whom, like Sayyid Qtub, were executed. They were the enemy, and they were prosecuted to the end, while official religious leaders were co-opted into the regime. Repression worked as long as it was concentrated on one particular segment of polity. But legitimacy was eroded by military failure and the fall of Nasser, and more importantly by the inability of a statist economy to adapt to the new environment of economic globalization. Moreover, whatever development was generated was appropriated by the regime's crony capitalists, by the top brass of the military, and by high-level government bureaucrats. Widespread poverty and the deterioration of living standards for an increasingly educated middle class prompted many youth to turn to Islamism, both in its moderate and radical versions. Elections were introduced as an image-making ploy to satisfy the new, Western allies of the regime, but each time that independent candidates (Islamic or secular) had some success, they were dismissed or curtailed in their voice and in their vote. In the first decade of the twenty-first century, the monopoly of violence, and the actual use of violence with total impunity, became the main pillar sustaining the regime.

But there is more complexity to be accounted for. Power is multidimensional. Each one of the dimensions (economic, political, military, ideological, cultural) is enacted by specific networks of power. Yet, for power to be sustainable, it is essential that several of the key networks network with each other, with the help of switchers that establish the connection. In the case of Egypt, the military was always the key network of power but it remained autonomous while holding decisive power in the state. Mubarak was the chief of the prestigious Air Force, and as such he became the switcher between the state and the armed forces, and took control of the bureaucracy and of the NDP, the official party. The state generated its own network of bureaucracies (including the police) through which power was exercised over society. Economic power was in the hands of business elites that were traditionally dependent on the state and on the military, although in the last decade, globalized businesses, including foreign companies, built their own connections to the regime, gaining autonomy because of their international reach. Religious power was integrated and/or repressed depending on its level of submission to the state. Media were censored and controlled, although multiple private satellite television channels provided an opening that would become decisive in the crisis of the regime. The other fundamental network to which the state had to connect was the geopolitical network. After the fall of Nasser and the assassination of Sadat, the influence of the Soviet Union all but disappeared. Mubarak added to his switching capacities a privileged connection to the United States. This was a fundamental source of stability for the dictatorship both in terms of fake democratic credentials, and in its ability to withstand economic difficulties and domestic challenges.

This complex network of power networks is what the social protesters and political opponents of the regime had to face in 2005, in 2008 and in 2010, with the ensuing outcome of their submission by force. Any semblance of legitimacy or consensus had disappeared among the overwhelming majority of Egyptians. But fear was instilled in their minds, and in the minds of the few opponents who dared to use institutional openings to counter the dictator. No organized opposition could match the formidable repressive machine networked with all domestic and international sources of power in a maze of intertwined economic, geopolitical, political and personal interests.

Then, the revolution happened, without warning and strategy, as the first calls for demonstrations were not different from those that took place in previous years, only to be easily dissolved by thugs and police. Why? Because fear had been overcome by large numbers. How? And why then? People overcome fear by being together. And they were, in the Internet social networks and in the urban networks formed in the squares. But to come together in throngs they needed a strong motivation, a mobilizing force. Outrage induces fearless risk-taking, and there was extreme outrage against police abuse, against hunger rising in the country and against the desperation that led people to immolate themselves. However, outrage had been there for quite a long time. The key difference was that another potent, positive emotion was present: Hope. Tunisia epitomized the hope for change. It showed that it was possible to topple a well-entrenched regime if everybody would come together and fight uncompromisingly, to the end, regardless of the risks. The Internet provided the safe space where networks of outrage and hope connected. Networks formed in cyberspace extended their reach to urban space, and the revolutionary community formed in public squares this time successfully resisted police repression, and connected through multimedia networks with the Egyptian people and with the world. Tahrir was the switcher that linked together the multiple networks of counterpower in spite of their diversity. Under the pressure of grassroots resistance and international public opinion, the switches connecting the networks of power were turned off, one after another, from the central connector, the dictator and his clique at the top of the state. First, and foremost, the army regained its autonomy trying to preserve remnants of its legitimacy and to recover control of the country by disconnecting the dictator and the police from the military network. The business elites split, with domestic groups siding with the army, a major business group in itself, against the growing threat of globalized business led by Gamal's boys. While the state media remained until the last minute in the hands of the censors, segments of the media, particularly private television channels, global satellite channels and Internet companies, disconnected themselves from the media networks that were appendages of state power. The political networks of the state (and particularly the official party) lost any capacity to influence people without the backing of decisive force, and so they remained in the state but isolated from key sources of economic, military or cultural power.

Most importantly: the geopolitical network, dominated by the United States, switched off its connection with Mubarak's network to strengthen its privileged connection with the military network. Obama's Cairo speech calling the Arab world to embrace and mobilize for democracy, and Hillary Clinton's speech in January 2010 arguing for the democratizing role of the Internet in the world, could not be openly contradicted by continuing support for a shaken dictator. Thus, the last critical switching off, the one from the geopolitical network, left Mubarak's state disconnected from any significant source of power, other than its central security forces and the camelback brigade of the *bagatiya*.

By connecting networks of counterpower, the protesters became powerful enough to induce the disconnection between major networks of power, weakening the system of domination and making violence an increasingly difficult means of keeping the country under control. This is why the military network, and its connected geopolitical network, tried to regain legitimacy by apparently moving towards democratic elections, legalizing Islamic political forces, promising a new constitution, and prosecuting the dictator and a few individuals of his immediate clique. However, the military quickly moved to switch all the networks of power, including the new network of parliamentary politics, around its command and control capacities, thus voiding in practice the promise of democracy. As the networks of counterpower remained fully active, and since they had broadened their connections internationally and nationally, the military went back to stern repression as a way of political life. Indeed, 2011 was a much more bloody and repressive year than any of the preceding years under Mubarak. Accordingly, the military lost the last of their legitimacy, and set the stage for a long, protracted battle between the networks of power and counterpower formed in the process of the Egyptian revolution.

NOTES

1 For a detailed account of the background and events of the January 2011 revolution in Egypt, see Mona El-Ghobashy, "The praxis of the Egyptian Revolution," in MER258, Middle East Research and Information Project (2011) (www.merip.org/mer/mer258/praxis-egyptian-revolution).

2 Official website for the 6 April Movement (in Arabic): <http://6april.org>. Esraa Abdel Fattah Ahmed Rashid was one of the co-founders of the movement who later split from the group. See PBS's Frontline "Inside April 6th Movement" for further details: <http://www. pbs.org/wgbh/pages/frontline/revolution-in-cairo/inside-april6-movement/>.

3 In summer of 2009, Adel traveled to Serbia to study non-violent strategies for revolution. "What Egypt learned from the students who overthrew Milosevic" by Tina Roseberg for *Foreign Policy* (<http://www.foreignpolicy. com/articles/2011/02/16/revolution_u?page=full>) and PBS's Frontline Profile page on the 6 April Movement from "Revolution in Cairo" documentary <http://www. pbs.org/wgbh/pages/frontline/revolution-in-cairo/inside-april6-movement/>.

4 On the "Silent Revolution" envisioned by "We are All Khaled Said" group members: "Reclaiming Silence in

Egypt" by Adel Iskandar, *Egypt Independent*, July 22, 2010, <http://www.egyptindependent.com/node/58021>.

5 The significant role of al-Ahly soccer club fans in the protests against Mubarak was not forgotten by the central security police. On February 1, 2012, in a game in Port Said between the local team and al-Ahly, hundreds of armed thugs, posing as fans of the Port Said team attacked the players and fans of al-Ahly without any opposition from the police present in the stadium. Seventy four people were killed and hundreds wounded. The obvious complicity of the old Mubarak's police, and the permissiveness of the military regime in the aggression, led to violent demonstrations in Cairo on February 2 and 3, with thousands charging police buildings branding the flag of al-Ahly. Several people were killed and hundreds wounded.

6 There were some tensions among Copts and radical Islamic groups during the occupation in Tahrir square. But the sharing of risks and goals in the movement created an atmosphere of tolerance and cooperation between Muslims, Copts and seculars. For instance, on February 6, 2011, a multi-faith mass was celebrated in Tahrir, with thousands of believers attending. There was, however, one major incident of violence against the Copts on October 9, during a demonstration by Copts in front of the State television building to protest against media reporting, and asking for the resignation of Tantawi, head of the Supreme Council of the Armed Forces, with the result of 25 demonstrators killed and 200 wounded. The media tried to portray the attack as conducted by Islamists, but reliable sources pointed out the police responsibility in planning the attack to stir sectarian violence. On November 21, while Muslims in Tahrir were in their Friday prayers, Copts kept guarding

the square against potential attackers, in a clear sign of inter-religious solidarity.

7 Egypt's great disconnection was an entirely different situation from the limited Internet manipulation that took place in Tunisia, where only specific routes were blocked, or Iran, where the Internet stayed up in a rate-limited form designed to make Internet connectivity extremely slow. Disconnecting the Internet in Egypt was relatively easy, compared with what would be necessary in democratic countries. In Egypt there were only four major ISPs, each of which had relatively few routers connecting them to the outside world. A similar shutting down of the Internet in the United States would have to deal with many different companies. And while Egypt can legally disable telecom companies by decree, US regulations limit the federal government's power to intervene in communication channels. However, we should be aware that members of the US Congress have proposed making plans for a "kill switch" that would shut down the Internet at the push of a button in the case of a "cybersecurity emergency."

8 BGP (border gateway protocol) is the protocol at the heart of the Internet's routing mechanism, and is used by routers to share information about the paths data traffic uses to "hop" from one network to another as it moves from a source to its destination.

9 Al-Nour Party official website, "FAQ" (<http://www.alnourparty.org/page/answer>) and "Who we are" (<http://www.alnourparty.org/about>).

10 Flock, E. (2011) Samira Ibrahim is the woman behind Egypt's ban of virginity tests. *The Washington Post.* <http://www.washingtonpost.com/blogs/blogpost/post/samira-ibrahim-is-the-woman-behind-egypts-ban-of-virginity-tests/2011/12/27/gIQACKNgKP_blog.html>.

11 Moore, H. (2012) Experts weigh in on low female representation in parliament. *Daily News Egypt*. <http://www.thedailynewsegypt.com/egypt-elections-2011/experts-weigh-in-on-low-female-representation-in-parliament.html>.

12 *Egyptian Independent*. (2011) Brotherhood sticks to ban on Christians and women for presidency. <http://www.egyptindependent.com/node/352738>.

13 Komsan, N.A. (ed.) (2011) Press Release: Women's Status Report of 2011: The Egyptian Women between the Wings of the Revolution and Stripping the Reality. *The Egyptian Center for Women's Rights*. <https://docs.google.com/viewer?url=http%3A%2F%2Fwww.ecwronline.org%2Fenglish%2Fpress%2520reless%2F2011%2FPress%2520Release-%2520English-%2520Women's%2520Status%2520Report%25202011.pdf>.

14 Adib, M. and Waziri, H. (2011) The Brotherhood in their first TV appearance: "We are not opportunists and reject the Iranian Model." *Al-Masry Al-Youm*. <http://www.almasry-alyoum.com/article2.aspx?ArticleID=288427>.

15 *Egyptian Independent*. (2011) Muslim Brotherhood to establish "Freedom and Justice Party." <http://www.egyptindependent.com/node/325599>.

16 Adib, M. and Waziri, H. (2012) The Brotherhood: "We respect all the treaties signed Between Egypt and Israel." *Al-Masry Al-Youm*. <http://www.almasry-alyoum.com/article2.aspx?ArticleID=288347>.

REFERENCES AND SOURCES

Note: The titles of texts originally written in Arabic and used as sources have been translated into English for the convenience for the reader. The referred texts are in Arabic.

On the background and events of the Egyptian revolution

6 April Youth Movement (Official Site). (2011) <http://6april. org/>.

Al Jazeera, Arabic. (2011a) Egyptian protests continue and high death toll. <http://www.aljazeera.net/news/ pages/585df5cd-4ee1-46d3-ae2e-bb82d15221ce>.

Al Jazeera, Arabic. (2011b) Dead and wounded: Demonstrations in Egypt. <http://aljazeera.net/news/ pages/9b5f8d6d-afed-4584-a502-cabf184ec070>.

Al Jazeera, Arabic. (2011c) Round up: Developments in Egypt. <http://aljazeera.net/news/pages/fc20dc11-146b-4081-b745-a1222bba2953>.

Al Jazeera, Arabic. (2011d). Mobilization of two million in Tahrir Square. <http://www.aljazeera.net/news/pages/ b35ad6ba-80e2-4105-a310-35b980547b04>.

Al Jazeera, English. (2011) Timeline: Egypt's Revolution. <http://www.aljazeera.com/news/middleeast/2011/01/201 112515334871490.html>.

Al-Khalsan, M. (2011) The Army and the economy in Egypt. *Jadaliyya*. Available at: <http://www.jadaliyya.com/pages/ index/3732/the-army-and-the-economy-in-egypt>.

Cook, S. O. (2011) *The Struggle for Egypt: from Nasser to Tahrir Square*. Oxford University Press, Oxford.

El-Gobashy, M. (2011) The praxis of the Egyptian Revolution. *Middle East Report*, Spring edition (volume 41) (MER258).

Elmeshad, M. & Sarant, L. (2011) Violence erupts as pro-Mubarak forces pour into Tahrir. *Al Masry Al Youm*. <http://www.almasryalyoum.com/node/308110> (Arabic).

Ghonim, W. (2012) *Revolution 2.0: The Power of the People is Greater than the People in Power. A Memoir*. Houghton-Mifflin-Harcourt, Boston, MA.

Hosni Mubarak announced that he would step down and hand over power to the Supreme Council of Armed Forces. (2011) *Al Arabiya*. <http://www.alarabiya.net/arti cles/2011/02/11/137168.html>.

Kouddous, S. A. (2012) Tahrir one year later: The fight for Egypt's future. *The Nation*, [online]. Available at: <http://www.thenation.com/article/165735/tahrir-one-year-later-fight-egypts-future>.

Shatz. A. (2012) Whose Egypt? *London Review of Books*, January [online]. Available at: <http://www.lrb.co.uk/v34/n01/adam-shatz/whose-egypt>.

PBS Frontline. (2011a) Inside April 6th Movement. *Revolution in Cairo*. <http://www.pbs.org/wgbh/pages/frontline/revolution-in-cairo/inside-april6-movement>.

PBS Frontline. (2011b) "Day to Day" Timeline. <http://www.pbs.org/wgbh/pages/frontline/revolution-in-cairo/d ay-to-day>.

On the interaction between Internet networks, social networks, and public space in the process of the revolution

Allagui, I. and Kuebler, J. (2011). The Arab Spring and the role of ICTs. *International Journal of Communication*. [Online] Vol. 5, 1435–42. Available at: <http://ijoc.org/ojs/index.php/ijoc/article/view/1392/616>.

Aouragh, M. and Alexander, A. (2011). The Egyptian experience: Sense and nonsense of the Internet Revolution. *International Journal of Communication*. [Online] Vol. 5, 1344–58. Available at: <http://ijoc.org/ojs/index.php/ijoc/article/view/1191/610>.

Eltantawy, N. and Wiest, J. B. (2011) Social media in the Egyptian Revolution: reconsidering resource mobilization theory. *International Journal of Communication*. [Online]

Vol. 5, 1207–24. Available at: <http://ijoc.org/ojs/index. php/ijoc/article/view/1242/597>.

Harlow, S. and Johnson, T. (2011) Overthrowing the protest paradigm? How the New York Times, Global Voices and Twitter covered the Egyptian Revolution. *International Journal of Communication*. [Online] Vol. 5, 1359–74. Available at: <http://ijoc.org/ojs/index.php/ijoc/article/ view/1239/611>.

Iskander, E. (2011) Connecting the national and the virtual: Can Facebook activism remain relevant after Egypt's January 25 uprising? *International Journal of Communication*. [Online] Vol. 5, 1225–37. Available at: <http://ijoc.org/ ojs/index.php/ijoc/article/view/1165/598>.

Lotan, G., Graeff, E., Ananny, M., Gaffney, D., Pearce, I. & boyd, d. (2011) The revolutions were tweeted: Information flows during the 2011 Tunisian and Egyptian revolutions. *International Journal of Communication*. [Online] Vol. 5, 1375–405. Available at: <http://ijoc.org/ojs/index.php/ ijoc/article/view/1246>.

Rinke, E. M. and Röder, M. (2011) Media ecologies, communication culture, and temporal-spatial unfolding: Three components in a communication model of the Egyptian regime change. *International Journal of Communication*. [Online] Vol. 5, 1273–85. Available at: <http://ijoc.org/ ojs/index.php/ijoc/article/view/1173/603>.

Russell, A. (2011) Extra-national information flows, social media, and the 2011 Egyptian uprising. *International Journal of Communication*. [Online] Vol. 5, 1375–405. Available at: <http://ijoc.org/ojs/index.php/ijoc/article/view/93/630>.

Wall, M. and El Zahed, S. (2011) "I'll Be Waiting for You Guys": A YouTube Call to Action in the Egyptian Revolution. *International Journal of Communication*. [Online] Vol. 5, 1333–43. Available at: <http://ijoc.org/ ojs/index.php/ijoc/article/view/1241/609>.

On media in the Egyptian Revolution

Iskandar, A. (2012) A year in the life of Egypt's media: A 2011 Timeline. *Jadaliyya*. <http://www.jadaliyya.com/pages/index/3642/a-year-in-the-life-of-egypts-media_a-2011-tim eline>.

On women in the Egyptian Revolution

Abdel-Fattah, B. (2012) Egyptian women victims of the revolution and the election. *Al Jazeera, Arabic*. <http://www.aljazeera.net/NR/EXERES/4A52E5A7-B70A-4CD 6-B64A-83B12CADC5CA.htm>.

Carr, S. (2011) Women march against SCAF brutality, hope for a nascent movement. *Al-Masry Al-Youm*. <http://www.almasryalyoum.com/en/node/559926>.

Egyptian Center for Women's Rights, Arabic. <http://www.ecwronline.org/>.

Egyptian Center for Women's Rights, English. <http://www.ecwronline.org/english/index.html>.

Elsadda, H. (2012) Exclusive Egypt – the revolution will continue. *The Women's Media Center*. Available at: <http://www.womensmediacenter.com/feature/entry/egypt-the-revolution-will-continue>.

Elwakil, M. (2011) Women's demo outlines controversial demands. *Egypt Independent*, March 8. <http://www.egyptindependent.com/node/344981>.

Komsan, N. A. (ed.) (2011) The Egyptian women between the wings of the revolution and stripping the reality. Press Release: The Status of Egyptian Women in 2011. *The Egyptian Center for Women's Rights*. Available at: <http://www.ecwronline.org/english/press%20reless/2011/Press%20Release-%20English-%20Women's%20Status%20Rep ort%202011.pdf>.

On political Islamism in Egypt

Adib, M. & Waziri, H. (2011a) The Brotherhood Renewed Demands for Mubarak's Departure and For a Peaceful Transition of Power. *Al-Masry Al-Youm*. <http://www. almasry-alyoum.com/article2.aspx?ArticleID=287453>.

Adib, M. & Waziri, H. (2011b) The Brotherhood in their first TV appearance: "We are not opportunists and reject the Iranian Model." *Al-Masry Al-Youm*. <http://www. almasry-alyoum.com/article2.aspx?ArticleID=288427>.

Adib, M. & Waziri, H. (2012) The Brotherhood: "We respect all the treaties signed between Egypt and Israel." *Al-Masry Al-Youm*. <http://www.almasry-alyoum.com/ article2.aspx?ArticleID=288347>.

Al-Nour Party, Arabic site. (2012a) <http://www.alnour-party.org>.

Al-Nour Party, Arabic site. (2012b) Who we are. <http:// www.alnourparty.org/about>.

Al-Nour Party, Arabic site. (2012c) FAQ. <http://www. alnourparty.org/page/answer>.

Ashour, A. (2011) Islamist parties in Turkey. *AL-AHRAM*. <http://weekly.ahram.org.eg/2011/1072/op42.htm>.

Bokhari, K. and Senzai, F. (2011) The many shades of Islamist. *The Huffington Post*. <http://www.huffingtonpost.com/ kamran-bokhari/the-many-shades-of-islami_b_1102063. html>.

Egypt Independent. (2011) Muslim Brotherhood to establish "Freedom and Justice Party." <http://www.egyptinde-pendent.com/node/325599>.

El-Shobaki, Amr. (2011) Where does the Brotherhood's strength lie? *Egypt Independent*. <http://www.egyptinde-pendent.com/node/470381>.

Freedom and Justice Party ("hurryh"), Arabic site. <http:// www.hurryh.com>.

Freedom and Justice Party, English site. <http://www.fjp online.com>.

Iskander, A. (2010) "We are All Khaled Said" group members: Reclaiming silence in Egypt. *Egypt Independent.* <http://www.egyptindependent.com/node/58021>.

Muslim Brotherhood, Arabic site. <http://www.ikhwan online.com>.

Muslim Brotherhood, English site. <http://www.ikhwanweb. com>.

Party Platforms 2011. (2011) <http://www.fjponline.com/ articles.php?pid=80>.

On the relationship between Arab nationalism and political Islam

See my analysis on the issue, which provides the backdrop for the interpretation presented here:

Castells, M. (2010) *The Power of Identity*. Blackwell, Oxford, pp. 13–23.

See also:

Carre, O. (2004) *Le nationalisme arabe*. Payot, Paris.

Keppel, G. (2008) *Beyond Terror and Martyrdom: the Future of the Middle East*. Harvard University Press, Cambridge, MA.

Roy, O. (2007) *Secularism Confronts Islam*. Columbia University Press, New York.

DIGNITY, VIOLENCE, GEOPOLITICS:

THE ARAB UPRISINGS[1]

The Arab world is today witnessing the birth of a new
world, which tyrants and unjust rulers strive to oppose. But
in the end, this new world will inevitably emerge ... Our
oppressed people have revolted, declaring the emergence of
a new dawn in which the sovereignty of the people, and
their invincible will, will prevail. The people have decided
to break free and walk in the footsteps of civilized free
people of the world.

> Tawakkol Karman, statement on the occasion of
> receiving the 2011 Nobel Peace Prize for her work
> on peace and justice in Yemen and among Arab
> women at large.[2]

In the wake of the Tunisian and Egyptian revolutions,
Days of Rage (*Youm al-Ghadab*) surged across the Arab
world in 2011: January 7 in Algeria, January 12 in Lebanon,
January 14 in Jordan, January 17 in Mauritania, January
17 in Sudan, January 17 in Oman, January 27 in Yemen,

February 14 in Bahrain, February 17 in Libya, February 18 in Kuwait, February 20 in Morocco, February 26 in the Western Sahara, March 11 in Saudi Arabia, March 18 in Syria. In a few instances (Saudi Arabia, Lebanon, Kuwait and the United Arab Emirates, where little happened in fact), the protest fizzled out for a variety of causes.[3] In others, uprisings were quelled by a mixture of repression and concession from the regimes (Morocco, Jordan, Algeria, Oman), although the ashes of the movements are still hot and could be rekindled at any moment. In Bahrain, a Saudi Arabia-backed savage repression crushed in blood a massive, peaceful movement largely made out of the Shia population in the "Bloody Thursday" of February 17. In Yemen, Libya and Syria, initially peaceful movements were met with utmost violence from the dictatorships, degenerating in civil wars that transformed these countries into battlefields where geopolitical contenders fought to assert their influence. Indeed, foreign direct military intervention was decisive in Libya and foreign geopolitical influence became an essential factor in the evolution of the Syrian uprising. These various movements emerged from causes specific to each country, and evolved according to the conditions of their contexts and to the idiosyncrasies of each revolt. However, they were all spontaneous uprisings stimulated by the hope inspired by the success of the Tunisian and Egyptian revolutions, conveyed by images and messages arriving from the Internet and from Arab satellite television networks. Without any doubt, the spark of indignation and hope that was born in Tunisia and had brought down the Mubarak regime, bringing in a democratic Tunisia and a proto-democratic Egypt, extended quickly to other Arab countries, following the same model: calls on the Internet, networking in cyberspace and calls to occupy urban space to put pressure on the government to resign and open a process of democratization, from the Pearl

Roundabout in Bahrain to "Change Square" in Saana, or squares in Casablanca and Amman. States all over the Arab world reacted in different ways, from slight liberalization to bloody repression, out of fear of losing power. The interaction between the protests and the regimes depended on internal and geopolitical conditions.

To be sure, there were deep-seated grievances among a population that had been submitted to political oppression and kept in dire economic conditions for decades, without a chance to claim their rights under the threat of arbitrary violence from the state.[4] Furthermore, the majority of these countries' populations were composed of people under 30 years of age, many of them relatively educated, and most of them unemployed or underemployed. These youth were familiar with the use of digital communication networks, as the penetration of mobile phones exceeded 100 percent in half of the Arab countries, with most others over the 50 percent mark, and many in the urban centers had some form of access to social media (Howard 2011). Moreover, they felt daily humiliation in their lives, void of opportunities in their society and participation in their polity. They were ready to rise for their dignity, a more potent motivation than anything else. Some had done so in the last decade, only to be met with violence, imprisonment and often death. Then, the spark of outrage and the light of hope came to them simultaneously. The hope was provided by other Arab youth, like themselves, who had risen up in other countries, particularly in Egypt, known in the Arab cultural imagination as *um al-dunya* ("mother of the world"). The spark resulted from specific events in each country: self-immolations and symbolic martyrdoms as a form of protest, images of police torture and beatings of peaceful demonstrators, assassinations of human rights advocates and popular bloggers. These were no Islamists, or leftist revolutionaries, although anyone with a project to change society eventually participated in the movement. Initially they were of a middle class background,[5] albeit usually an impoverished middle class, and many were women. They were later joined by poor people hit by inflation and unable to buy their daily food staples as a result of policies of economic liberalization and the subjugation of their countries to increased food prices in the world market.[6] Dignity and bread were the original drivers of most movements, together with housing demands in the case of Algeria. But asking for bread meant actually to reverse economic policies, and to end corruption as a way of governance. The assertion of dignity became a cry for democracy. Thus all movements became political movements, asking for democratic reforms.

The evolution of each movement largely depended on the reaction of the state. When governments showed some semblance of accommodation to their demands, and hinted at political liberalization, movements were channeled into a process of democratization of the state within the limits of maintaining the essence of elite domination. Thus King Abdullah II in Jordan sacked his prime minister and dismissed his cabinet (the target of the protest against economic policies), establishing mechanisms of consultation with citizens, particularly with representatives of the Bedouin tribes. King Mohammed VI of Morocco proposed a few democratizing amendments in the Constitution, including a transfer of the power to appoint members of parliament to the prime minister. The amendments were approved by referendum in July 2011 with 98.5 percent voting in favor. He also freed dozens of political prisoners and held new elections on November 25, 2011 that saw the victory of Islamist candidates (most of them moderate), as in all other free elections held in the Arab world in recent years.

However, when the regimes resisted the demands for

political reform and resorted to sheer repression, the movements shifted from reform to revolution and engaged in a process of overthrowing the dictatorships. In such process, the interplay of internal factionalism and geopolitical influences led to bloody civil wars whose differential outcome is redefining the politics of the Arab world in the coming years.

VIOLENCE AND THE STATE

When states are challenged in their power, they respond according to their institutional rules, be they democratic, dictatorial, or a mix of both. When they fail to integrate the demands or projects of their challengers without jeopardizing the fundamentals of the power relationships they embody, they resort to their ultimate essence: their monopoly of violence in their sphere of action. Their willingness to use extreme violence depends on the extent of their legitimacy, the intensity of the challenge they have to face, and their operational and social capacity to use violence. When movements are determined enough to keep up their relentless pressure on the state regardless of the violence they endure, and the state resorts to extreme violence (tanks against unarmed demonstrators), the outcome of the conflict depends on the interplay between political interests in the country and geopolitical interests related to the country.

In Yemen, a fractured state, in a barely unified nation, split under the assault of a massive, variegated movement, with one part of the army siding with the demonstrators in their demand concerning the resignation of dictator Ali Abdullah Saleh. The tribal nature of Yemen, and the secessionist movements in the North and the South, led to a stalemate between Saleh, backed by Saudi Arabia, and the democratic movement calling for a new constitution and true democracy. The suspected presence of Al Qaeda, with greater intensity than in any other country, prompted the US to extreme caution, so that in spite of some rhetoric of support for the movement, the American diplomacy left the Saudis in charge of a controlled political transition. In February 2012, under a brokered agreement, Saleh stepped down after three decades in power, and his vice president, Abd Rabbuh Mansur al-Hadi, ran for an election that he won with 99.8 percent of the vote . . . to be continued.

In Libya, the nation-state, while incarnating the messianic pan-Africanist project of its charismatic founder, expressed in reality the domination of Western tribes over Eastern tribes. Ruthless suppression of any attempt from the Bengazhi elites or from subdued tribes to claim their share of the bounty of oil and gas, mainly found in the Eastern desert, led to the concentration of power in Gaddafi's family, their tribal supporters and a small circle of the elites in the Western areas of the country. Power was exercised by the control of a well-equipped, well-trained praetorian guard, backed when necessary by mercenaries from other countries. Thus, there was not a real national army that could embody the institutions of the nation independently of the designs of the dictator and his clique. The Libyan state was largely a patrimonial state. This meant that, on the one hand, large segments of the population, particularly in the East, were excluded from the riches of energy revenues. On the other hand, the clientelistic networks organized around the patronage system of the leader were extensive and treated with generosity. The regime had a certain social base, supported by tribal divisions, fears and animosities that the leader played skillfully against one another for his own benefit. Most of the youth of Libya were disaffected politically vis-à-vis the regime, but in Tripoli they had greater economic opportunities than their counterparts in Egypt. Under these conditions, the demonstrations that started on

February 17 in Bengazhi, following calls in social media and through mobile phone networks, had only limited repercussions in Tripoli, and expressed both democratic aspirations and a regional and tribal rebellion against the authoritarian, patrimonial state. As such they were backed by one segment of the armed forces with links to the East, and were protected by these armed units when Gaddafi tried to crush the movement by force. Thus, the rebellion quickly escalated to a civil war: by February 20, only three days after the beginning of the movement, the rebels had occupied Bengazhi and other towns in the East, and by February 23 they had taken Misrata, mid-way to Tripoli. The movement improvised a civilian administration in Bengazhi with the cooperation of most of the local bureaucrats, while enthusiastic ragtag militias, mounted on pickup trucks, hastily armed and without any combat experience, marched towards Tripoli only to be doomed in their unequal confrontation with a well-prepared private army, commanded by Gaddafi's sons with superior firepower. Hours before Gaddafi could implement his announced intention to occupy Benghazi and search and kill all of the rebels house by house, 20 French bombers stopped the assault and internationalized the Libyan conflict, draping the NATO intervention under the UN flag. Geopolitics took over. Obama's deep reluctance to engage in any form of military action was partly overcome by the insistence of Hillary Clinton, Susan Rice, and some members of the presidential team such as Samantha Power, to protect the rebels from massacre, perhaps remembering the terrible consequences of President Clinton's inaction in Rwanda. More decisive was the role played by France, the UK and Italy in the intervention, in order to secure the control of Libyan oil and gas, a critical supply for Western Europe. Russia and China were caught off guard and out-maneuvered by NATO in a lesson they would never forget. Since my main interest here is not about war games but about the fate of social movements, what appears clearly is that once the movement engages in military violence to counter military violence, it loses its character as a democratic movement to become a contender, sometimes as ruthless as its oppressors, in a bloody civil war. And any civil war may become an opportunity for geopolitical actors to increase their real estate, under whatever ideological mantle, just in case their competitors would be tempted to take advantage of the vacuum of power created in the aftermath of regime collapse. In a certain sense, civil wars not only kill people, they also kill social movements and their ideals of peace, democracy and justice.

The poignant contradiction between social movements and violence was also acutely present in the Syrian uprising, one of the most potent, determined social movements to shake up the Arab world. It too was ignited by the explosive coincidence of hope and outrage. Hope: the example of Egypt, a historical reference for Syrians. Outrage: on February 27, 2011, in the Southern city of Daraa, 15 children, aged 9 to 14, were arrested. Their crime? Inspired by the images from other countries, they wrote on walls of the city "*As-shaab yureed askot an-nizam*" ("The people want to overthrow the regime"). They were jailed and tortured. When their parents protested in the streets they were shot and a few were killed. When a funeral was held for them, the mourners were shot and many were killed. Bashar Al-Assad thought that he could simply follow the lessons of his father when he crushed the Muslim Brotherhood rebellion in the city of Hama in 1982 by shelling the entire town with over 20,000 people killed. It was different this time. People had their networks among themselves and with the world. In Damascus, four women, three human rights lawyers and one blogger, called over the Internet for a "Family Vigil for Prisoners" to be held in front of the Ministry of Interior on

March 16. Only 150 persons came, and they were beaten and jailed. But calls to demonstrate against the regime's brutality then came from Daraa, Homs, Hama, Damascus, Baniyas and many other towns, and on March 18 tens of thousands of people marched nationwide, confronting with their hands and their will the police and the thugs shooting at them. No one came to their rescue. They were not asking for it; they refused the notion of foreign intervention. But they wanted the world to know. Their original demands were about lowering food prices, stopping police brutality and putting an end to political corruption. They wanted political reform. Assad replied with vague promises of constitutional reform in the parliament, dismissing the governor of Daraa, sacking his cabinet, lifting the ban on *niqab* for teachers, closing the only casino in the country and giving Syrian nationality to Kurds, among other concessions. Yet, in the perception of the people, these limited gestures could not offset the extreme violence unleashed by the regime, which escalated to the use of combat troops and tanks against unarmed demonstrators. The movement became uncompromising: people wanted to overthrow the regime; Assad should go. Then, after six months, 5,000 dead, and tens of thousands injured and imprisoned, the movement evolved towards a combination of demonstrations, occupations of urban space and limited armed resistance. People started to arm themselves, a few military units deserted and formed a mysterious Free Syrian Army, of unknown origin and allegiance, and a civil war began. This time, however, it was not like in Libya. The dictator had some social support, particularly among the business elites of Damascus and Aleppo, and among the minority Alawites, who are the ethnic base of the Baath party and of the state's leadership. Some social groups were influenced by Assad's propaganda and were afraid of the possibility that an Islamist takeover could curtail their religious freedom; a fear that Assad instilled, and provoked, including by setting up car bombs and blaming the Islamists. Moreover, the core of the dictatorship is the Baath party, which controls a powerful, modern army that takes orders only from the party leaders, led by the Assad family. Thus the fracture in the society did not permeate into the state that remained, at least for the first year of the movement, unified around the party. Yet, the decisive factor in the fate of the Syrian revolution was its geopolitical environment, as Syria occupies a key position in the entangled power games of the Middle East. Russia and China have supported wholeheartedly the dictatorship and were not ready to repeat the Libyan scenario. Thus, they blocked any military action from the UN and warned NATO and the US against intervention, while supporting negotiations. Russia has its only military base outside Russia in Tartus, a Syrian naval base, and sells considerable amounts of weapons to Assad, its last ally in the Arab world. China is a supporter of Iran, its main supplier of oil, and Iran is the protector of Assad. On the other hand, Saudi Arabia, together with Qatar and Jordan, is engaged in a major fight with Shia Iran over Syria, to claim the power for its majority Sunni population and to undermine a fundamental position for its archrival Iran for influence in the region. Informed circles considered that, in 2012, the Free Syrian Army was in fact bankrolled and trained by the Saudis who had called openly in the Arab League for intervention in Syria. At the time of this writing, Kofi Annan was leading a United Nations mission to engage in political negotiations in Syria, where the movement continued to occupy the streets, in spite of shelling, and an uneven combat went on between army troops and armed rebels. Yet, here again, regardless of the outcome of this process in political terms, one of the most extraordinary democratic movements of the Arab uprising would become

entangled in the maneuvers of a fragmented political opposition, in the realignments of power in the corridors of the
state, and in the web of geopolitical strategies, losing its grip
on the promise of democracy that people had defended with
their lives. However, freedom and autonomous deliberation
continue in the occupied squares and in the digital networks
where the movement was born. There is no going back for
the Syrian people, who did not yield to sectarian confrontation, and did not accept dictatorship under different names
in their determination to choose their right to be.

A DIGITAL REVOLUTION?

As in Tunisia and as in Egypt, most of the Arab uprisings
started with organization, debate and calls to rise up on the
Internet, and continued and formed in the urban space.
Thus, Internet networks provided a space of autonomy
from where the movements emerged under different forms
and with different results depending on their social context.
As in all of the other cases of social movements I studied
in this volume, there is also a raging debate in the media
and in academia about the precise role of digital networks in
these movements. Fortunately, in the case of the Arab uprisings, we can rely on a rigorous assessment of their role on
the basis of social science research, thanks to the work that
Philip Howard, Muhammad Hussain and their collaborators have been conducting on this matter for some time. I
will summarize here their main findings because I think they
have put to rest a meaningless debate about the causal role of
social media on social movement. Of course technology does
not determine social movements or for that matter any social
behavior. But Internet and mobile phone networks are not
simply tools, but organizational forms, cultural expressions
and specific platforms for political autonomy. Let's look at

the evidence collected and theorized by Howard, Hussain and their team.

First of all, in his book *The Digital Origins of Dictatorship and Democracy: Information Technology and Political Islam* (2011), written before the Arab uprisings, Philip Howard, on the basis of a comparative analysis of 75 countries, either Muslim or with significant Muslim populations, finds that, while framed by a number of contextual factors, the diffusion and use of ICTs favor democratization, strengthen democracy and increase civic involvement and autonomy of the civil society, paving the way for the democratization of state and also for challenges to dictatorships. Furthermore, involvement of civic young Muslims was favored by Internet use. He wrote: "Countries where civil society and journalism made active use of the new information technologies subsequently experience a radical democratic transition or significant solidification of their democratic institutions" (2011: 200). Particularly significant, before the Arab Spring, was the transformation of social involvement in Egypt and Bahrain with the help of ICT diffusion. In a stream of research conducted in 2011 and 2012 after the Arab uprisings, Howard and Hussain, using a series of quantitative and qualitative indicators, probed a multi-causal, statistical model of the processes and outcomes of the Arab uprisings by using fuzzy logic (Hussain and Howard 2012). They found that the extensive use of digital networks by a predominantly young population of demonstrators had a significant effect on the intensity and power of these movements, starting with a very active debate on social and political demands in the social media *before* the demonstrations' onset. In their words:

> Digital media had a causal role in the Arab Spring in that they provided the fundamental infrastructure of a social movement unlike the others that have emerged in recent

years in these countries. In the first few weeks of protest in each country, the generation of people in the streets – and its leadership – was clearly not interested in the three major models of political Islam ... Instead, these mostly cosmopolitan and younger generations of mobilizers felt disenfranchised by their political systems, saw vast losses in the poor management of national economies and development, and most importantly, a consistent and widely shared narrative of common grievances – a narrative which they learned about from each other and co-wrote on the digital spaces of political writing and venting on blogs, videos shared on Facebook and Twitter, and comment board discussions on international news sites like Al Jazeera and the BBC.

The Arab Spring is historically unique because it is the first set of political upheavals in which all of these things [alienation from the state, consensus among the population in the protest, defence of the movement by the international public opinion] were digitally mediated ... It is true that Facebook and Twitter did not cause revolutions, but it is silly to ignore the fact that the careful and strategic uses of digital media to network regional publics, along with international support networks, have empowered activists in new ways that have led to some of the largest protests this decade in Iran, the temporary lifting of the Egyptian blockade on Gaza, and the popular movements that ended the decades long rule of Mubarak and Ben Ali. Digital media had a causal role in the Arab Spring in the sense that it provided the very infrastructure that created deep communication ties and organizational capacity in groups of activists before the major protests took place, and while street protests were being formalized. Indeed, it was because of those well-developed, digital networks, that civic leaders so successfully activated such large numbers of people to protest.

In every single case, the inciting incidents of the Arab Spring were digitally mediated in some way. Information infrastructure, in the form of mobile phones, personal computers, and social media were part of the causal story we must tell about the Arab Spring. People were inspired to protest for many different, and always personal reasons. Information technologies mediated that inspiration, such that the revolutions followed each other by a few weeks and had notably similar patterns. Certainly there were different political outcomes, but that does not diminish the important role of digital media in the Arab Spring. But even more importantly, this investigation has illustrated that countries that don't have a civil society equipped with digital scaffolding are much less likely to experience popular movements for democracy – an observation we are able to make only by accounting for the constellation of causal variables that existed before the street protests began, not simply the short-term uses of digital technologies during the short period of political upheaval.

In my words: the Arab uprisings were spontaneous processes of mobilization that emerged from calls from the Internet and wireless communication networks on the basis of the pre-existing social networks, both digital and face-to-face, that existed in the society. By and large, they were not mediated by formal political organizations, which had been decimated by repression and were not trusted by most of the young, active participants that spearheaded the movements. Digital networks and occupation of the urban space, in close interaction, provided the platform for autonomous organization and deliberation on which the uprisings were based, and created the resilience that was necessary for the movements to withstand ferocious assaults from state violence until the moment that, in some cases, out of a self-defence instinct, they became a counter-state.

There was another meaningful effect of the movements' presence on the Internet networks that has been pointed out to me by Maytha Alhassen: artistic political creativity. The movements, particularly in Syria, were supported by the innovative graphic design of avatar images, mini-documentaries, YouTube web series (such as Beeshu), vlogs, photographic montages and the like. The power of images, and creative narrative-activated emotions, both mobilizing and soothing, created a virtual environment of art and meaning on which the activists of the movement could rely to connect with the youth population at large, thus changing culture as a tool of changing politics.

Political blogs, in the time before the uprisings, were essential in creating, in many countries, a political culture of debate and activism that contributed to the critical thinking and rebellious attitudes of a young generation that was ready to revolt in the streets. The Arab uprisings were born at the dawn of the explosion of the digital age in the Arab world, albeit with different levels of diffusion of these communication technologies in various countries. Even in countries with low levels of Internet access, the core of activists that, as a network, networked the movement and the movement with their nation and the world, was organized and deliberated on the social networking sites. From that protected space, extensive mobile phone networks reached out to society at large. And because society was ready to receive certain messages about bread and dignity, people were moved and – ultimately – became a movement.

NOTES

1 This chapter largely relies on the contribution of information, data gathering and advice of journalist and scholar Maytha Alhassen. For her own analysis of the

Arab uprisings, see Alhassen, Maytha and Ahmed Shihab-Eldin (eds.). (2012) *Demanding Dignity: Young Voices from the Arab Revolutions*. White Cloud Press, Ashland, OR.

2 http://www.democracynow.org/2011/12/13/the_arab_people_have_woken_up

3 The context of each country partly explains the cases in which protests were limited in 2011 (still to be seen in the future). Thus, in Lebanon and Algeria, the memory of atrocious civil wars had a paralyzing effect, although active protests did take place in Algeria, and were reproduced in January 2012. In Iraq, the painful period of war, occupation, civil war and lingering terrorism left the population exhausted and yearning for peace. In Saudi Arabia, the limited protest that took place on March 11 was largely confined to the Shia minority in the Eastern part of the country, and so its movement was isolated from the Sunni majority, and easily repressed by an effective security apparatus. The most significant social movement in Saudi Arabia was the women's campaign for their right to drive, a movement still in process, with the potential of extending to other women's rights. In the United Arab Emirates, the fact that most residents are not citizens, and most citizens enjoy affluent subsidized lives creates a context in which the lack of liberty does not necessarily appear as a burden to the citizens, and is a factor of intimidation for the immigrants.

4 For a discussion on Arab dictatorships, see Marzouki (2004); Schlumberger (2007).

5 For the social background of Syrian activists, as well as a firsthand account of the uprising, see the excellent analysis by Mohja Kahf: <http://www.jadaliyya.com/pages/index/4274/the-syrian-revolution-on-four-packs-a-day>.

6 For the impact of the rise of food prices in the world on the social situation of the Arab countries (they import

more food than any other region in the world), see: <http://www.economist.com/node/21550328?fsrc=scn/tw/te/ar/letthemeatbaklava>.

REFERENCES AND SOURCES

Council of Foreign Affairs. (2011) *The New Arab Revolts: What Happened, What it Means, and What Comes Next.* Council of Foreign Affairs, New York.

Howard, P. (2011) *The Digital Origins of Dictatorship and Democracy. Information Technology and Political Islam.* Oxford University Press, Oxford.

Hussain, M. M. and Howard, P. (2012) *Democracy's Fourth Wave? Information Technology and the Fuzzy Causes of the Arab Spring*, unpublished paper presented to the meeting of the International Studies Association, San Diego, April 1–4.

Marzouki, M. (2004) *Le mal arabe. Entre dictatures et integrisme: la democratie interdite.* L'Harmattan, Paris.

Noland, M. (2011) *The Arab Economies in a Changing World.* Peter G. Peterson Institute for International Economics, Washington, DC.

Schlumberger, O. (2007) *Debating Arab Authoritarianism: Dynamics and Durability in Nondemocratic Regimes.* Stanford University Press, Stanford, CA.

A RHIZOMATIC
REVOLUTION:

INDIGNADAS[1] IN SPAIN[2]

February 2011. The euro-crisis is in full swing in Spain. Unemployment reaches 22 percent, with youth unemployment at 47 percent. After ignoring the severity of the crisis for a long time, under the pressure of Germany and the IMF, the Socialist Government, reversing its electoral promises of 2008, is engaged in ever deeper budget cuts in health, education and social services. Priority is given to recapitalizing the financial institutions and to reducing the skyrocketing public debt for the sake of preserving Spain's membership in the eurozone. Labor unions are in disarray, and politicians and political parties are despised by a large majority of citizens. A small network of concerned citizens from Madrid, Barcelona, Jerez and other cities create a Facebook group under the name "Platform of Coordination of Groups Pro-Citizen Mobilization." Some of them have been at the forefront of the campaign to defend a free Internet against the Sinde Law, approved by the government to impose control and censorship of Internet Service Providers (ISPs) and

Internet users. Networks such as x.net, Anonymous and Nolesvotes were among the participants. Others were veterans from the movements for global justice. Still others, such as Estado del Malestar, Juventud Sin Futuro, Juventud en Accion, Plataforma de Afectados por la Hipoteca and others were inspired by the struggles spreading throughout Europe against the social consequences of the rampant financial crisis, although in Spain the main criticism focused on the mismanagement of the crisis by a dysfunctional, unresponsive political system. They were encouraged by the example of Iceland; by the possibility of successfully confronting the collusion between bankers and politicians through grassroots mobilization. This platform evolved quickly into a Facebook group of debate and action under the name of "*Democracia Real Ya*" (Real Democracy Now!), which created a forum, a blog and an email list.[3] However, as one of the initiators of DRY, Javier Toret, puts it:

> The campaign was anonymous, Democracia Real Ya was nothing. It was a conglomeration of blogs, different groups, some people that came from the Ley Sinde or the Nolesvotes groups. Democracia Real was a brand that did not have anyone behind it, there were no people behind it.[4]

The group was based on a decentralized network with autonomous nodes in different cities. In some cases, such as in Barcelona, they met in person every Sunday morning. Hundreds joined the Facebook group, and some participated in the meetings. They denounced the lack of representative democracy under its current form in Spain. In their view, the main political parties were at the service of the bankers and were not responsive to the interests of citizens. Following the example of the Arab revolutions, they decided to call for action in the streets. They seized the opportunity of the municipal elections that were scheduled throughout the country on May 22, 2011. Thus, on March 2, they called for citizens to demonstrate their protest in the streets on Sunday, May 15, under the slogan "Real Democracy Now! Take the streets. We are not merchandise in the hands of politicians and bankers," and published a manifesto:

> We are normal people. We are like you: people who get up in the morning to study, to work or to look for a job, people with family and friends. People who work hard every day to live and get a better future for those we are with . . . Yet in this country most of the political class does not even listen to us. Its functions should be to bring our voice to the institutions, facilitating citizen's political participation, aiming at achieving the greatest benefit for the majority of society instead of just enriching themselves on our back, paying attention only to the instructions of the great economic powers, and maintaining a partytocratic dictatorship . . . We are people, not merchandise. I am not only what I buy, why I buy it, and for whom I buy it. For all these reasons, I am indignant. I believe I can change it. I believe I can contribute. I know together we can. Come with us. It is your right.

The call was not supported by any political party, labor unions or civil society associations, and was ignored by the media. It was diffused primarily over the Internet's social networks, Facebook, Twitter, tuenti, etc. On May 15, without any formal leadership but with a careful preparation of the demonstrations that went on for weeks, tens of thousands of people demonstrated in Madrid (50,000), Barcelona (20,000), Valencia (10,000) and 50 more cities, peacefully, without any major incident anywhere.

At the end of the demonstration in Madrid, a few dozen

protesters went to the Puerta del Sol, the most symbolic square of the city, and spent the night in balmy weather to discuss among themselves what Real Democracy meant. At that point they decided they were not going to leave Puerta del Sol until they came to a consensus about the meaning of Real Democracy – a lengthy process, as it turned out. The following night, May 16, many people gathered in Barcelona's Catalunya Square. In both places they decided to occupy the square to debate the issues that had not been discussed in the meaningless campaigns of political candidates for the municipal elections to be held in a few days. They tweeted their friends. Hundreds came, who then tweeted their networks, and so thousands came. Many of them came with sleeping bags, to spend the night in the occupied space. The *acampadas* (camps) were born. Many more people came during daytime. They participated in debates, activities and demonstrations. Commissions of all sorts sprung up spontaneously. Some took care of the logistical problems, including sanitation, water and food supply. Others set up webs, deployed Wi-Fi networks, and connected to occupied spaces around the country and around the world. Many others facilitated debates, on any theme anyone wanted to propose and for anyone who was interested. No leaders were recognized: everybody represented just her/himself, and decisions were left in the hands of the General Assembly meeting at the end of every day, and in the commissions that were formed on every issue that people wanted to act upon. Over 100 Spanish cities followed suit, triggering a massive occupy movement that spread in a few days to almost 800 cities around the world, although, interestingly enough, its impact was limited at that point in the United States. National and international media reported on the movement, albeit usually misrepresenting it. The police tried, unsuccessfully, to evict the occupiers twice. The Electoral Court declared occupations unlawful as they were interfering with the "day of reflection" before the elections, as established by the law. Yet, on the two occasions there was a threat against the occupied spaces, thousands joined in, blocking police action. Political parties were mindful of adverse consequences for their electoral prospects if they would engage in all-out police operations, and so the occupations continued, as per the decision of the assemblies, beyond election day. The movement had taken on a life of its own. It was first known as the 15-M, a name derived from the date of the first demonstration, but soon the media popularized the label of "*indignados*," which some in the movement had adopted, perhaps inspired by the title of a pamphlet ("*Indignez-vous!*") published a few months earlier by a 93-year-old French philosopher and former diplomat, Stephane Hessel, who struck a nerve among young people in Spain (more so than in France).[5] Indeed, there was a general climate of indignation in the country (as in most of the world) against politicians who cared only about themselves, and against the bankers who had wrecked the economy with their speculative maneuvers, only to be bailed out, and to receive handsome bonuses, while citizens suffered dearly from the consequences of the crisis in their jobs, salaries, services and foreclosed mortgages. The movement went on under different forms for several months, although most of the occupations of public space ended in early July. During July, several marches started from different points in Spain and converged on Madrid on the 22nd. The marchers walked, passing through towns and villages, explaining the reasons for the protest, and were joined by many others during their journey. When they reached Madrid after hundreds of kilometers by foot, they were greeted by supportive crowds, who joined them for the final lap. On July 23 in the Puerta del Sol, a demonstration of about 250,000 people reaffirmed the determination of the movement to keep fighting for democracy and against the unfair management of the economic crisis. Actions of protest continued during August, including some attempts to reoccupy Sol in Madrid, to the point that hundreds of policemen occupied the square themselves for several days, to preempt a new occupation by the *indignadas*. At the end of August, the Socialist Party government and the opposition Partido Popular (Conservative) agreed to bow to the ultimatum from Merkel to amend the Spanish Constitution to forbid the possibility of budget deficits as a way to appease the financial markets speculating against the Spanish debt (this in fact did not work). The country was on vacation and the vote took place almost in secrecy. The *indignadas* protested in front of the Parliament, calling for a referendum, and staged demonstrations in many cities, receiving some support from the trade unions and from a left-wing party that also opposed amending the Constitution under the gun of Germany. The *indignadas* carried a banner saying, "Unions, thanks for coming."

It is estimated that a minimum of 2.2 million people participated, and participation in the protests increased from May to October (Blanco 2011).

On October 15, 2011 a global demonstration, convened over the Internet at the initiative of a network of activists who met in Barcelona in early September, gathered hundreds of thousands of demonstrators in 951 cities and 82 countries around the world under the slogan "United for Global Change." There were almost 500,000 demonstrators in Madrid and about 400,000 in Barcelona.

Who were these determined protesters? While at the origin of the movement there were many university students and unemployed college graduates in the 20–35 age group (as there were in the Arab revolutions), they were joined later by people from all social backgrounds and ages, with an active participation of elderly, under direct threat of deteriorating living conditions. Moreover, the movement received the overwhelming support of the public opinion throughout 2011, with at least three quarters of the Spanish people, according to different surveys, declaring their agreement with the critiques and statements of the movement. Some sources put the degree of identification with the movement at 88 percent (see Table 1).

Yet, in early 2012 there was uncertainty about the path ahead for those who "worried about our future because this is the place where we will spend the rest of our lives," as a banner in the occupied square stated. This is why the search and the debates continued on the Internet social networks, the safe space from which the movement was imagined and where new projects were and are being conceived.

A SELF-MEDIATED MOVEMENT

While the occupation of public space was essential to make the movement visible, and to provide support to the key organizational form of the movement – the local assemblies – the origin of the movement, and its backbone throughout the protest can be traced back to the free spaces of the Internet. This is the account of Javier Toret, a psychologist and researcher on techno-politics, who was one of the first members of the network that created *Democracia Real Ya*:

> What the 15-M has shown is that people can overcome a media block. The capacity of mass self-communication and self organization online has allowed people to overcome a media block. In Barcelona there was only one media outlet that did come to the press conference we organized around the 15-M demonstrations, BTV (Barcelona TV). All the media outlets knew that the 15-M demonstrations were going to take place. We had written to them, everything

Table 1: Public opinion towards the 15M mobilizations in Spain

	Percentage of the total surveyed	Scale from 1 to 10 (where 1 is completely disagree and 10 is completely agree)
Metroscopia survey conducted June 1-2, 2011		
Do the 15M mobilizations inspire a sense of sympathy or rejection in you?		
They inspire a sense of sympathy.	66%	
They inspire a sense of rejection.	21%	
Do you think the motivations for protesting are right?		
Yes, they are right.	81%	
No, they are not right.	9%	
Which of the following opinions do you agree with most?		
The 15M movement deals with problems that only affect a few people.	11%	
The 15M movement deals with problems that affect the entire society.	84%	
The 15M movement is politically left leaning.	31%	
The 15M movement is politically right leaning.	2%	
The 15M movement does not have a definite political tendency.	58%	
The 15M movement deals with real problems that exist in our society.		
Agree/Strongly Agree	80%	
Disagree/Strongly Disagree	15%	
The 15M movement is something that is widely discussed, but will soon be forgotten.		
Agree/Strongly Agree	57%	
Disagree/Strongly Disagree	38%	

Table 1: (continued)

	Percentage of the total surveyed	Scale from 1 to 10 (where 1 is completely disagree and 10 is completely agree)
The 15M movement will evolve into a political party.		
Agree/Strongly Agree	21%	
Disagree/Strongly Disagree	69%	
The 15M movement will become radicalized and engage in violent acts.		
Agree/Strongly Agree	19%	
Disagree/Strongly Disagree	74%	
The 15M movement will become integrated into an existing political party.		
Agree/Strongly Agree	22%	
Disagree/Strongly Disagree	68%	
The Cocktail Analysis survey conducted May 31, 2011		
Have you heard of the Democracia Real Ya movement, also known as the 15M movement or the movement of the Indignados?		
Yes	97%	
No	3%	
Would you say that you agree or disagree with the Democracia Real Ya/15M movement?		
Agree	88%	
Disagree	12%	
Do you think that the Democracia Real Ya/15M movement should continue?		
Yes	83%	
No	17%	

On a scale of 1 to 10, where 1 is completely disagree and 10 is completely agree, what do you think of the following?

The electoral law needs to be reformed.	8.7
Corruption needs to be fought by implementing rules aimed at full political transparency.	9.3
There needs to be an effective separation of political powers.	8.6
Mechanisms for effective citizen control need to be created to keep effective political responsibility.	8.7

Simple Lógica survey conducted June 1-6, 2011

Do you approve or disapprove of the protests that have been occurring in many plazas throughout Spain?

Approve	73%
Disapprove	19%

Do you agree with the ideas that are being defended by the movement?

Agree	72%
Neither Agree nor Disagree	10%
Disagree	10%

To what extent do you think that this movement will help improve things in Spain?

A lot	12%
Somewhat	27%
Not at all	53%

Source:
1) Metroscopia available at www.metroscopia.es/portada.html
2) The Cocktail Analysis available at http://www.tcanalysis.com/2011/06/03/movimiento-15mdemocraciarealya-representatividad-movilizacion-social-y-canales-de-informacion/
3) Simple Lógica available at http://www.simplelogica.com/iop/iop11002.asp

had been announced via Twitter, Facebook, email lists . . . but nothing appeared. Television stations ignored us completely, newspapers also ignored us. There were individual journalists who did accompany the movement, for example Lali Sandiumenge, who has a blog in La Vanguardia [http://blogs.lavanguardia.com/guerreros-del-teclado/] . . . But generally, the mainstream media either ignored, or blocked the proposal we put forth . . . What this shows is a type of movement that is postmedia. It's postmedia because there is a technopolitical reappropriation of tools, technologies and mediums of participation and communication that exist today. This is where people are today. There are a lot of people in these mediums. It's an online viral campaign that is sufficiently open for anyone to get involved and participate . . . For something to be viral online, for it to be mimetic, slogans have to resonate. For example, "we are not merchandise in the hands of bankers." This has resonated, and it has circulated. It was something that anyone could relate with. People have created videos, and all sorts of signs with these slogans. The initial slogans had wide circulation because they were anonymous and because they were common sense. Slogans were not coming from a left-leaning group that had certain ideologies. It just had a viral capacity, that was mimetic, and had the capacity to use web 2.0 tools. This caused everyone to be their own media. It caused thousands of people to be their own media distributors. That's why it's a postmedia movement. It has the capacity to overcome the media and create an event, and communicate this event . . . Some media outlets have taken the tweets or what was said in the Facebook page of Acampadasol or DRY to inform the public. This could be because with a movement that is networked, that does not have leaders, it is hard for the media to be able to tell the story of what is happening. The media initially ignored the

movement, but when all of the plazas of Spain were full
with people, they had no choice but to explain what was
happening ... A lot of spaces were created that functioned
as media outlets, for example there were a lot of personal
blogs that had good coverage of the movement. We became
a collective that had the capacity to speak each one for themselves without the filters of the media. The media outlets
amplified what we did, be it for better or worse. There was
a lot of autonomy for each person to say what they thought
and felt. The 15-M movement positioned itself against
intermediaries, be it political, media, or cultural. It directly
attacks the idea that someone has to do things for me. This
is a paradigm shift in the relationship between citizen and
governments, unions, media outlets ... If this is a movement that is being created equally by thousands of people, it
creates contradictions to have one person speaking. There
has been an internal debate on whether there should be
spokespeople. The movement's idea is that everyone spoke
for themselves. It's not a person who decides anything. This
makes it hard for media outlets to cover what is happening. In 2001, when we started Indymedia, we had a saying
that said: "Don't hate the media, become the media." This
is what the 15-M has shown. When people join together,
they become more powerful than any other media outlet.
For example, on the 27 May when they hit us in the plaza
Catalunya, the movement had an incredible capacity to
communicate what was happening ... Everyone became a
reporter even if it is for a few moments. Everyone has been
at some point the primary source of the news. When you
have a lot of people reporting, you have a collective account
of what is happening. People can follow what is happening
via streaming, online, on television, live. People who were
there were tweeting, "come help us," and people came. This
has permitted people to take things from a digital medium,

be it at their homes, or through a cell phone and be able to move in the city.[6]

Yet, even a new medium, as powerful and participatory as the Internet's social networks, is not the message. The message constructs the medium. As Toret argues, the message went viral because it resonated with people's personal experiences. And the key message was a rejection of the entire political and economic institutions that determine people's lives. Because as one banner in Madrid said, "This is not a crisis, it is that I do not love you any more."

But how is new love found?

WHAT DID/DO THE *INDIGNADAS* WANT?

The movement did not have a program. The main reason for this was that there never was a formal organization known as "the movement." But there were many demands approved by the assemblies in many occupations. Every possible demand, critique and proposal was present in the movement. It was certainly a movement against the bankers and speculators, and against people paying the consequences of a financial crisis they were not responsible for. A deep feeling of unfairness was boiling in the population at large and came to be expressed in the movement. They felt that the banks in trouble should not be bailed out but nationalized, just as they were in Iceland, a constant reference of the movement. They thought that the fraudulent executives should be prosecuted. They were unanimously opposed to the government's budget cuts, and asked instead for taxation of the rich and of the corporations. There was widespread denunciation of the unemployment of millions of young people who had no prospects of finding a decent job. On April 7, 2011, thousands of youth had demonstrated in Madrid following the call of "Youth Without a Future," an Internet-based campaign to defend their rights to education, work and housing. There had also been a protest against the housing crisis in general and against the shortage of affordable housing for young people in particular. One important contingent of the 15-M movement came from the youth involved in the "*V as Vivienda* (Housing)" campaign in the months preceding the movement. There were particularly virulent protests against mortgage foreclosures and evictions of elderly and families in need, who had been trapped by the banks in subprime loans that they would have to continue to pay for the rest of their lives, even after having lost their homes. There was a clear criticism of capitalism as such: "This is not a crisis, it is the system." But there were no specific proposals to either overcome capitalism or restore economic growth. The reason was that many in the movement opposed the very notion of growth for the sake of growth. Environmental concerns were paramount. The opposition to a consumption-driven society was running deep. So, while the criticism of capitalism in general and of the kind of financial capitalism that led to the crisis in particular was shared almost unanimously, there was no consensus about which kind of economy would provide jobs, housing and decent living conditions to everybody in ways that were environmentally sustainable and ethically just. This is not to say that the movement was incapable of generating very specific, highly sophisticated policy proposals. In fact, there was a wealth of such proposals that were elaborated and debated in assemblies and commissions. Yet, since the movement was not organized to agree on any detailed program, there were multiple proposals from various people in various places, and so they were as diverse as the movement's composition.

However, in spite of the vast array of critiques and demands on economic and social issues, my deep conviction, from my own observation, is that this movement was essentially political. It was a movement for the transformation of pseudo-democracy into real democracy. In spite of the fact that the original call from Real Democracy Now! was later diluted in the ocean of demands and dreams present in the movement, and that Real Democracy Now! was the trigger but not the movement itself, its original manifesto was the implicit or explicit common core of the *Indignadas* movement. Yes, the crisis was an expression of the capitalist system, and the banks were the culprits. But politicians of all affiliations, parties, parliaments and governments were accomplices of the bankers whose interests they defended above those of the citizens they represented. There was a general opinion in the movement that politicians lived in their own, closed, privileged world, indifferent to people's needs, manipulating the elections and the electoral law to perpetuate their power as a political class. "They do not represent us" is probably the most popular and certainly the most fundamental slogan from the movement. Because if there is no real representation, there is no democracy, and the institutions have to be reconstructed from the bottom up, as they were in Iceland. Starting with the judiciary, fully politicized, and part of the system of reciprocal support between bankers, politicians and the high levels of the Magistracy.

This rejection of the current form of democracy has deep consequences in the project of the movement because it implies that elections and parties are useless and irrelevant to defending citizens' interests and values. Thus the movement was indifferent to electoral participation as long as there was not a deep reform of the system, starting with the reform of the electoral law that had been tailored to the convenience of the largest parties through a system of non-proportional representation favoring the majority vote getters (the D'Hondt method). In positive terms, the movement agreed to move to different models of participatory democracy, starting with deliberative democracy over the Internet to ensure a fully conscious participation of citizens in the process of consultative decision-making. The forms of deliberation and decision-making in the movement itself, which I will discuss below, aimed explicitly to prefigure what political democracy should be in society at large. Fully aware of the difficulty of affecting politics and policies within the limits of existing institutions, the movement, in its large majority, positioned itself in the long haul. It was not a matter of creating a program to be approved in the next election, since they did not recognize any political party as their interlocutor. In the view of the movement, a long march had to be undertaken from the negation of the system to the reconstruction of the institutions that would express people's will through the process of raising consciousness and participatory deliberation.

This is why the project(s) of the movement can be better found in the discourse of its actors, rather than in specific demands, which only represented the momentarily predominant view in the local assemblies that voted on them.

THE DISCOURSE OF THE MOVEMENT

The *Indignadas* is a movement of multiple, rich discourses. Imaginative slogans, punchy terms, meaningful words and poetic expressions constituted a language ecosystem expressive of new subjectivities. Although I cannot speak of one single discourse, there are a number of terms, connotating ways of thinking, that appeared regularly in the slogans and debates that took place, both in the camps and on the Internet.

Eduardo Serrano (2011) constructed, on the basis of his observation, a list of key terms widely present in the discourse of the movement, characterizing each term by both its implications and its cancellations. His analysis, whose terms I have translated, is presented in Table 2, providing a profile of the movement in its orientations as revealed in its discourse.

What is evident in this analysis is the depth of the cultural transformation embodied in this movement. Although partly prompted by the precarious lives of millions of young people (54 percent in the age group 18–34 still were living with their parents because of lack of housing and work), the discourse of the movement expresses the rise of a new economic and political culture: an alternative economic culture, which our research team studied in Barcelona in 2009–12. It is expressed in everyday life practices that emphasize the use value of life over commercial value and engage in self-production, cooperativism, barter networks, social currency, ethical banking and networks of reciprocal solidarity. The economic crisis helped to extend the appeal of this alternative economic culture to a significant proportion of the population of Barcelona. These practices were present in the lives of thousands of people, precisely in the same age group as most of the *indignadas* (20–35) for quite some time. It was the search for a meaning of life that explains why a majority of the Barcelona population would prefer to work less even if this meant being paid proportionally less (Conill et al. 2012a, 2012b). The movement extended the values present in this alternative economy project to the formation of an alternative political project. In both cases, the construction of autonomy of the individual and the networking of these autonomous individuals to create new, shared forms of life are paramount motivations.

A sample of popular slogans express this dream of freedom and democracy in the movement's own words: "Another politics is possible," "People united function without parties," "The revolution was in our hearts and now it flies in the streets," "We carry a new world in our hearts," "I am not anti-system, the system is anti-me."

Table 2: Implications and cancellations of meaning in the shared terms of discourse in the Indignados movement

Term	Implies	Cancels
Common	Self-management of community, shared space	Restricted property, dichotomy of public/private, seizing of power by a few
Consensus by Assembly	Decisions result from interaction between different proposals, respect of all ideas, non-linear process of decision-making, no vote but synthesis, qualitatively superior outcome of the decision-making process	Opposition consensus/dissent, averaging propositions, linear decision-making, outcome inferior to the quality of the original proposals debated
Anybody	Singularity, anonymous citizens	Everybody, totality
Future-less	Right now	Delayed fulfillment, separation between means and goals
No bosses	Self-regulation, distributed network, full involvement of everybody (as in the Internet interaction), anonymity, rotation of responsibilities	Assignment of rigid social roles, pre-definition of subjects, command and submission
Non-representation	Participation, direct democracy, politics of expression	Delegation
Non-violence	Legitimacy, exemplarity, actual self-defence, intangible field of force by de-legitimizing violence from others	Efficacy of violence, tyranny of the testosterone
Respect	Reciprocity, dignity, self-limitation, true citizenship	Security, enemy

Table 2: (continued)

Term	Implies	Cancels
Money-less	Wealth is not monetary, disconnection with the financial system, local currencies, decommodification	Economy of scarcity, financial tyranny, inevitable austerity, zero sum games
Fearless	Together we can, you are not alone, the crisis can be overcome (as in Iceland), creativity	Fatality, paralysis
Slowness	Co-evolution, processes of gradual maturation	'Fast life' subordination of life to the acceleration of capital

Source: Eduardo Serrano, 2011. El poder de las palabras: glosario de términos del 15M. [online] Available at: <http://madrilonia. org/2011/06/el-poder-de-las-palabras-glosario-de-terminos-del-15m/> [Accessed 8 February 2012]. My translation.

How can this political transformation be achieved? By being together, by thinking together, by pursuing the struggle, by calling the majority to join the movement: "Love to the world is what moves revolutionaries. Join us!" There will be difficulties, but it is worthwhile: "The barricade closes the street but opens the way," "Sorry for the inconvenience, we are changing the world." And a warning to the powers that be: "If you steal our dreams, we will not let you sleep."

However, the most critical issue for the movement has been how to put into its own practice the principles of democracy that they had proposed for society at large.

REINVENTING DEMOCRACY IN PRACTICE: AN ASSEMBLY-LED, LEADERLESS MOVEMENT

There was no formal decision, but everybody agreed in practice, from the onset of the movement. There would be no leaders in the movement, either locally or nationally. For that matter, not even spokespersons were recognized. Everyone would represent him/herself, and no one else. This drove the media crazy, as the faces of any collective action are necessary ingredients in the media's storytelling technique. The source of this ancient, anarchist principle, usually betrayed in history, was not ideological in the case of this movement, although it became a fundamental principle, enforced by the large majority of the movement's actors. It was present in the experience of Internet networks in which horizontality is the norm, and there is little need for leadership because the coordination functions can be exercised by the network itself through interaction between its nodes. The new subjectivity appeared in the network: the network became the subject. The rejection of leaders was also the consequence of the negative experiences that some of the veteran activists had suffered in the movement for global justice and in the various radical organizations of the extreme left. But it resulted as well from the deep distrust of any organized political leadership after observing the corruption and cynicism that characterized governments and traditional parties. This search for authenticity by a new generation that came into politics by rejecting *realpolitik* defines fundamentally the movement, although this was at times criticized within the movement itself, by unreconstructed militants, as "*buenismo*" (naïve goodness). Yet, the claim for legitimacy in constructing a new form of politics could only be credible if practiced in the daily activity of the movement.

The organizational concretion of this principle was to give all power of decision-making for matters that would imply the whole collective to the General Assembly that would represent the people camping in a given location, as well as anyone joining the camp at the time of the assembly. Assemblies would usually meet daily, except when an

emergency meeting had to be called. The number of participants varied with the size of the encampment, but in Madrid
and Barcelona attendance would range from hundreds to
two or three thousand in special moments. Decisions of the
assembly held merely symbolic power, as each person was
always free to make her own decision. But the main issue was
how to reach a decision. In many of the camps, the movement tried to reach a decision by consensus, conversing and
debating until everybody would agree, after arguments and
counter-arguments were exchanged politely and respectfully
(for hours). To avoid excessive noise and interruptions, a hand
language was adopted (adapted from the deaf language) to
signal approval and disapproval, or to ask the speaker to wrap
it up. Assemblies were moderated by volunteers who rotated
regularly in these roles, not so much to prevent the rise of
leaders as to care for the exhaustion derived from such a task.
Although the debates did not have the acrimony often found
in discussions within social movements in most cases that our
team observed, there was a collective pressure exercised by
the participants against any attempt by ideologues and self-
proclaimed leaders to use the assembly for their propaganda.
After many days of experience, some in the movement began
to debate the need to reach a collective decision on specific
proposals by a simple majority vote, after integrating as many
different contributions as possible. Indeed, the principle of
decision by consensus allowed some minority groups to block
any decision by engaging in obstruction to impose a preconceived position. The movement re-learned old historical
lessons, such as the importance of recognizing the rights of
minorities without submitting to their blackmail.

The contradiction between deliberation and efficient
implementation was addressed by creating multiple commissions that would enact the general orientations derived from
the assembly into specific initiatives. In fact, the commissions

were fully autonomous, and they also had to deliberate different proposals to reach agreement on what was to be done.
Furthermore, anyone could propose the creation of a commission on a specific topic, from agro-ecological initiatives
to child care or the reform of the electoral law. Some were
functional, to take charge of the needs of the movement (sanitation, security, communication, etc.). Others focused on
elaborating proposals on different issues to be submitted to
the assembly. Still others would organize action to put some
of these proposals into practice, such as the commission to
block housing evictions. Commissions would remain active
as long as there were people attending them, so they would
appear and disappear depending on the evolution of the
movement. In the case of Barcelona, those that lasted longer
were the commissions reflecting on the forms of the movement, elaborating strategies on how to implement principles
of participatory democracy in the practice of the movement.

However, the possibility for the movement to organize
this new polity was materially dependent on the occupation
of public space: on the existence of camps that, even if only
a small minority would stay overnight, provided the setting
for the counter-society that materialized the dreams of real
democracy. Yet, it was clearly impossible to maintain such
occupation indefinitely. This was not only due to logistical problems and harassment by the police, but also to the
process of degradation of life in the camp. Homelessness
is a dramatic reality in Spanish cities like everywhere in
the world. Only a fraction of homeless people have serious
psychiatric problems, but this fraction is highly visible, and
many of them ended up in the camps where they felt protected. This created a major problem in the movement, in
Spain as in almost every occupation I have experienced in
other countries. On the one hand, the image that the presence of the homeless in the camp projects to the 99 percent

(who are the reference of the movement) makes it impossible for people at large to identify with the *indignadas* camps. On the other hand, very few people among the occupiers would be ready to forbid the presence of anyone in the encampment, as this would contradict the inclusive principles of the movement.

Yet, the most important problem that the movement faced in continuing with the occupation of public space is that, over time, only full-time activists could actually participate in the assemblies and manage the day-to-day tasks of the movement. They were usually young men without family responsibilities, jobless and increasingly devoted almost exclusively to the movement. The more the occupations would continue, the more the movement would become identified with a tiny minority of activists, hardly representative of the citizenry they wanted to mobilize. This is why after six or eight weeks, on average, most of the assemblies voted to lift the camps and continue the movement in other forms. A few opted to stay in the squares but they became an easy target for the police, who ultimately removed all occupations by mid-August.

In many towns, the movement decided to decentralize its action to the neighborhood level, and organize assemblies at the local level, representing the interests of the residents according to the same pattern of democratic deliberation and decision-making. Commissions continued to be formed spontaneously to conduct campaigns or to simply elaborate proposals that would be diffused over the Internet, and discussed in different forms and venues. Yet, the key organizational principles – refusal of elected leaders, sovereignty of the assemblies and spontaneity and self-management of the commissions – continued to operate everywhere. So did the same problems of functionality and efficiency that had plagued the movement, inducing a deep reflection on what was the meaning of efficiency and achievement in a collective practice aiming to change lives, in addition to achieving demands and defending rights.

FROM DELIBERATION TO ACTION: THE QUESTION OF VIOLENCE

A popular hacker slogan says "Do not propose, do!" This is what the movement attempted. It started by voicing its indignation in street demonstrations, the oldest form of collective action. Thereafter, by occupying public space in many cities around the country, it affirmed its determination to stand up to the arrogance of power that had responded to the protest with a combination of disdain and police operations. The question quickly arose about the ways and means of affecting the goals of the movement. Since there was total distrust in the political system, the movement did not issue any advice about what to do in the elections, not even whether to abstain or cast a blank ballot. Everybody was free to follow her own assessment on tactical voting decisions. With formal politics absent from the movement's horizon, it had to resort to other forms of action. There were numerous street demonstrations, as well as marches crisscrossing Spain and Europe. There were also a number of actions against injustice: physically blocking evictions from homes whose mortgages had been foreclosed; protecting immigrants harassed by the police; refusing to pay for the subway to protest against excessive fare hikes; engaging in civil disobedience in different forms and demonstrating in front of government buildings, European Commission offices, bank headquarters, rating agency services, and the like. Yet, from the early stages of the movement it was clear that the main action concerned raising consciousness among its participants and in the population at large. The assemblies and commissions were not gatherings to prepare revolutionary actions: they were not a means, but a goal in themselves. Coming together to fully realize the inequity of the system, to dare to confront it from the safety of a shared space, on the Internet and in the squares, was the most meaningful form of action of the movement. If there was a long march to be undertaken, it was critical to share feelings and knowledge among occupiers themselves and with people at large. The first assemblies were very emotional: people were able to freely express themselves, receive attention and feel respected. I personally witnessed an old woman calling home from a bench near the assembly of Catalunya Square in Barcelona, reporting, almost in tears, that she had actually spoken in the meeting and that they had listened to her. She added: "never before in my life, this was the first time I spoke in public." Just saying loudly and collectively what everybody had been keeping inside for years was a liberating gesture that made the movement more expressive than instrumental in the short term. Since we know that emotions are the drivers of collective action, this could in fact be a key for future social change, a major issue that I will discuss below.

For the movement to go further in non-institutional action, engaging fully in civil disobedience, it had to dare to deal with the possible consequences of confrontation: the possibility of violence. By occupying public space, protesters exposed themselves to police repression. There were several violent police actions in different cities. A particularly vicious one took place in Barcelona on May 27. A combined operation between the Catalan Government police (under orders from councillor Felip Puig, from the nationalist party) and the Municipality police (under orders of Socialist councilwoman Assumpta Escarp) attacked in the early morning the camp of Plaza Catalunya with the pretext of cleaning the square. Occupiers sat peacefully and refused to leave. They were clubbed repeatedly for six hours, with the result of 147 injured, scores of them seriously. The scene, with people being bloodied mercilessly without opposing resistance, was streamed live on the Internet and broadcast on TV, inducing massive, renewed indignation. In the afternoon, over 20,000 people came in solidarity and reoccupied the square while the police withdrew. Feeling strong with such a display of support, some in the Barcelona movement decided to step up the offensive by blocking the entrance to the Catalan parliament on June 11, the day the MPs would meet to vote on the budget cuts they had prepared. Several hundred demonstrators tried to block the entrance and they insulted, pushed and threw paint on some of the parliamentarians. The police had infiltrated the demonstrators, disguised as protesters, and some observers considered this a provocation. A violent police repression ensued, ending with people injured, arrested and later charged and brought to trial. These incidents were distorted and widely reported in the media, portraying the movement as radical and violent. Many thought this was the end of the movement. In fact, these demeaning tactics backfired. A few days later, on June 19, the movement called for a demonstration in protest of police violence and in support of its demands, which attracted 200,000 people in the streets of Barcelona. The movement survived the acid test of its popularity. Yet, a debate surged within the movement about the role of self-defence, including physical defence, as a form of action. After all, some argued, violence is in the system: it is in systematic police brutality against the youth; it is in the torture that, according to some judicial sentences, the police practices occasionally; it is in the refusal of decent jobs and affordable housing for the youth; and it is in the unresponsiveness of government and parliamentarians to citizens' serious grievances. And yet, it was reaffirmed as an axiom of the movement that non-violence was essential. First, because violence, amplified in the media, even when not provoked by the protesters, would alienate the support of the population. But more fundamentally, opposing violence, under all its forms, and regardless of the origin, is a basic principle of the new culture of peace and democracy that the movement wants to propagate. Thus, civil disobedience is appropriate, including some daring forms such as blocking buildings by sitting in entranceways, or chaining bodies to gates. But it is never okay to engage in active violence or even respond to violent attacks from the police. The question of violence was debated in the assemblies, and received always the same answer from the large majority of the movement. To engage in violence, even if justified, contradicts the very essence of what the movement is about, and goes back to the old tactics of revolutionary actions that gave up ethical integrity for the sake of expressing rage, becoming in the process the same evil as the one they were opposing.[7] The *Indignadas* was and is a peaceful movement whose courage allowed for the de-legitimization of violent repression, thus achieving a first and major victory in the citizens' hearts.

A POLITICAL MOVEMENT AGAINST THE POLITICAL SYSTEM

If we were to identify a unifying goal of the movement, it is the transformation of the political democratic process. Many different versions of democracy, and how to achieve it, were envisioned. One of the most popular themes was the reform of the electoral law, to make it proportional, and to make feasible an adequate representation of political minorities. But there were also proposals for mandatory referendums, for consultation and participation in decision-making both locally and over the Internet. Control of corruption, term limits for elected officials, salary caps, privilege elimination (including the lifting of judicial immunity for MPs) and a flurry of measures to clean up and open up the political system were debated and proposed in assemblies and commissions. The notion was that without truly democratic political institutions, any progressive policies or decisions adopted would not be implemented, as politicians would not be responsible to their citizens, and would continue to serve the powers that be. Thus, this was a political movement, but a non-partisan political movement, with no affiliation with or sympathy for any party. It was ideologically and politically plural, even if in its ranks there were individuals of many ideologies, as well as a majority of young people with little prior political experience and a total distrust of organized politics. However, if the movement was political, its intent was not to work through the institutional system, since the large majority considered the institutional rules of representation to have been manipulated. Thus, even if some reforms were proposed, it was more of a pedagogic exercise to connect with the population at large than a real hope of changing the political system. Creating a party, or parties, to express the aspirations of the movement was never considered. Yes, other politics would be possible, but not yet, and not through the channels established by those who wanted to limit within narrow boundaries the process of democratic representation.

Political parties did not know how to deal with the movement. In practice they were hostile and used police repression, with varying degrees of violence, against occupation of public space. They were particularly incensed by the attempts to block the parliament, going even so far as to denounce these actions as a fascist attack on democracy. At the same time, particularly for the Socialists and for the United Left (ex-Communists), the massive mobilizations appeared to be a chance to re-supply their meager contingents, since the young generation had given up any hope of being represented by the traditional parties. The Socialists, the government party at the onset of the movement, declared somewhat ambiguous verbal support during the electoral campaign for some of the demands of the movement, but did not follow up after its crushing defeat in the elections of November 2011. The conservative party, Partido Popular, after a cautious attitude during the electoral period so as not to alienate any constituency, insulted the *indignadas* once it came into power, labeling them as "a mixture of radical revolutionaries, violent anarchists and naïve followers." The United Left did express some sympathy and attracted votes as a result of this benevolent attitude. It appeared purely tactical to most in the movement, since they knew there was a deep distrust in the Communist tradition against any movement without leaders or program, a libertarian brand that was historically at odds with the vanguard role of the party. In sum, there was almost total exteriority between the movement and the political system, both organizationally and ideologically.

However, even if the movement did not care at all about the electoral process (other than intervening in the debates to raise consciousness among citizens), and dismissed the election results as irrelevant for the future of democracy, it did appear to have had an impact on the elections. There were two elections in Spain in 2011: municipal elections on May 22 – precisely the elections that were used by the nascent movement to trigger its critique of democracy – and parliamentary elections on November 20. There are few rigorous studies on the electoral impact of the movement at the time of this writing. However, there are a number of observations that are relevant for our analysis. The study of Jimenez Sanchez (2011) on the municipal elections shows that there was the largest increase of blank and nullified votes since

1987, with an increase of 37 percent and 48 percent respectively from the prior municipal election in 2007. There was also an increase in the vote for the United Left. These trends were correlated with the cities where the movement had the strongest presence. Conservatives, Moderate Catalan nationalists and Basque pro-independence candidates also increased their votes. The combined impact of these votes negatively affected the Socialist party, which lost 19 percent of its votes in 2007, suffering the most serious defeat in municipal elections of its history, losing in particular the municipality of Barcelona that it had governed for three decades.

The parliamentary elections of November 20 were a resounding victory for the Partido Popular (PP), which obtained an absolute majority in terms of seats in the Parliament. This was considered by the conservatives, as well as their supporting media, as a rejection of the values of the movement by the silent majority of voters. In fact, a closer look at the election results tells a different story (Molinas 2011). The key factor in the election was the collapse of the Socialist party, which lost 4,300,000 votes compared to the prior election in 2008, while the Partido Popular won only 560,000 more votes than in 2008. The remaining votes went to minor parties that, with one exception, increased their votes substantially. Indeed, with the number of votes it obtained in 2011, the Partido Popular would have lost the election in 2004 and in 2008. It was the loss of the Socialists, not the victory of the conservatives, that gave the PP control of the parliament because of the distorted electoral law in favor of majority vote getters. Thus, although this analysis has to be confirmed with future studies, it seems that the main impact of the movement in the political system was to inflict major, lasting damage to the Socialist PSOE, the party that, in most elections, had dominated Spanish politics since 1982. This was not a deliberate strategy on the part of the movement. It was the consequence of a spontaneous reaction of withdrawal from the young electorate that made possible the Socialist victory in 2004, in the wake of the movement against the Iraq war, and against the manipulation of information on terrorist attacks by the Conservative Prime Minister Aznar (Castells 2009: 349–61). The conservative vote was not affected by the movement because of the fidelity of conservative voters to their party, and their general ideological distrust of popular protests. Indeed, parties such as the Socialists, which have based their historical legitimacy around claims of representing workers and civil society rather than the business and social elites, are dependent on their electoral base believing that they can still count on them. Since it became clear, through the protest of the movement, that the Socialist government was more interested in bailing out banks and following Merkel's instructions than helping the youth and preserving the welfare state, political disaffection against the system concentrated on the Socialists. They lost most of the institutional power they held around the country, and most observers believe that it will take a long time, if ever, for them to recover from this crushing defeat. The United Left (ex-Communists) considerably improved their electoral results, more than tripling their seats. However, this impressive display of Communist resilience actually translated into 11 seats in a Parliament of 350. Indeed, what the elections show is that the new politics, present in the movement, and the old politics, present in the institutions, are disconnected in the minds of citizens who will ultimately have to decide if they dare to reconcile their feelings with their vote.

A RHIZOMATIC REVOLUTION[8]

After months of intense activity, of mobilizing hundreds of thousands in the streets, of camping by the thousands, of networking around the world with similar movements, the measurable impact of the *Indignadas* in Spain appeared to be scant: few of their proposals have become policy, their main political impact was to contribute to the quasi-destruction of the Socialist party, and their dreams remained dreams.

A number of actions opposing evictions or denouncing institutional abuses found sympathy in the public opinion, but were not able to change the greed of landlords, the cold determination of lenders to execute their contracts, or the bureaucratic application of law and order by the authorities. Yes, there were, and there are, hundreds of autonomous assemblies in cities and neighborhoods around the country that meet with variable periodicity. There is relentless buzz on the Internet – debates, ideas, projects – but no coordination between the different voices of the movement. But a certain uneasiness became pervasive among the most active components of the movement.

On December 19, 2011, the Commission of the international extension of the Acampada Sol in Madrid made a symbolic decision: they declared themselves "on strike" from their activity and in a situation of "indefinite active reflexion." The reason:

> The 15-M is losing participation, we see it in the demonstrations, in assemblies, in the neighborhoods, in activities, in the Internet. . . . This is the time to stop and ask ourselves some deep questions . . . Have we forgotten to listen to each other? Are we reproducing the forms of old activism that have been shown to be useless because they exclude so many people? . . . The success of the movement depends of being again the 99% . . . We live in a unique historical moment when we can change the world, and we cannot miss it . . . We hope to be able to get out of our assemblies, to join each other again, without the constraints

of our commissions and working groups, to breathe fresh
air again and build a common path. A path that could allow
us to recover the force we had and that shook up those
above   (www.actasmadrid.tomalaplaza.net/?p=2518,   my
translation).

This was a clear manifestation of the self-reflexive character of a movement that was re-inventing politics and would
not yield to the temptation of becoming another political
force while refusing to accept the marginality of a critical
voice without influence in society at large. The question
for many was: what is next? Proposals started to circulate,
one of them targeting May 12, 2012 as a day for a coordinated global action to rekindle the struggle against an unjust
social order. But there was a prior question to be considered:
what has this movement, the largest autonomous mobilization in Spain in many years, been able to accomplish? The
most direct answer is that the true transformation was taking
place in people's minds. If people think otherwise, if they
share their indignation and harbor hope for change, society
will ultimately change according to their wishes. But how do
we know that such a cultural change is actually happening?
A very rough approximation can be derived from opinion
polls gauging the Spanish population's attitude regarding
the movement (*Zoom Politico* 2011; Metroscopia several surveys 2011; SimpleLógica 2011). Since the first survey in May
2011 to the latest at the time of this writing, conducted in
November 2011 and accessed on January 18, 2012, consist-
ently about three quarters of Spaniards were in sympathy
with the movement and shared its main ideas concerning the
critique of the political system, the responsibility of the banks
in the crisis, and a number of other themes. Seventy-five
percent considered the movement a source of regeneration
of democracy. However, 53.2 percent of respondents did not

think that the movement had helped to change the situation: the crisis continued, and nothing changed in politics as usual (<http://www.simplelogica.com/iop/iop11002.asp>). Indeed, this was a fair assessment of the situation.

Thus, the movement clearly voices the feeling and opinion of people at large. It is not a marginal protest, and refuses to be enclosed in a radical, ideological ghetto. Its ideas diffuse and are accepted by most people because they connect with the movement's frustration. But the ways to link these feelings with action, leading to material change in people's lives and social institutions, are still to be explored. Because this is exactly what new politics is. This sincere search undertaken by most in the movement is still a work in progress.

However, there is also a meaningful debate in some of the movement's circles. This is the critique of what many call a "productivist vision of social action." If nothing concrete is accomplished, there is failure. They argue this is the reproduction of the capitalist logic in the evaluation of the movement. By internalizing the productivity imperative, they actually engage in a self-defeating perspective in relation to the original goals of deep social transformation. Because if a precise outcome has to be obtained, then there is no way out of the need for a program, a strategy, an organization and an action plan going from A to B. These are all of the things that the *indignadas* have refused because they know by experience or they feel by intuition where they lead: to a new form of delegated democracy and to surrendering the meaning of life to economic rationality. So, a serene feeling of patience settled in many activists. Let us rebuild ourselves, they said, from the inside out, not waiting for the world to change to find the joy of living in our daily practice. It is winter now, and spring will come. Spring is the season of life and revolution. We will be there. There will be moments: moments of crisis, moments of struggle, moments of sorrow, moments of heroism, and exhilarating moments when new avenues open up and millions join out of their own desire, not because they have alienated their freedom to whatever flag was raised on their behalf. For a deep, self-reflexive current in the movement, what matters is the process, more than the product. In fact, the process is the product. Not that the ultimate product (a new society) is irrelevant. But this new society will result from the process, not from a preconceived blueprint of what the product should be. This is the true revolutionary transformation: the material production of social change not from programmatic goals but from the networked experiences of the actors in the movement. This is why inefficient assemblies are important, because these are the learning curves of new democracy. This is why commissions exist and die depending not on their effectiveness but on the commitment of people contributing their time and ideas. This is why non-violence is a fundamental practice, because a non-violent world cannot be created out of violence, let alone revolutionary violence. Because they think this non-productivist logic in the movement is the most important mental transformation, they accept the slowness of the process, and they place themselves in the long haul, because slowness is a virtue: it allows for self-reflection, makes it possible to correct mistakes, and provides space and time to enjoy the process of changing the world as a prelude to celebrating the new world in the making. "We are slow because we go far" was one of the most popular banners in the movement. In this long journey, the tempos alternate: sometimes accelerating, and then calming down in other moments. But the process never stops, even if it remains unseen for a while. There are roots of the new life spreading everywhere, with no central plan, but moving and networking, keeping the energy flowing, waiting for spring. Because these nodes are always connected. There are nodes of Internet networks, locally and globally, and there are personal networks, vibrating with the pulse of a new kind of revolution whose most revolutionary act is the invention of itself.

NOTES

1 There is some debate within the Spanish movement about its labeling. Most people in the movement simply talk about "the movement." The most frequent name used in the movement is the "15-M," a neutral term simply designating the date of the first large demonstration that ushered in the protest throughout Spain on May 15, 2011. I have retained the name of "*Indignadas*" because this is the term most often used in Spain and around the world among people at large to designate the Spanish movement, after the initial name circulating on the Internet – #spanishrevolution – ceased to be used. *Indignadas* was largely used by the media because it is a catchy term. Some activists do not like it because it refers only to indignation, and not to the positive, propositional dimension of the movement, but this double character is clear in the text of my analysis. In my observation, most people sympathizing with the movement in Spain would refer to the "*indignados*," because this term echoed their own feelings. Finally, I have used the name *Indignados/as* systematically in feminine to follow the cultural habit of the movement, to reverse the traditional male-dominated connotation of language.

2 The study presented in this chapter is largely based on fieldwork research, participant observation, and interviewing by our research team on alternative cultures at the Open University of Catalonia, Barcelona, a team formed by Amalia Cardenas, Joana Conill and myself. Amalia and

Joana did most of the fieldwork and interviewing. We also followed the movement through reports and accounts on the Internet. Two interviews have been essential for my understanding of the movement, conducted by Amalia Cardenas and Joana Conill in February 2012. One with Javier Toret, and another with Arnau Monterde, both self-reflexive activists in the movement, who played a significant role in the origins of *Democracia Real Ya*. My own prior conversations with Javier and Arnau were also key sources of ideas and analysis. Other sources of information, both in print and on the web, are cited in the references, without being attributed to any specific statement, as they have been mixed in my narrative.

3 On the origins of *Democracia Real Ya*, and the subsequent development of the movement in Barcelona, I have relied on the excellent analysis by Monterde (2010–11).

4 Interview and translation by Amalia Cardenas, Barcelona, February 2012.

5 The pamphlet by Hessel (2010) was translated in Spanish and widely read by many in Spain in the months prior to the movement. It has sold over three million copies worldwide. Most activists do not acknowledge his direct influence, attributing it to the media obsession to find sources of inspiration from outside the movement itself. However, I found in most cases a deep respect and appreciation for the stern denunciation of the system by someone of a much older generation, even if its reference to the values of the French Resistance in War World II did not really connect with the movement. In fact, Hessel called for the necessity of leadership if the movement were to succeed, in clear dissonance with the philosophy of the movement. Yet, there was a tender affection for this dignified man appealing to the defence of principles that were being sullied by European governments. His

main contribution was probably to find a word that could resonate.

6 Javier Toret, Barcelona, February 2012, interview and translation by Amalia Cardenas.

7 In 2012, a number of demonstrations, particularly in Barcelona, were followed by violent confrontations between the police and small groups of youth burning garbage containers and breaking windows of banks and shops. Although the origin of these actions remains unclear, there is certainly a propensity among some youth, outraged by their living conditions, without any positive response to their claims, to engage in violence. These violent actions are magnified by the media and used by the authorities to de-legitimize the movement, going as far as denouncing the rise of urban guerrillas, an obvious exaggeration if we consider the international experience of what urban guerrillas are. Yet, while this particular movement is overwhelmingly non-violent, there is an ambiguity among actors of social change throughout history concerning the question of violence, including Karl Marx: "Force is the midwife of every society which is pregnant with a new one. It is itself an economic power." *Capital*, cited in Bruce Lawrence and Aisha Karim (eds.) (2007) *On Violence: A Reader*. Duke University Press, Durham, NC, p. 17. This volume is an excellent compendium of debates about violence in the processes of social change.

8 The concept of rhizomatic revolution was suggested to me by Isidora Chacon. According to Wikipedia, a rhizome is "a characteristically horizontal stem of a plant that is usually found underground, often sending out roots and shoots from its nodes ... If a rhizome is separated into pieces, each piece may be able to give rise to a new plant."

REFERENCES

Bennasar, S. (2011) *La primavera dels indign@ts*. Meteora, Barcelona.

Calvo, K., Gomez-Pastrana, T. and Mena, L. (2011) Movimiento 15M: quienes son y que reivindican? *Zoom Politico*, 4/11: 4–17. Laboratorio de Alternativas: Salamanca.

Castells, M. (2009) *Communication Power*. Oxford University Press, Oxford.

The Cocktail Analysis. (2011) *Movimiento #15M/Democracia Real Ya: Representatividad, movilizacion y canales de informacion*. Madrid: The Cocktail Analysis (www.tcanalysis.com, accessed January 18, 2012).

Conill, J., Cardenas, A., Castells, M. and Servon, L. (2012a) Another life is possible: the rise of alternative economic cultures. In Castells, M., Caraca, J. and Cardoso, G. (eds.) *Aftermath. The Cultures of the Economic Crisis*. Oxford University Press, Oxford.

Conill, J., Cardenas, A., Castells, M., Servon, L. and Hlebik, S. (2012b) *Otra vida es posible: practicas economicas alternativas en la crisis*. Ediciones UOC Press, Barcelona.

Fernandez-Planells, A. and Figueras, M. (2012) *Plaza en red. Características del seguimiento informativo de la @acampadaBCN por parte de los/las jóvenes participantes en Plaza Cataluña*. (Informe). Available at: <http://hdl.handle.net/10230/16284>.

Hessel, S. (2010) *Indignez-vous!* Indigene, Montpellier.

Jimenez Sanchez, M. (2011) Influyo el 15M en las elecciones municipales? *Zoom Politico*, 4/11: 18-28. Laboratorio de Alternativas, Salamanca.

Lawrence, B. and Karim, A. (eds.) (2007) *On Violence: A Reader*. Duke University Press, Durham, NC.

Metroscopia. (2011) Opinion de los Espanoles ante el 15 M. June 22, 2011.

Molinas, C. (2011) La izquierda volatil sigue decidiendo pero . . . *El Pais*, November 22.

Monterde Mateo, A. (2010–11) *Movimients moleculars a la ciutat-xarxa, produccio de noves subjectivitats connectedes y emergencia dels "commons."* Un preludi del 15M. Barcelona: Universitat Oberta de Catalunya, Master Thesis del Programa de Master en Societat de la Informacio i el Coneixement (unpublished).

Serrano, E. (2011) *El poder de las palabras*. Madrilonia.org (blog), June.

Simple Lógica. (2011) *Indices de opinión publica sobre el movimiento 15 M*, Madrid. Available at: <http://www.simplelogica.com/iop/iop11002.asp> [Accessed January 18, 2012].

Taibo, C. (2011) *El 15-M en sesenta preguntas*. Los libros de la Catarata, Madrid.

Various Authors. (2011a) *Nosotros los Indignados*. Destino, Barcelona.

Various Authors. (2011b) *Las voces del 15-M*. Del Lince, Barcelona.

Various Authors. (2011c) *La rebelion de los indignados*. Popular, Madrid.

Velasco, P. (2011) *No nos representan. El Manifiesto de los Indignados en 25 propuestas*. Temas de Hoy, Madrid.

Web resources

Evolution of the movement

15October.net. (2011) October 29 #Robinhood global march. [Online] Available at: <http://15october.net/> [Accessed February 25, 2012].

Acampadasol. (2011) Cómo fue #acampadasol, texto para difusión internacional. [Online] Available at: <http://madrid.tomalaplaza.net/2011/07/16/como-fue-acampadas

ol-texto-para-difusion-internacional/> [Accessed February 25, 2012].

Antibanks. (2011) September 17th everywhere. [Online] Available at: <http://antibanks.takethesquare.net/2011/08/15/september-17th-everywhere/> [Accessed February 25, 2012].

Bcnhubmeeting. (2011) 15SHM statement. *Bcnhubmeeting*, [blog] September 18. Available at: <http://bcnhubmeeting. wordpress.com/> [Accessed February 25, 2012].

Blanco, J. L. (2011) Análisis estadístico del movimiento 15M: ¿Cuántos y quiénes se han manifestado?. *Ciencia explicada*, [blog] October 26. Available at: <http://www. ciencia-explicada.com/2011/10/analisis-estadistico-del-mo vimiento-15m.html> [Accessed January 18, 2012].

Bretos, D. (2011) Democracia Real Ya convoca una manifestación internacional para el 15 de octubre. *Nación Red*, [Online] May 30. Available at: <http://www.nacionred. com/sociedad-civil-digital/democracia-real-ya-convoca-una-manifestacion-internacional-para-el-15-de-octubre> [Accessed February 25, 2012].

Buentes, P. (2011) ¿Como se gestó el 15M? [Online] Available at: <http://storify.com/pablobuentes/que-es-y-como-se-gesto-el-movimiento-15m> [Accessed February 25, 2012].

Democracia Real Ya. (2011) Datos de participación oficiales de DRY. [online] Available at: <http://www.face book.com/notes/democracia-real-ya/datos-de-participaci% C3%B3n-oficiales-de-dry/139427826133836> [Accessed February 25, 2012].

De Soto, P. (2011) Los mapas del 15M al 15O. *Periodismo Humano*, [blog] October 15. Available at: <http://tomalapalabra.periodismohumano.com/2011/10/1 5/los-mapas-del-15m-al-15o/> [Accessed February 25, 2012].

Fernández-Savater, A. (2011) Apuntes de AcampadaSol. *Publico.es Fuera de lugar blog*, [blog] June 9. Available at: <http://blogs.publico.es/fueradelugar/531/apuntes-de-aca mpadasol-8> [Accessed February 25, 2012].

Galarraga, N. (2011) 951 ciudades en 82 países (por ahora) se suman a la protesta planetaria del 15-O. *El País*, [online] October 14. Available at: <http://politica.elpais.com/p olitica/2011/10/13/actualidad/1318509855_468846.html> [Accessed February 25, 2012].

Kaosenlared. (2011) Inside 15M: 48 horas con l@s indignad@s. [video online] Available at: <http://www. portaloaca.com/videos/documentales-/3194-documental-inside-15m-48-horas-con-ls-indignads.html> [Accessed February 25, 2012].

Lenore, Victor. (2011) 15 datos que explican el 15M. *Madrilonia.org*, [blog] September 19. Available at <http:// madrilonia.org/2011/07/15-datos-que-explican-el-15m/> [Accessed February 25, 2012].

Letón, H. and Sanz D. (2011) ¿Quién es quién en las protestas de la red?. *Diagonal Web*, [Online] May 4. Available at: <http://www.diagonalperiodico.net/Quien-es-quien-en-la s-protestas-de.html> [Accessed February 25, 2012].

Noor, O. (2011) Espagne labs: Inventer la démocratie du futur. *Owni*, [Online] June 6. Available at: <http://owni. fr/2011/06/06/espagne-labs-inventer-la-democratie-du-fu tur/> [Accessed February 25, 2012].

Saleh, S. (2011) El núcleo del 15-M acuerda irse el domingo. *El Pais*, [Online] June 8. Available at: <http://www.elpais.com/articulo/madrid/nucleo/15-M/ac uerda/irse/domingo/elpepiespmad/20110608elpmad_1/T es> [Accessed February 25, 2012].

Sánchez J. (2011) El 15M rompe otro tópico y llena Madrid en verano. *Periodismo Humano*, [Online] July 25. Available at: <http://periodismohumano.com/sociedad/

el-15m-rompe-otro-topico-y-llena-madrid-en-verano.htm l> [Accessed February 25, 2012].

Sandiumenge, L. (2011) La calle (y la red) es nuestra. *La Vanguardia.com Los guerros del teclado*, [blog] May 2. Available at: <http://blogs.lavanguardia.com/guerreros-del-teclado/2011/05/02/la-calle-y-la-red-es-nuestra/> [Accessed February 25, 2012].

Taylor, A. (2011) Occupy Wall Street Spreads beyond NYC. *The Atlantic*, [Online] October 7. Available at: <http://www.theatlantic.com/infocus/2011/10/occupy-wall-street-spreads-beyond-nyc/100165/> [Accessed February 25, 2012].

Versus Sistema. (2011) ¿Qué ha pasado con la Spanish Revolution?. *Versus Sistema*, [blog] September 23. Available at: <http://www.versussistema.com/2011/09/%C2%BFque-ha-pasado-con-la-spanish-revolution/> [Accessed February 25, 2012].

On violence

Hotmatube. (2011) ¿Quiénes son los violentos?. [video online] Available at: <http://www.youtube.com/watch?v=pbhuEVgU9mI&feature=player_embedded> [Accessed February 25, 2012].

Teclista. (2011) Quince de mayo no tuvimos miedo. [video online] Available at: <http://vimeo.com/29544229> [Accessed February 25, 2012].

On Internet in the camps

Map of interactions
BifiUnizar. (2011) Interacciones entre usuarios 15m. [video online] Available at: <http://15m.bifi.es/index.php> [Accessed February 25, 2012].

Twitter in the occupied squares

15October.net, 2011. Reports. [Online] Available at: <http://map.15october.net/> [Accessed February 25, 2012].

Algo grande. (2011) Clasificación de las acampadas por el volumen de su conversación. *Algo grande*, [blog] May 23. Available at: <http://algogrande.org/seccion/analisis/> [Accessed February 25, 2012].

Comscore. (2011) El tiempo en la Red crece en España un 17% en mayo, influido por los acontecimientos nacionales e internacionales. [Press release] July 7, 2011. Available at: <http://www.comscore.com/esl/Press_Events/Press_Rele ases/2011/7/comScore_Releases_Overview_of_European_ Internet_Usage_for_May_2011> [Accessed February 25, 2012].

Congosto, M. L. (2011) Evolución de la propagación del 15M en la plaza de Twitter. *Barri blog*, [blog] May 21. Available at: <http://www.barriblog.com/index.php/2011/05/21/evo lucion-de-la-propagacion-del-15m-en-la-plaza-de-twitter /> [Accessed February 25, 2012].

On media and the movement

Ibarrondo J. (2011a) Medios de comunicación y 15-M: un avispero fuera de control. *Diagonal Web*, [Online] July 14. Available at: <http://www.diagonalperiodico.net/Medios-de-comunicacion-y-15-M-un.html> [Accessed February 25, 2012].

Ibarrondo, J. (2011b) Medios de comunicación y 15M. *Análisis Madrid 15M*, [blog] July 18. Available at: <http://analisismadrid.wordpress.com/2011/07/18/medios-de-co municacion-y-15m-juan-ibarrondo/> [Accessed February 25, 2012].

Público.es. (2011) Los manifestantes de "Occupy Wall Street" son como los nazis. *Público.es*, [Online] October 5.

Available at: <http://www.publico.es/internacional/399995
/los-manifestantes-de-occupy-wall-street-son-como-los-
nazis> [Accessed February 25, 2012].

On leadership

Balblogger, R. (2011) Cómo se hace una asamblea en Wall
Street. *Tuamiguelturrayyoafiladelfia*, [blog] October 12.
Available at: <http://tuamiguelturrayyoafiladelfia.blogspot.
com/2011/10/como-se-hace-una-asamblea-en-wall.html>
[Accessed February 25, 2012].

General sources

15m.cc. (2011) Project. [online] Available at: <http://
www.15m.cc/> [Accessed February 25, 2012]. (Set of
documents and interviews available on the web with free
licenses. It is a documentary project in the making.)
Centro de documentación Ciudadana. (2011) Available at:
<http://www.archive.org/details/centrodedocumentacionc
iudadana> [Accessed February 25, 2012].

Websites of the movement

Acampadabcn. (2011a) [Online] Available at: <http://acam-
padabcn.wordpress.com/> [Accessed February 25, 2012].
Acampadabcn. (2011b) Actes de l'Assemblea. [Online]
Available at: <http://acampadabcn.wordpress.com/docu
ments/actes-de-lassemblea-general/> [Accessed February
25, 2012].
#Acampadasol. (2011) Available at: <http://madrid.tomal
aplaza.net/> [Accessed February 25, 2012].
Acampadatrs. (2011a) Available at: <http://acampadatrs.
net/> [Accessed February 25, 2012].

Acampadatrs. (2011b) Acampadatrs – Pads. [Online] Available at: <http://agora.acampadatrs.net/es/node/3/content/pads> [Accessed February 25, 2012].

Acampadatrs. (2011c) Agora. Available at: <http://agora.acampadatrs.net/> [Accessed February 25, 2012].

Análisis Madrid. (2011) Available at: <http://analisismadrid.wordpress.com/> [Accessed February 25, 2012].

Democracia Real Ya. (2011) Available at: <http://www.Democracia Real Ya.es/> [Accessed February 25, 2012].

Marchapopularindignada. (2011) Available at: <http://marchapopularindignada.wordpress.com/> [Accessed February 25, 2012].

N-1. (2011) Available at: <https://n-1.cc/> [Accessed February 25, 2012]. This is a critical source; it reports on internal documents and interactions in the movement not available anywhere else.

Occupy Wall Street. (2011) Available at: <http://occupy-wallst.org/> [Accessed February 25, 2012].

Tomalaplaza.net. (2011a) Actas de #acampandasol. Available at: <http://actasmadrid.tomalaplaza.net/> [Accessed February 25, 2012].

Tomalaplaza.net. (2011b) Grupo Pensamiento. Available at: <http://madrid.tomalaplaza.net/category/grupos-de-trabajo/pensamiento/> [Accessed February 25, 2012].

OCCUPY WALL STREET:

HARVESTING THE SALT OF

THE EARTH

THE OUTRAGE, THE THUNDER, THE SPARK

There was outrage in the air. At first, suddenly, the real estate market plunged. Hundreds of thousands lost their homes, and millions lost much of the value they had traded their lives for. Then, the financial system came to the brink of collapse, as a result of the speculation and greed of its managers. Who were bailed out. With taxpayers' money. They did not forget to collect their millionaire bonuses, rewarding their clumsy performance. Surviving financial companies cut off lending, thus closing down thousands of firms, shredding millions of jobs and sharply reducing pay. No one was held accountable. Both political parties prioritized the rescue of the financial system. Obama was overwhelmed by the depth of the crisis and quickly set aside most of his campaign promises – a campaign that had brought unprecedented hope for a young generation that had re-entered politics to revitalize American democracy.

The hardest was the fall. People became discouraged and enraged. Some began to quantify their rage. The share of US income of the top 1 percent of Americans jumped from 9 percent in 1976 to 23.5 percent in 2007. Cumulative productivity growth between 1998 and 2008 reached about 30 percent, but real wages increased only by 2 percent during the decade. The financial industry captured most of the productivity gains, as its share of profits increased from 10 percent in the 1980s to 40 percent in 2007, and the value of its shares increased from 6 percent to 23 percent in spite of employing only 5 percent of the labor force. Indeed, the top 1 percent appropriated 58 percent of the economic growth in this period. In the decade preceding the crisis, hourly real wages increased by 2 percent while the income of the richest 5 percent increased by 42 percent. The pay of a CEO was 50 times higher than that of the average worker in 1980, and 350 times more in 2010. These were no longer abstract figures. There were faces, too: Madoff, Wagoner, Nardelli, Pandit, Lewis, Sullivan. And they were interspersed with politicians and government officials (Bush, Paulsen, Summers, Bernanke, Geithner and, yes, Obama) who were rationalizing people's pain and arguing for the need of saving finance to save people's lives. Moreover, the Republican Party went on a vengeful offensive to bring down a popular president who came to power advocating for an active role of government in improving the welfare of society. The electoral success of this suicidal strategy allowed the Republican dominated Congress to block most reform initiatives, thus aggravating the crisis and increasing its social costs. The first expression of popular outrage was the rise of the Tea Party, a mixture of populism and libertarianism that offered a channel of mobilization to a variety of indignant opposition to government in general and to Obama in particular. Yet, when it became clear that it was bankrolled by Koch Industries, among other corporations, and captured by the right of the Republican Party as storm-troopers to be sacrificed in the final stage of the electoral process, it lost appeal for many of its participants. Diehard Tea Partiers became militants of a manipulated cause: to undo government, so to free the hands of corporate business. A sense of despair set throughout the land. Then, there was thunder.

It came from Tahrir Square; an irony of history considering that for most Americans, only oil and Israel are of any relevance in the Middle East. Yet, images and sounds of people's determination to bring down dictatorships against all odds, at whatever cost, rekindled faith in people's power, at least in some activists' quarters. The echo of the Arab revolts was amplified by the news coming from Europe, and particularly from Spain, proposing novel forms of mobilization and organization, based on the practice of direct democracy as a way to further the demand for real democracy. In a world connected live by the Internet, concerned citizens became immediately aware of struggles and projects they could identify with.

The Obama campaign had left an imprint on thousands who had believed in the possibility of real change, and had enacted a new form of political mobilization in which the Internet networks became crucial, as far as they connected people meeting face-to-face in neighborhoods and living rooms, to form an insurgent political movement. I documented the power of this truly new form of politics, inspired by hope and powered by the Internet, in my book *Communication Power* (2009).[1]

Many former Obamists, together with thousands of people who have been at the forefront of struggles against social injustice for quite some time, including the public sector unions that mobilized in and around the Wisconsin campaign for bargaining rights, were receptive of the buzz surrounding the #spanishrevolution and of the Greek demonstrations against the crisis. Some of them traveled to Europe. They saw the camps, participated in the General Assemblies and experienced a new form of deliberation and decision-making, actually connecting with a historical tradition of assembly-led movements on both sides of the Atlantic. They participated in meetings in which the call for a global demonstration on October 15, 2011, under the slogan "United for Global Change," was discussed and decided. In this way, the global networks of hope extended decisively to the United States in the summer of 2011. Then came the spark.

On July 13, 2011, Adbusters, a Vancouver-based journal of cultural critique, posted the following call on its blog:

> #occupywallstreet
> Are you ready for a Tahrir moment? On September 17th, flood into lower Manhattan, set up tents, kitchens, peaceful barricades and occupy Wall Street.

And they went on to elaborate:

> A worldwide shift in revolutionary tactics is underway right now that bodes well for the future. [There is a] spirit of this fresh tactic, a fusion of Tahrir with the acampadas of Spain.
>
> The beauty of this new formula . . . is its pragmatic simplicity: we talk to each other in various physical gatherings and virtual people's assemblies. We zero in on what our one demand will be, a demand that awakens the imagination and, if achieved, would propel us toward the radical democracy of the future . . . and then we go out and seize a square of singular symbolic significance and put our asses on the line to make it happen. The time has come to deploy

this emerging stratagem against the greatest corrupter of our democracy: Wall Street, the financial Gomorrah of America.

On September 17, we want to see 20,000 people flood into lower Manhattan, set up tents, kitchens, peaceful barricades and occupy Wall Street for a few months. Once there, we shall incessantly repeat one simple demand in a plurality of voices ... Following this model, what is our equally uncomplicated demand? ... [It is the one] that gets at the core of why the American political establishment is currently unworthy of being called a democracy: we demand that Barack Obama ordain a Presidential Commission tasked with ending the influence money has over our representatives in Washington. It's time for DEMOCRACY NOT CORPORATOCRACY, we're doomed without it.

This demand seems to capture the current national mood because cleaning up corruption in Washington is something all Americans, right and left, yearn for and can stand behind ... This could be the beginning of a whole new social dynamic in America, a step beyond the Tea Party movement, where, instead of being caught helpless by the current power structure, we the people start getting what we want whether it be the dismantling of half the 1,000 military bases America has around the world to the reinstatement of the Glass-Steagall Act or a three strikes and you're out law for corporate criminals. Beginning from one simple demand – a presidential commission to separate money from politics – we start setting the agenda for a new America. Post a comment and help each other zero in on what our one demand will be. And then let's screw up our courage, pack our tents and head to Wall Street with a vengeance September 17. **For the wild, Culture Jammers HQ.**

The date selected was symbolic: September 17 is the anniversary of the signing of the American Constitution, although few people are aware of it. And so, the initial call to occupy was aimed at restoring democracy by making the political system independent from the power of money. To be sure, there were other networks and groups involved in the origins of the occupy movement, and some in the movement have resented the attribution of the first call to Adbusters. For instance, AmpedStatus, a network of activists organized around a website, had been posting for quite a while analysis and information on the financial destruction of the US economy. On February 15, 2010, David DeGraw posted the first of a six-part series on the financial crisis in America whose first sentence read "It's time for 99% of Americans to mobilize and aggressively move on common sense political reforms."[2] The AmpedStatus website came under repeated cyber attacks by mysterious aggressors. Anonymous came to the rescue and the website, and the network behind it, survived and started to build a 99% movement, planning for an "Empire State Rebellion" and calling for the occupation of Wall Street. A subgroup within Anonymous joined forces with AmpedStatus and they created an A99 platform presented in AmpedStatus's social network. On March 23, 2011, Anonymous called for a Day of Rage, in the wake of similar calls in the Arab world. The A99 coalition also called, unsuccessfully, to occupy on June 14 Liberty Park (later named Zuccotti Park), two blocks from Wall Street. They came together with a group of New York activists protesting against budget cuts who had set up a camp known as Bloombergville. These activists' networks evolved to form the New York City General Assembly, building the protest on grassroots mobilization and community-based organizing. It is in this context of rampant activism in New York that Adbusters issued its call to occupy on September 17. All

of the pre-existing networks did not see any problem in joining the call and preparing jointly the occupation. A paternity
test would have been contradictory to the spirit of a collaborative, decentralized movement, and so everybody called
for people to "rebel against the system of economic tyranny
in a non-violent manner," and to come to Wall Street on
September 17. About 1,000 people came, demonstrated in
Wall Street and occupied Zuccotti Park. The spark had lit
a fire.

THE PRAIRIE ON FIRE

The September 17 demonstration on Wall Street, with the
subsequent occupation of Zuccotti Park, was followed by
several demonstrations in New York, in spite of the police
making hundreds of arrests under several pretexts. The
more the police resorted to repression, the more the images
posted on YouTube of these actions mobilized protesters.
Solidarity with the occupiers came from many quarters.
Anonymous revealed the name of an NYPD police officer
who maced, without any reason, young women marching
in a demonstration. On September 27, 2,000 people gathered in the General Assembly at the occupied camp, with
New York Councilman Charles Barron, intellectuals such
as Cornel West and others addressing the assembly, as
Michael Moore had done two days earlier. The New York
Local of the Transport Workers Union of America voted
to support the movement and to join in the demonstrations. The AFL-CIO also declared its support and called
upon its membership to demonstrate. On October 1, 5,000
people took over the Brooklyn Bridge and the police set
up a trap on the bridge and proceeded to arrest over 700.
In response, on October 5, following a call from Occupy
Wall Street together with the labor unions, 15,000 people

demonstrated from Foley Square, in Lower Manhattan, to Zuccotti Park. The occupation was consolidated. With images and news spreading over the Internet, occupations started spontaneously in many other cities during the first few days of October: Chicago, Boston, Washington DC, San Francisco, Oakland, Los Angeles, Atlanta, Fort Lauderdale, Tampa, Houston, Austin, Philadelphia, New Orleans, Cleveland, Las Vegas, Jersey City, Hartford, Salt Lake City, Cincinnati, Seattle and even outside the White House, as well as countless neighborhoods and small towns around the country. Maps 1 and 2 show the *speed* and the *spread* of the occupy movement. Moreover, the data represented in the maps are incomplete, as there is no reliable, unified database on the occupation, although the activists who are building the directory section of the website occupy.net are making good progress toward this goal. However, it is safe to estimate that the number of demonstrations throughout the United States was over 600. For instance, according to a study conducted by a team directed by Christopher Chase-Dunn at the University of California Riverside, out of 482 towns in California, 143 had Occupy groups on Facebook, usually indicating the existence of an occupied space.[3] Not all occupy camps were permanent; many of them were daily gatherings in assemblies and working groups. Thus, Occupy Youngstown, Ohio would hold regular weekly meetings to discuss issues, post on their Facebook page, and then go home for the night. In other words, there was considerable diversity in the forms of protest and in the shape of the occupations. But what is clear is the fast spread of the movement throughout the entire geography of the country: Mosier, Oregon, population 430, may have been the smallest town to have an occupation, and every state had at least one occupied site – even North Dakota, the last one to start a camp.

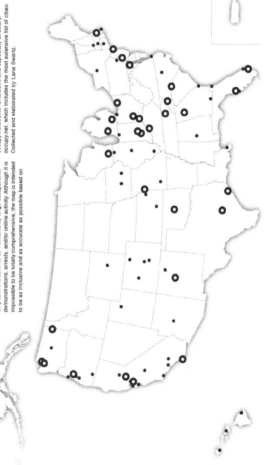

Spread of Occupations in the United States, September 17– October 9, 2011

This map depicts the location of occupations that began by October 9, 2011. It demonstrates the rapid spread of the movement after the initial spark in New York City on September 17, 2011. Larger circles represent particularly active locations, as indicated by large occupations, demonstrations, arrests, and/or online activity. Although it is impossible to be totally comprehensive, the map is intended to be as inclusive and as accurate as possible based on existing information. It was compiled by cross-referencing data pulled from the Facebook, API, news coverage, and lists produced by Chase-Dunn and Curran-Strange (2011), collectivedisorder.com, firedoglake.com, occupylist.org, occupywallstreetevents.com, and especially directory. occupy.net, which includes the most extensive list of cities. Collected and elaborated by Lana Swartz.

Map 1: Spread of occupations in the United States, September 17–October 9, 2011

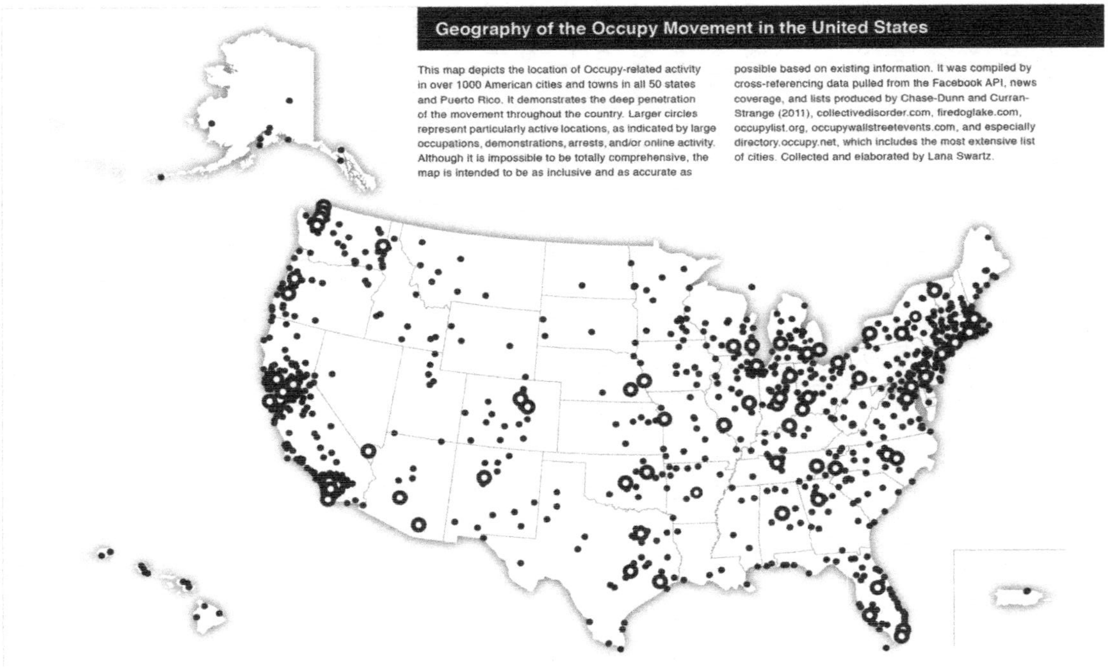

Geography of the Occupy Movement in the United States

This map depicts the location of Occupy-related activity in over 1000 American cities and towns in all 50 states and Puerto Rico. It demonstrates the deep penetration of the movement throughout the country. Larger circles represent particularly active locations, as indicated by large occupations, demonstrations, arrests, and/or online activity. Although it is impossible to be totally comprehensive, the map is intended to be as inclusive and as accurate as

possible based on existing information. It was compiled by cross-referencing data pulled from the Facebook API, news coverage, and lists produced by Chase-Dunn and Curran-Strange (2011), collectivedisorder.com, firedoglake.com, occupylist.org, occupywallstreetevents.com, and especially directory.occupy.net, which includes the most extensive list of cities. Collected and elaborated by Lena Swartz.

Map 2: Geography of the Occupy movement in the United States

The rapid propagation of the Occupy fire across the American prairie is full of meaning. It shows the depth and spontaneity of the protest, rooted in the outrage felt by the majority of the population across the country and in society at large. It also shows the seizing of the opportunity by many to voice their concerns and to discuss alternatives in the midst of a generalized crisis of trust in the economy and in the polity. This was not a campus revolt or a cosmopolitan counter-culture. It was spoken with as many voices and accents as there are present in a highly diverse and multicultural society.

Who, then, were these occupiers? There was in fact a great deal of social and political diversity among those participating in the movement. There was also a wide variation depending on the level of involvement in the movement, from full-time presence in the camps to participating in the assemblies or engaging in demonstrations or actions of protest. At the time of this writing, the various data-gathering efforts in process are still not available. Yet, I have been able to use some preliminary results from what appears to be a reliable data source: the online survey coordinated by MIT's Sasha Costanza-Chock and the Occupy Research Network[4] of occupy activists in the country. I have also compared his data with the findings of Baruch College's Hector Cordero-Guzman's non-representative sample of visitors to OccupyWallSt.org.[5] On the basis of these surveys, and personal observation from participants in the movement, it appears that the majority of those fully engaged in most camps were young professionals and students in the 20–40 age group, with a slightly higher percentage of women than men. About one half of them had a full-time job, with a significant number being unemployed, underemployed, temporarily employed or employed part-time. The income level of the majority seemed to be around the median income level of Americans. They were an educated group, with half of them holding a college degree, and many more having finished some college. Thus, as in similar movements in other countries, the Occupy participants appear to be relatively young, educated people whose professional expectations are limited in the current economy. They are white/Caucasian in their large majority, although there is a presence of minorities, particularly African Americans, who often organized their own caucuses within the movement. However, only about one fifth of the occupiers actually slept in the camps. The large majority participated in daily activities, and about three quarters in street demonstrations. Thus, to apprehend the diversity of the movement, we must include many other stakeholders who were present in its activities, particularly middle-aged union members, as well as working class people in their fifties, some unemployed and bearing the brunt of the recession on their lives. Numerous veterans were in the camps and at the forefront of the demonstrations. And, as the occupations lengthened, most sites became havens for homeless people who could find food, shelter and protection. Yet, their proportion among the occupiers was limited, in spite of their high social visibility. There was often tension among occupiers about how to handle their presence, yet it was ideologically impossible to reproduce the same kind of prejudice towards the homeless that permeates the mainstream society.

The diversity within the occupiers was even greater in terms of their ideological and political preferences: anarchists were the most vocal, but Libertarians (some of them Republican) were present, as were some disappointed former Tea Party activists, and a few fringe leftists. But by and large the movement was made up of a large majority of democratic voters, as well as of politically independent-minded people who were in search of new forms of changing the world and/or fending off the threat of the crisis on their lives.

Perhaps the most significant characteristic of the occupiers is that this movement did not come out of the blue, even if it was spontaneous and leaderless. Preliminary findings from the Occupy Research Network survey indicate that the vast majority of the active persons in the movement had participated in various social movements, and had been involved in non-governmental organizations and political campaigns. They had also been present in networks of activism on the Internet, posting videos and participating in animated political forums. By converging on Occupy Wall Street from multiple streams of resistance and alternative politics, they formed a wide river of protest and projects that flooded the plains, climbed the mountains and nested in the towns of the entire country.

The rapid geographical spread of the movement reflected its viral diffusion on the Internet. The movement was born on the Internet, diffused by the Internet, and maintained its presence on the Internet, as most occupations set up their own websites, as well as their specific groups and other social networks.

Yet, at the same time, the movement's material form of existence was the *occupation of public space*. A space where the protesters could come together and form a community beyond their differences. A space of conviviality. A space of debate, to move from contesting an unjust system to reconstructing society from the bottom up. In sum, a space of autonomy. Because only by being autonomous could they overcome multiple forms of ideological and political control and find, individually and collectively, new ways of life.

Thus, the Occupy movement built *a new form of space*, a mixture of space of places, in a given territory, and space of flows, on the Internet. One could not function without the other; it is this hybrid space that characterized the movement. Places made possible face-to-face interaction, sharing the experience, the danger and the difficulties as well as facing together the police and enduring together rain, cold and the loss of comfort in their daily lives. But social networks on the Internet allowed the experience to be communicated and amplified, bringing the entire world into the movement, and creating a permanent forum of solidarity, debate and strategic planning.

Occupied spaces also created *a new form of time*, which some in the camps characterized as a feeling of "forever." The routine of their daily lives was interrupted; a parenthesis was open with an undefined time horizon. Many thought that the occupation would last as long as the institutions remained unresponsive to their critiques and requests. Given the uncertainty of when and if the eviction would come, the occupations lived on a day-by-day basis, without deadlines, thus freeing themselves from time constraints, while rooting the occupation in everyday life experience. This made the timeless time of the occupation an experience that was exhausting and exhilarating at the same time because, as one occupier in Washington DC put it:

> We are tired, and get wet and cold. Sharing Porta-Potties, walking 13 blocks to the showers the CWA lets us use and brushing our teeth and spitting into a soggy paper coffee cup takes its toll . . . But we show up [for General Assembly] and listen to everyone who has an opinion or proposal and eventually we do reach consensus . . . As I sat there, watching the fully engaged occupiers, one more time I marveled. This is the way it is supposed to be. We've got a long way to go, but every so often I get to feel the chill running up and down my spine telling me that this is what hope looks like.[6]

This hope was born from the material verification that another life is possible in the makeshift community rising from the protest.

In the large occupations, such as New York, Los Angeles or Oakland, daily life was organized with great care. Tents were set up, then toilets, kitchens, daycare centers, children's play spaces, a community garden, a people's library, an Occupy University where lecturers were invited to address the occupiers, and media centers, sometimes powered by bicycles. Medical assistance provided by volunteer medical personnel was organized, legal teams were on hand, Wi-Fi networks were constructed, a website was developed, security of the camp was taken care of, conflicts were mediated, and even a hosting team would offer tours of the occupation to visitors who were curious about the movement, and perhaps also interested in joining. There was also the thorny issue of managing donations. Money was necessary to buy supplies for hundreds of people, but also to bail out those who were arrested, and to support the activities of the movement. In fact, the Occupy movement received hundreds of thousands of dollars in donations. The question then became how to manage them, since there was no legal entity able to set up a bank account. In some cases those in charge of the donations committee just put it in their own personal accounts. But of course this raised issues of paying personal taxes as well as potential embezzlement of the funds. It is striking that there are few known cases of undue appropriation. However, in many cases there was an incorporation of the camp as a legal entity to set up financial accountability. The issue then was the need to pay taxes for the money deposited in these accounts, something that the libertarian branch of the movement would oppose. Yet, all these decisions to be made are what constituted the process of experimentation that was at the heart of the movement.

As important as the material organization of the occupation was, it was the process of communication that enabled
the movement to find internal cohesion and external support. Communication networks were the blood vessels of the
Occupy movement.

A NETWORKED MOVEMENT

Occupy Wall Street was born digital. The cry of outrage
and the call to occupy came from various blogs (Adbusters,
AmpedStatus and Anonymous, among others), and was
posted on Facebook and spread by Twitter. Adbusters registered the hashtag #occupywallstreet on June 9, 2011 and
included it in its first call to demonstrate on its blog, which
was linked to its Facebook group on July 13. Groups and
networks of activists around the Internet heard and distributed the call, and commented in support of the initiative.
A good share of the first wave of tweets in July came from
Spain, where the *indignants* movement found new hope in
the direct confrontation planned against the core of financial capitalism. As the movement expanded, Twitter became
an essential tool for internal communication in the camps,
as well as for linking to other occupations and for planning
specific actions. An unpublished study by Kevin Driscoll
and François Bar at the University of Southern California
Annenberg Innovation Lab collected Occupy tweets con-
tinuously beginning on October 12, 2011 by comparing
them against an evolving set of approximately 289 related
keywords and phrases. During the month of November, they
observed approximately 120,000 Occupy-related tweets on a
typical day with a peak of over 500,000 during the raid of
Zuccotti Park on November 15. The analysis by Gilad Lotan
on Twitter traffic related to the movement shows that the
peaks are associated with crucial moments in the movement,

such as the first attempt to evict the occupation of Zuccotti Park on October 13.[7] In most instances of threatened police action against occupations, Twitter networks alerted thousands, and their instant mobilization in solidarity played a role in protecting the occupiers. Using Twitter from their cell phones, the protesters were able to constantly distribute information, photos, videos and comments to build a real-time network of communication overlaid on the occupied space.

The 99% theme was popularized, in large part, by the "We are the 99%" Tumblr page, started in mid-August, in advance of the September 17 protests, by Chris (who chose not to give his last name) and Priscilla Grim, who both work professionally in media in New York, and were involved in social activism. At first, both chose to remain anonymous, writing "Brought to you by the people who will Occupy Wall Street." Tumblr, a social network started in 2007, has been characterized by *The Atlantic*'s Rebecca Rosen as a "collaborative confessional" that can, in the case of social movements, be used to create "self-service history" and demonstrates that "the power of personal narrative, whether on the radio, in a book, on YouTube, or on a Tumblr, can cut through the noise and cynicism of punditry and give shape and texture to our national story" (Rosen 2011). Posts on Tumblr can consist of a quote, a picture, a video or a link, instead of a long text as in a traditional blog post. Many Tumblr blogs consist of pictures and other media expressions around a particular theme. Topics are often humorous and playful. Users "follow" other Tumblr blogs and can see from their account an aggregation of all followed Tumblr blog posts together. Tumblr allows users to be part of collaboratively produced group blogs. They can "reblog" others' posts to post them onto their Tumblr blog and share the post with their own followers. And it is easy to implement a form that allows users to submit anonymous messages. This was crucial for the spread of the "We are the 99%" group because Tumblr provided a platform for personal storytelling in anonymity, with most people hiding their faces in the video, yet narrating their personal drama in coping with an unjust society. In October 2011, the group site was receiving about 100 submissions a day. As of February 2012 there were 225 pages of posts. Emphasizing the role of Tumblr as a distinctive feature of the Occupy Wall Street movement, Graham-Felsen (2011) wrote:

> Why has Tumblr become the go-to platform of this moment? As we saw in Iran, Twitter can be a powerful broadcast tool for delivering minute-by-minute accounts of breaking news and amplifying concrete messages ("Down with Ahmedinejad"). And in Egypt, Facebook was pivotal for recruiting protesters and scheduling rallies in Tahrir Square. But Tumblr has served neither of these purposes for Occupy Wall Street, a diffuse and leaderless movement with a deliberately undefined goal. Instead, Tumblr has humanized the movement. Tumblr is a powerful storytelling medium, and this movement is about stories – about how the nation's economic policies have priced us out of school, swallowed us in debt, permanently postponed retirements, and torn apart families. "We Are the 99 Percent" is the closest thing we've had to the work of Farm Security Administration – which paid photojournalists to document the plight of farmers during the Great Depression – and it may well go down as the definitive social history of this recession.

In a telling comment, Ezra Klein wrote in *The Washington Post*: "It's not the arrests that convinced me that 'Occupy Wall Street' was worth covering seriously. Nor was it their press strategy, which largely consisted of tweeting journalists to cover a small protest that couldn't say what, exactly, it hoped to achieve. It was a Tumblr called, 'We Are The 99 Percent'" (2011).

Internet social networks mobilized enough support for people to come together and occupy public space, territorializing their protest. Once the camps were organized, they established their presence as specific occupations on the Internet. Most camps created their own website, set up a group on Facebook, or both. Members of the web committee created hot spots in the camp, and people tethered their phones to computers to go online. The diversity of the occupy movement could be detected in its existence on the web, sometimes with very rich web pages in terms of content and graphics. Most large or particularly active occupations had their own website. These served as sites to organize the movement, but also to create a public presence for it. Most had the following sections: contact (to get in touch with members of the Press Relations committees, etc.), how to get involved (a list of committees, times and locations of General Assemblies), supplies requested for donation, resources (a set of documents explaining how to occupy, the protocols of the General Assembly, how to deal with the police), calendar of events and announcements, and message boards (some open, some password-protected). Also, most of these websites had a forum on which a visitor could create an account. Some message boards could be viewed by any visitor, but others were password-protected and open only to registered users. Minutes, proposals and ratified documents (including lists of demands) were posted on the web, usually with a comment thread beneath. This was an essential practice to ensure transparency within the movement.

Most occupations also had a Facebook group. These were used to complement the websites of larger occupations, and served as primary sites of organizing for smaller or less tech-savvy occupations. They also served as directories to help members stay in touch with each other, send private messages, or post on each other's walls. The groups were also used for organizing: to make announcements, post calendar items and send messages to all members of the group. Despite its utility, Facebook has been criticized within the movement for being a proprietary platform and thus at odds with the openness valued within the movement. Also, new Facebook facial recognition software can automatically tag people in photographs, and this was resented, given the lack of trust in that Facebook will not protect privacy if subpoenaed by authorities. Therefore, some skilled occupiers were trying to use alternatives to Facebook, such as N-1, Ning or Diaspora. Others engaged in working on an "Occupy Facebook" called Global Square, widely publicized by WikiLeaks. A functional prototype was supposed to be available sometime in 2012. In the words of the developers:

> The aim of the platform should not be to replace the physical assemblies but rather to empower them by providing the online tools for local and (trans)national organization and collaboration. The ideal would be both to foster individual participation and to structure collective action. The Global Square will be our own public space where different groups can come together to organize their local squares and assemblies.[8]

However, overall, the movement relied mainly on commercially available platforms that were ready to be used. So doing, activists became vulnerable to subpoenas trying to obtain information on tweets, violating the privacy of the users with potentially serious consequences.[9]

Livestreams, a collection of tools that allows users to

broadcast real-time video content over the Internet, was also an important technology for the movement. Livestreams are ephemeral, but they are essential during moments of police repression. During raids, there was often a blackout on mainstream media, which did not apply to livestreamers. For instance, in the early hours of October 11, Occupy Boston faced a wave of police violence and arrests. Over 8,000 people were reported to be watching the livestream at 3am. When the livestream of an occupation stopped broadcasting, it became a symbol that the demonstration had been effectively shut down, which can be a mobilizing experience for those watching at home. However, livestreaming is in fact controversial within the movement. Because livestreamers show the occupation from their own point of view, narrating the events as they see them, many have achieved some degree of celebrity within the movement and have been identified as spokespeople by those outside of it. This has lead to criticism that some are exploiting the movement for personal gain, including sponsorship from livestreaming service companies. Most of the time, the occupations were very boring, with repression, violence and other "action" relatively infrequent. Livestreamers have been criticized for gravitating toward sensationalism and misrepresenting the actual experience of most present at the occupations. They also were blamed for being, as one livestreamer put it, "dry snitches," that is, people who unintentionally provide evidence to the police of people engaged in the occupation.[10]

Thus, the occupy sites were nodes of communication networks toward the world at large and within the occupation. These networks were a hybrid of communication forms, both digital and face-to-face, based on community building, interpersonal interaction, social networking and posting on the Internet. Thus, SMS was important, particularly for coordinating actions and staying in touch, as were email listservs to diffuse information. Conference calls, using Mumble and other VOIP technologies, allowed deliberation between distant sites. But print publications were also a significant medium with journals such as *Occupied WJS, Occupy! N+1* or *Tidal*, as well as a multitude of local print bulletins. People's deliberation and decision-making in the camp were based on direct human interaction, such as hand signals in the General Assemblies and the widespread use of People's Mic, in which someone says something to an audience who repeats each sentence loudly so that everybody can hear without amplification equipment. Besides its practical uses, People's Mic symbolizes belonging and community experience, reproducing forms of communication used in past movements of civil disobedience.

After the occupied sites were vacated under pressure from police and winter, the movement did not disappear: it went on in the diverse forms of the Internet networks, always buzzing with proclamations and ideas, and always ready to land again with a vengeance from the space of flows into the space of places. Indeed, the Occupy Wall Street movement is a hybrid networked movement that links cyberspace and urban space in multiple forms of communication.

Furthermore, to be autonomous vis-à-vis the mainstream media without accepting isolation from the 99%, the movement is self-mediated, both over the Internet and within its autonomous public space, mixing in its messages both grievances and hope. Indeed, the hand signals used in the General Assemblies are shaped to facilitate their viral diffusion on the Internet. The entire activity of the camp and in the demonstrations is largely staged for their expression in social media, connecting in this way to society at large. There is a constant practice of storytelling in the movement, with everybody taking pictures and making videos, and uploading them to YouTube and to multiple social networking sites. This is the first kind of movement that tells every day its own story in its multiple voices in a way that transcends both time and space, projecting itself in history and reaching out to the global visions and voices of our world.

In deeper terms, the movement set out to occupy Wall Street, the key node of the global networks of financial domination of the world, by occupying surrounding territories and making free communities. The occupiers used the autonomous space of flows of Internet networks to seize symbolic spaces of places, from where they could challenge, by their presence and their messages, the financial space of flows from where global powers dominate human life.

DIRECT DEMOCRACY IN PRACTICE

From its onset, the Occupy movement experimented with new forms of organization, deliberation and decision-making as a way of learning, by doing, what real democracy is. This is a fundamental feature of the movement. Instrumentality was not paramount. Authenticity was. The occupiers did not want to reproduce in their practice the kind of formal democracy and personalized leadership they were opposing. They invented, incrementally, a new organizational model that, with variations, was present in most of the occupations. It originally came from experiences in Egypt and Spain, and then it co-evolved between the many occupied sites through cross-fertilization, mutual consultation and feedback. Since most occupations created their own website, all the guidelines for organization and the experiences in collaborative decision-making were posted and communicated throughout the network of occupations. This is how a largely common organizational pattern emerged.

Its most important characteristic was the deliberate

absence of formal leadership. There were no leaders in the
movement, not locally, not nationally, and not globally. This
was a fundamental principle that was enforced by the multitude of occupiers with utmost determination at any instance
when someone tried to assume a prominent role. This was
truly an experiment in social movement organization. It
belied deep-seated assumptions that no socio-political process could work without some sort of strategic guidance and
vertical authority. In the Occupy movement, there was no
traditional leadership, no rational leadership and no charismatic leadership. And certainly no personalized leadership.
There were leadership functions, but these were exercised
locally by the General Assembly meeting regularly in the
occupied space. There were also coordinating functions
that would help to shape collective decisions, and these
were assumed by networks of iterative consultation over the
Internet.

However, to ensure some form of effective initiative in a
compatible way with the principle of sovereign assemblies
with no delegation, more complex organizational forms
emerged. Since this was one of the fundamental social inno-
vations of the movement, it is worthwhile to analyze it in
some detail. It goes without saying that the diversity of
organizational experiences cannot be reduced to one single
pattern. Yet, in what follows I will try to convey the key features that were often repeated in the largest occupations, so
that we can consider that there is an implicit model of direct
democracy emerging from the practice of the movement.
To construct this ideal type of Occupy organization with
my team, we have relied on the websites of the occupations
that often post guides explaining how to participate and how
to organize. The description here relies on direct quotes
from these guides. This is because since these documents
have circulated freely within the movement and between

the occupations, many of them include similar wording and images. This is another example of the importance of the Internet in the practice of the movement.

The decision-making power for a given occupied site is exclusively in the hands of the General Assembly. It is a "horizontal, leaderless, consensus-based open meeting" (this description is used on almost every Occupation website and GA guide). Everyone present at the GA has the ability to participate in the GA. Anyone can make a proposal or address a proposal. Everyone, except for those who choose to stand aside or observe, is expected to participate in the decision-making process through hand-signals. Although there is no leader in the GA, it is facilitated or moderated by individuals from the Facilitation Committee and usually rotates each time.

Most occupations follow the same general rules, although some may have slightly different norms: "There is no single leader or governing body of the GA – everyone's voice is equal. Anyone is free to propose an idea or express an opinion as part of the GA." Ideally, only decisions that affect the entire group are brought to the GA. Smaller actions that happen outside the occupation can be planned in smaller groups without the GA's approval. Affinity groups and working groups can make decisions within themselves but must bring matters that affect the entire occupation to the GA for approval. Each proposal follows the same basic format: an individual describes the proposal and explains why it is being proposed and how it can be carried out. Other members of the GA express their support, ask questions, or react to the proposal. After sufficient discussion, and when it seems that the group may be near consensus, the facilitator will call for the entire GA to express, through a series of hand gestures, their opinion of each proposal (see figure 1). If there is positive consensus for a proposal, it is accepted and direct action

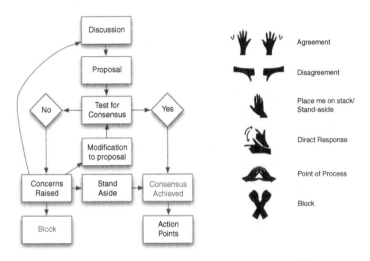

Figure 1: Consensus flow and hand signals in Occupy Movement
Source: Occupy Atlanta

begins. If there is not consensus, the individual making the proposal is asked to revise and resubmit it to the GA until a consensus is achieved. Some GAs required full consensus, but others adopted modified or partial consensus, such as 90 percent. This has been a controversial issue at many occupations. Because reaching consensus is so difficult, the members of the GA express different kinds of disagreement: Stand-aside – for reasons including non-support, reservations and personal conflict – and Blocking. Blocking consensus is something that should, in theory, only be done in extreme situations. In practice, it was used quite frequently.

To implement decisions of the General Assembly, organize the camp, and engage in a practice, committees are formed. Most occupations include some combination of the following committees, although some may use different names or have slightly different categories: Facilitation, Media, Outreach, Food, Direct Action, Peace Keeping/Security, Sanitation/

Sustainability, Finance/Resources, Legal, Medical, Social Media, Programming, People of Color, Press Relations, etc. In order to be officially recognized, committees must be agreed upon by the GA, but less formal groups, called Affinity Groups, need not be. The role of the committees is to figure out specifics and formulate proposals to present to the GA for general consensus and to identify and communicate information that everyone needs to take into consideration. Membership and leadership within the working groups is open to anyone, but actually formed by those who show up regularly and take on responsibility and deliver on promises. Eventually these roles become associated with particular individuals who become the point persons for the committee.

To be more operative without betraying the principle of leaderlessness, many occupations adopted the Spokes Council model in an attempt to ensure better communication among working groups and committees, create more accountability and limit the power of visitors to derail the consensus process. Spokes are individuals designated by committees and affinity groups to represent their views.[11] The main tasks for the Spokes Council are described as: effectively coordinating between Operations Groups and Caucuses; making budgetary decisions; and enabling the GA to engage in broader movement discussions, rather than being "bogged down" with time-consuming decisions on implementing its general orientations.

The Spokes Council has been considered controversial among many in the movement, and some do not recognize it. As one occupier told *The Village Voice*, "I think through the Spokes Council process, working groups become organizations and they become parties. What's the reason for us to marginalize ourselves?"[12] However, no occupation can adopt a Spokes Council without the approval of the GA. The

Spokes Council was designed to facilitate productive, expeditious decision-making among those who are actively working on behalf of the movement. It is open to all to witness, but to participate one must be an active participant in a Working Group or Caucus. However, measures have been taken to ensure that these decisions are open-access and transparent: all decisions made in the Spokes Council take place in a well-publicized indoor location with amplified sound so all can hear, and are broadcast over the Livestream: furthermore, all decisions, meeting minutes and budget details must be completely transparent and posted on the website.

There are different kinds of groups that participate in the Spokes Council:

(a) Working Groups, which engage logistical work on behalf of the occupation. Some Occupations split these into Operations Groups, which work on the material and financial organization of the movement on a daily basis, and Movement Groups, which work on the actions and campaigns of the movement, often on a project basis.

(b) Caucuses, self-determined groups based on the common experience of being marginalized in society on bases including, but not limited to, race, gender identity, sexuality, physical ability or homelessness status. Caucus Clusters have the same powers as Working Group Clusters. In addition, they have the ability to halt proposals that may have disproportionately adverse consequences for their constituency.

(c) In addition, a Spoke is allotted to represent those who are camping full-time but not involved in any Working Group or Caucus.

In terms of process, before each Spokes Council, each Working Group and Caucus decides on a Cluster to align with. Prior to meeting in the Spokes Council, each Cluster meets to discuss and craft proposals. Each Cluster chooses a person to serve as a "Spoke." The Spokes sit in a circle in the middle of the meeting space, with the rest of the Cluster sitting directly behind them. Individuals in multiple Working Groups and Caucuses are free to sit with any Cluster they are a part of. The Spoke rotates every meeting. Spokes are the only individuals to speak at the Spokes Council, but they must confer with and accurately reflect the members of their Cluster before speaking for them. Cluster can recall their Spoke at any time if they are failing to accurately reflect the will of the Cluster. Spokes present proposals crafted by the Clusters to the Spokes Council. Clusters discuss the proposal among themselves, and the Spoke presents those discussions to the entire group. After sufficient discussion, the Spokes call for modified consensus on the proposal. The Spokes Council model makes it more difficult for individuals to Hard Block a proposal without consensus from their Cluster.

The complexity of this organizational model expresses the tension between the principle of integral democracy, based on the non-delegation of power in decision-making, and the instrumental need to reach consensus leading to action. While many of the observed practices deviated from the interactive, multilayered flows of decision presented in this synthetic view of an assembly-led and committee-implemented movement, it conveys the depth of the search for new political forms within the movement that could prefigure new forms of democracy in society at large. So doing, the Occupy movement is challenging the current practice of political institutions in the US, while reaching back to the founding principles of community-based democracy as one of the sources of the American Revolution.

A NON-DEMAND MOVEMENT:
"THE PROCESS IS THE MESSAGE"[13]

The movement surged as a largely spontaneous expression of outrage. It was infused with hope for a better world, which began to materialize in the daily life of the camps, in the dialogue and cooperation of social networks, and in the courageous street demonstrations where the bonding was enacted. But for what? For most observers, the difficulty of assessing the Occupy Wall Street movement came from the absence of precise demands that could be won or negotiated. There was a concrete demand in the initial call to demonstrate: the appointment of a presidential commission to enact the independence of government in regard to Wall Street. Indeed, former Wall Street executives have been at the key posts of the cabinets of all recent presidents, including Obama. An IMF study found a significant statistical association between the money spent by financial industry lobbyists in 2000–6 and Congressional votes in favor of the financial industry on 51 important bills.[14] If the outrage was directed at Wall Street, it appeared logical that the demand to separate money and politics would be the unifying goal of the movement. It was not. The movement demanded everything and nothing at the same time. In fact, given the widespread character of the movement, each occupation had its local and regional specificity: everybody brought in her own grievances and defined her own targets. There were multiple proposals of various natures, voted on in the General Assemblies, but little effort to translate them into a policy campaign going beyond combating the effects of mortgage foreclosures or financial abuses on borrowers and consumers. The list of most frequently mentioned demands debated in various occupations hints at the extraordinary diversity of the movement's targets: controlling financial speculation, particularly high frequency trading; auditing the Federal Reserve; addressing the housing crisis; regulating overdraft fees; controlling currency manipulation; opposing the outsourcing of jobs; defending collective bargaining and union rights; reducing income inequality; reforming tax law; reforming political campaign finance; reversing the Supreme Court's decision allowing unlimited campaign contributions from corporations; banning bailouts of companies; controlling the military-industrial complex; improving the care of veterans; limiting terms for elected politicians; defending freedom on the Internet; assuring privacy on the Internet and in the media; combating economic exploitation; reforming the prison system; reforming health care; combating racism, sexism and xenophobia; improving student loans; opposing the Keystone pipeline and other environmentally predatory projects; enacting policies against global warming; fining and controlling BP and similar oil spillers; enforcing animal rights; supporting alternative energy sources; critiquing personal leadership and vertical authority, beginning with a new democratic culture in the camps; and watching out for cooptation in the political system (as happened with the Tea Party). As Sydney Tarrow wrote: "That is hardly a policy platform. But policy platforms are not the point of this new kind of movement" (2011: 1).

Some occupations, such as Fort Lauderdale and New York, approved elaborate documents providing the rationale for a long list of demands. The Declaration of the Occupation of New York City (see Appendix) was the most widely distributed document from the movement, approved by the New York City General Assembly on September 29, 2011, and translated into 26 languages. But it presented more grievances than demands. And the demands included in the document were of generic character. Other documents, such as the "99% Declaration" from New York, or draft statements from Chicago, Washington DC and many others, did not reach consensus and could not represent the views of the movement as such. Indeed, the movement was popular and attractive to many precisely because it remained open to all kinds of proposals, and did not present specific policy positions that would have elicited support but also opposition within the movement, as shown in the divisiveness that emerged in most occupations each time a committee put forward specific programs for reform. For many people in the movement, and for almost all external observers, particularly those intellectuals on the left always looking for the politics of their dreams, the lack of specific demands by the movement was a fundamental flaw. In a dire economic and social situation, there is an urgent need for a change of course, and this can only be achieved by channeling the energy liberated by the movement into some achievable, short-term goals that, in return, would empower the movement.

The problem, though, is that "the movement" is not a single entity, but multiple streams that converge into a diverse challenge to the existing order. Furthermore, a very strong sentiment in the movement is that any pragmatic approach to achieving demands would be required to go through the mediation of the political system, and this would contradict the generalized distrust of the representativeness of political institutions as they presently exist in America. I think that a statement retrieved from the discussions in the Demands Committee of the New York General Assembly expresses a widespread feeling in the movement:

> I wanted to introduce a different way of thinking about this. The movement doesn't need to make demands, because this movement is an assertive process. This movement has the power to affect change. It does not need to ask for it. The OWS does not make demands. We will simply assert

our own power to achieve what we desire. The more of us gather to the cause, the more power we have. Make no demands for others to solve these problems. Assert yourself.[15]

While this position is controversial, and considered suicidal outside the movement by the old political left, it does correspond to two fundamental trends: (a) most people simply do not trust the political process as it is currently framed, so they only count on themselves; (b) the movement is wide and strong because it unites outrage and dreams while skipping politics as usual. This is its strength and its weakness. But this is what this movement is, not a surrogate for an old left always looking to find fresh support for its unreconstructed view of the world. No demands, and every demand; not a piece of this society, but the whole of a different society.

VIOLENCE AGAINST A NON-VIOLENT MOVEMENT

The Occupy movement was overwhelmingly non-violent, both in philosophy and in its practice. But it was confrontational, because its tactics of occupying space to build autonomy, and of demonstrating in the streets against functional nodes of the system, were bound to be met with police action. This was anticipated by the participants in the movement. Challenging the system outside the institutionalized channels of dissent meant taking risks of police repression. But there is always a gray zone of legality and political calculation that the movement tried to use to its advantage. For instance, the occupation of Zuccotti Park was paradoxically protected for a while because it is private property and the owning company took some time to proceed with the cost/benefit analysis of calling for an eviction.

In city after city, the local authorities in control of the territory had to evaluate the potential backlash for their political futures in terms of the different options they would take relating to the movement. For instance, in Los Angeles, Mayor Villaraigosa, nurturing political ambitions for higher office, issued a statement, with the majority of the City Council, supporting the goals of the movement but falling short of supporting a long-term occupation of the lawn in front of City Hall (it is often used as a stand-in for Washington DC in Hollywood movies, so the city would lose revenue if it allowed it to be used too long just for the purpose of exercising democracy). Los Angeles was the last major occupation to be evicted, which was done with a Hollywood-style display of force (hundreds of policemen in full riot gear emerging by surprise from the building), but without any major incident. On the other hand, the City of Oakland unleashed its ferocious attack police, well known in the city and around the country for numerous incidents of unjustified killings, detentions and violent charges on demonstrators. Oakland witnessed several major, violent confrontations in repeated attempts to dislodge the occupied square, with dozens of injured, hundreds of arrests, and two veterans seriously injured and hospitalized. This police action radicalized the movement in Oakland, to the point that on November 3 demonstrators succeeded in shutting down the Port of Oakland, the second largest on the US Pacific Coast, at the price of pitched street battles with the police. New York oscillated between its initial tolerance of the occupation and several instances of harsh repression. Many university campuses, including some of the elite universities such as Yale, Berkeley and Harvard, were occupied. At one point, campus security only allowed those with Harvard identification cards to enter the occupied Harvard Yard. Response from the academic authorities varied. In one instance at the University of

California at Davis, the campus police pepper sprayed, without justification, peacefully seated demonstrations, inducing outrage around the world and a disciplinary suspension of the provocative officers.

In general terms, the movement was calm but determined, and local police forces everywhere were ready to club and arrest at the slightest legal possibility of doing so, although some policemen privately expressed their agreement with the goals of the movement. The violence that often ensued had two different effects: on the one hand, it increased solidarity with those occupiers subject to violence, prompting wider mobilization beyond the localities where the repression took place. On the other hand, any broadcast of violence on television drew a wedge between the movement and the 99% they aspired to represent. A critical element in protecting the movement from violence is the massive practice of video reporting by hundreds of people branding their cell phones in every demonstration. The mainstream media only reported what their editors wanted, but the movement self-reported everything, posting on the Internet all the actions that took place in every confrontation. In some cases, the vision of police brutality re-energized the demonstrators and induced popular sympathy countering the prejudice against the movement, which was portrayed as violent in some media. There were some radical, organized groups (particularly the Black Bloc) as well as "autonomous actors" participating in demonstrations who attacked the police, public buildings, banks and stores. They were only effective in creating violence in situations where the police had provoked a violent atmosphere. This was particularly the case in Oakland, where demonstrators invaded City Hall and burned an American flag on January 28, 2012. However, the General Assemblies often debated the issue of violence and were systematically opposed to it, devising several strategies to diffuse police violence as well as provocations of the radical fringe of the movement, including provocateurs external to the movement itself. By and large, they succeeded. Yet, police presence was constantly felt around the occupied sites and street marches, increasing both the radicalism of the movement and the separation between the movement's actions and the perception of a majority of people whose life is dominated by fear.

In mid-November 2011, 18 mayors of cities with active occupations reportedly took part in conference calls to discuss how they were handling the movement. In what seemed to many like a coordinated action, many sites all over the US were evicted in the weeks following. The pretext used for the forced eviction was the same everywhere: concern for public hygiene, in spite of the cleaning and sanitation efforts that had been made daily in most occupied sites. In a few weeks local police forces succeeded in dislodging the occupiers from their camps, usually with limited violence, since in most cases the remaining people had decided to hibernate elsewhere, regroup and strategize for a spring offensive under new forms. To be continued.

WHAT DID THE MOVEMENT ACHIEVE?

Since the movement did not mobilize in support of specific policies, no major policy changes resulted directly from the movement's action. However, there were multiple campaigns everywhere that obtained partial corrections in a number of unfair practices. This was particularly the case of the housing campaigns, a major issue in the Occupy movement. Occupy groups "occupied" foreclosed homes in many areas of the country on the December 6 Day of Action, with the goal of pressuring lenders to offer loan modifications with substantial reductions. They succeeded in some cases, even reinstating mortgages that had previously been canceled. They showcased especially poignant foreclosures of aged persons or invalid veterans as a way to denounce the unfairness of the system in the public light.

There were also widespread attempts to put pressure on the major banks using customers' power with the "Bank Transfer Day" initiative. It drew on pre-existing campaigns that encouraged individuals and institutions to divest from the nation's largest Wall Street banks and move to local financial institutions and non-profit credit unions. Among these were Arianna Huffington's "Move Your Money" in 2009, and the 2010 Valentine's Day movement to "Break up with your Bank." Then in September 2011, after Bank of America announced that it would impose a $5 monthly fee on debit card and checking accounts, there was a wave of protests, with many customers canceling their accounts. After the backlash, Bank of America rescinded the increased fees, but other fees are quietly coming back. As of October 15, 2011, a Facebook page devoted to the effort had drawn more than 54,900 "likes." November 5, 2011 was declared "Bank Transfer Day," calling people to switch their accounts from commercial banks to not-for-profit credit unions. According to the Credit Union National Association (CUNA), the association's website aimed at informing customers about credit union services saw traffic double in this period. CUNA estimated that nearly 650,000 consumers had opened new accounts at credit unions between late September and the November 5 target date.[16] In other instances of starting up new financial institutions, some Occupy movements, such as Occupy Orange County in Southern California, created their own credit unions. Similar efforts of new, community-based credit unions were reported in San Francisco, Boston and Washington State.

Yet, while these actions were exemplary in character, they

were mere drops in the ocean of injustice confronted by the movement. The hope was that these initiatives would give people the courage to resist, and would alert the public at large on a socially unbearable situation. In this sense, George Lakoff's characterization of Occupy Wall Street as a moral movement aiming to impact the public discourse seems to be supported by observation (2011). Indeed, in spite of its limitations, public opinion surveys seem to indicate a significant cultural change in America as a result of the movement's actions and proclamations. According to a *New York Times* poll of a national sample in November 9, 2011, almost 50 percent of the public thought that the sentiments at the root of the movement generally reflected the view of most Americans.[17]

A Pew Institute Survey on the attitudes towards Occupy Wall Street among a national sample of 1,521 adults, released on December 15, 2011,[18] showed that 44 percent supported the movement, while 39 percent opposed it (see Appendix). Moreover, 48 percent agreed with the concerns expressed by OWS while 30 percent disagreed. However, when it came to tactics (meaning occupations, demonstrations), 49 percent disagreed, while only 29 percent agreed. It seems that crossing the line towards non-institutional action is still a barrier for most citizens, even when they agree with the causes of the protest. The attitudes about the movement vary of course depending on income level, education, age and political ideology: older, conservative, more affluent and less-educated citizens opposed the movement, while the movement received widespread support from other demographic groups. However, the most salient point is that a movement that clearly places itself outside institutional politics and challenges up front the heart of global capitalism – namely Wall Street – has received significant support in mainstream America.

However, what is truly decisive in assessing the political effect of a social movement is its impact on people's consciousness, as I have argued throughout this book, and more thoroughly in previous works (Castells 2003; 2009). As a result of the movement, and of the debates it has generated on the Internet and in the mainstream media, the issue of social inequality, epitomized by the opposition between the 99% and the 1%, has come to the forefront of public discourse. Politicians (including President Obama), media commentators and comedians have embraced the term, claiming they represent the 99%. Regardless of the cynicism of such a statement in a political class usually defending the interests of the financial and corporate elites as a prerequisite for their political future, the simple fact of accepting this dichotomy has deep consequences in terms of trust in the fairness of the system. Indeed, the old American dream about equality of opportunities on the basis of personal effort has been shattered, if we are to believe the results of a Pew Institute Survey taken in December 2011, as shown in figures 2–4. Furthermore, 61 percent think that the country's economic system "unfairly favors the wealthy," and 77 percent agree with the statement that "there is too much power in the hands of a few rich people and large corporations," including 53 percent of Republicans.

Yet, what is relatively new and meaningful is that there are indications that Occupy Wall Street has shaped the awareness of Americans on the reality of what I would dare to call class struggle. Thus, according to a Pew Institute survey on a national representative sample of adults in the age group 18 to 34, released on January 11, 2012, 66 percent believe there are "very strong" or "strong" conflicts between the rich and the poor: *an increase of 19 percentage points since 2009.* Not only have perceptions of class conflict grown more prevalent; so, too, has the belief that these

Decreased Attitude that "Hard Work Leads to Success"

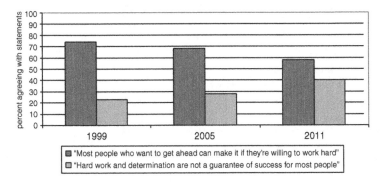

Figure 2: Decreased attitude that "hard work leads to success"
Source: Pew Research Center, 2011

Percent who say there are "very strong" or "strong" conflicts between . . .

	2009	2011
Rich and poor	47	66
Immigrants and native born	55	62
Black and whites	39	38
Young and old	25	34

Figure 3: Perception of social conflicts in society
Source: Pew Research Center, 2011

disputes are acute: 30 percent say there are "very strong conflicts" between poor people and rich people, double the proportion that offered a similar view in July 2009 and *the largest percentage expressing this opinion since the question was first asked in 1987.* Conflicts between rich and poor now rank ahead of three other potential sources of group tension: between immigrants and the native born, between blacks and whites, and between young and old. All major demographic groups now perceive significantly more class conflict than two years ago. However, the survey found

	Republicans	Democrats	Independents	Total
OWS overall	%	%	%	%
Support	21	60	46	44
Oppose	59	21	34	35
Neither	5	4	7	6
Don't know	15	15	14	16
Concerns raised by OWS protests				
Agree	31	62	50	48
Disagree	47	19	27	30
Don't know	22	19	23	22
Way OWS protests are conducted				
Approve	14	43	29	29
Disapprove	67	37	49	49
Don't know	19	20	22	23

Figure 4: Support and opposition to Occupy Wall Street, concerns raised by protests, and way protests are conducted
Source: Pew Research Center, December 7–11, 2011 and December 8–11, 2011. Figures may not add up to 100% because of rounding.

that younger adults, women, Democrats and African Americans are somewhat more likely than older people, men, Republicans, whites or Hispanics to say that there are strong disagreements between the rich and the poor. The biggest increase in perceptions of class conflicts occurred among political liberals and Americans who say they are not affiliated with either major party. In each group, the proportion who said there are major disagreements between rich and poor Americans *increased by more than 20 percentage points since 2009.* To quote the report:

> These changes in attitudes over a relatively short period of time may reflect the income and wealth inequality message conveyed by Occupy Wall Street protesters across the country in late 2011 that led to a spike in media attention to the topic. But the changes may also reflect a growing public

awareness of underlying shifts in the distribution of wealth in American society.[19]

However, it is to be noticed that perceptions of capitalism and socialism have changed little since 2010. Indeed, the majority of supporters of the Occupy movement are not openly critical of capitalism: there are as many positive as negative opinions about capitalism among its ranks. The criticism is focused on financial capitalism and on its influence on government, not on capitalism as such. The movement does not embrace ideologies of the past. Its quest aims at eradicating evil in the present, while reinventing community for the future. Its fundamental achievement has been to rekindle hope that another life is possible.

THE SALT OF THE EARTH[20]

How can people enact fundamental change when they do not trust their political institutions and refuse to engage in the violent overthrowing of said institutions? When the mechanisms of representation do not function properly, when unaccountable powers, such as financial institutions and corporate media, define the terms and outcomes of deliberation and decision-making within a framed field of options, and when major deviations of behavior from the biased rules of the game are subjected to intimidation by the security forces and a politically appointed judiciary? This was the dilemma confronting those who did not submit to resignation and passivity, those who took risks and dared to explore new avenues of political resistance and social change when forced to assume the hardship of a financial crisis unfairly imposed upon them. After deliberation on the Internet networks, with the help of occasional meetings face-to-face to connect with one another and exercise togetherness, they resorted to the oldest tactic of power when people do not yield to the temptation of becoming like the enemy in order to overcome the enemy: they engaged in civil disobedience. They targeted the most essential commodity shaping their lives, and everybody's life: virtual money. The value that does not exist materially and yet permeates everything. The value that has escaped into the computer networks of the global financial markets, but still lives out of territorial nodes that manage and control the space of financial flows from the places they inhabit. By challenging the inviolability of absolute financial power on the shores of the ocean of global capital, they materialized resistance, giving a face to the source of oppression that was asphyxiating people's lives and establishing its rule over the rulers. They set up a convivial community in the sites where before there were only headquarters of power and greed. They created experience out of defiance. They self-mediated their connection to the world and the connections among themselves. They opposed the threat of violence with peaceful assertiveness. They believed in their right to believe. They connected to each other and reached out to the others. They found meaning in being together. They did not collect money, nor did they pay their debts. They harvested themselves. They harvested the salt of the earth. And they became free.

NOTES

1 In concluding my analysis of the Obama campaign, after he won the election, I wrote:

> How much [Obama] will have to deviate from his original ideas when confronted with the harsh economic and geopolitical realities of our world is a matter for future

appraisal and further study. Yet, as I write this and you read it in another time/space warp, the fundamental analytical lesson to retain is how the insurgent politics of hope came to the forefront in the world's political scene at a critical moment when despair descended upon us. We will always have Berlin. Or for that matter Grant Park (2009: 412).

Thus, there was despair, then came hope, at least for enough people to elect president an African-American against the Clinton machine, and against the Republican machine. Then, rather quickly, there was widespread despair again in the country and among his most enthusiastic supporters. Yet, the seeds of hope planted in the hearts of the multitudes that cheered Obama in Berlin and Grant Park, were not washed away by the crisis of crisis management. They yielded new hope, under different forms, when the time came again to move beyond outrage. Indeed there are some indications that there was a transfer of energy from disappointment with Obama to the Occupy movement. According to the Fordham University Poll by Political Science professor Costas Panagopoulos from October 2011, 60 percent of occupiers voted for Obama in 2008 but 73 percent of occupiers now disapprove of the way Barack Obama is handling his job as president. A sign in Occupy Wall Street in NYC read, "The Barack Obama we elected would be out here with us." Another read, "Standing Up For The Change We Voted For," referring to Obama's 2008 campaign slogan. "The very people who supported Obama in '08 are the Occupy organizers. That same energy has shifted from the electoral arena to the streets," David Goodner, a volunteer with Occupy Des Moines, told the *LA Times* in December 2011. Shepherd Fairey, who made the famous and influential Obama Hope poster in 2008, made a new poster in the same style with the image of Guy Fawkes (representing Anonymous) that read, "Mr. President we HOPE you're on our side" and a small emblem that reads, "We are the 99%." The artist wrote on his website:

> I still see Obama as the closest thing to "a man on the inside" that we have presently. Obviously, just voting is not enough. We need to use all of our tools to help us achieve our goals and ideals. However, I think idealism and realism need to exist hand in hand. Change is not about one election, one rally, one leader, it is about a constant dedication to progress and a constant push in the right direction.

It must be noticed, nonetheless, that according to some polls on occupiers, the overwhelming majority were planning to vote in the 2012 presidential election, and about half of them were inclined to vote Democrat, with a very small number supporting a Republican candidate. But almost 40 percent were undecided about their potential vote. There are some cases of active members of the movement running for office in order to support the demands of the movement. For instance, Nate Kleinman, 29-year-old active member of the Occupy Philadelphia movement, is a candidate for congress in Pennsylvania's 13th district against Democratic incumbent Allyson Schwartz. However, the movement as such did not support his candidacy. In other words, most occupiers are political, and most of them are progressive. They simply do not trust that their goals can be fulfilled by elections without a previous transformation of the public mind among people at large.

2 DeGraw, D. (2010) The economic elite have engineered an

extraordinary coup, threatening the very existence of the middle class. AmpedStatus/Alternet. Available at: <http://www.alternet.org/economy/145667/?page=entire>.

3 Chase-Dunn, C. and Curran-Strange, M. (2011) Diffusion of the Occupy Movement in California. IROWS Working Paper # 74. Available at: <http://irows.ucr.edu/papers/irows74/irows74.h>.

4 Occupy Research Network. (2012) *General Demographic and Political Participation Survey.* Available at: <http://occupyresearch.net>.

5 Cordero-Guzman, H. (2011) *Main Stream Support for a Mainstream Movement: The 99% Movement Comes From and Looks Like the 99%.* Profile of web traffic taken from occupywallst.org. Available at: <http://occupywallst.org/media/pdf/OWS-profile1-10-18-11-sent-v2-HRCG.pdf>.

6 Zevon, C. (2011) "We're Still Here: This is what a holiday looks like at Occupy Washington DC." *OpenMike.* Available at: <http://www.michaelmoore.com/words/mike-friends-blog/were-still-here>.

7 Lotan, G. (2011) *#OccupyWallStreet Analyses.* Available at: <http://giladlotan.com/2012/02/occupywallstreet-analyses>.

8 The Global Square. (2011) *The Global Square: A project to perpetuate the creative and cooperative spirit of the occupations and transform them into lasting forms of social organization.* Available at: <http://theglobalsquare.org>.

9 On 14 December, Twitter received a subpoena from the Boston-area district attorney's office requesting all available information for accounts associated with two hashtags, two accounts, and one name, seemingly connected with Occupy Boston and members of Anonymous who had released online logins, physical addresses, and payroll information for 40 senior officers

of Boston Police Department. It was very confusingly worded, as if the DA does not really understand how Twitter works, as there is no specific account association with hashtags, and if they wanted user information for all users who used those hashtags, they would number in the hundreds of thousands. In addition, one account named @occupyboston, is fallow and not associated with the movement. It is Twitter's policy to send subpoenas to users in order to give that user a chance to fight it unless the company is specifically placed under a gag order. It seems that one targeted user received a copy from Twitter and posted it online. The ACLU filed to dismiss the subpoena but was rejected by Judge Carol Ball, who also issued an Impoundment Order, an extraordinary measure preventing either side from talking about arguments that is generally granted only in cases involving sensitive security issues, investigative issues, witness intimidation, or the possibility of the suspect running. In another instance, in January 2012, the Criminal Court of the City of New York requested "any and all user information" from September 15 to December 31, 2011 for the account @destructuremal, which belongs to Malcolm Harris, an Occupy protester who was arrested, along with 700 others, on the Brooklyn Bridge on October 5, 2011.

10 Dupay, T. (2012) The rise of the livestream: telling the truth about Occupy in real time. *AlterNet*. Available at: <http://www.alternet.org/occupywallst/154272/rise_of_the_livestreamer_telling_the_truth_about_occupy_in_real_time?page=1>.

11 The name "Spokes Council" refers both to the "spokespeople," who speak for their cluster and, more metaphorically, to "spokes" of a wheel, as the group sits in a circle and spokes are rotated each meeting.

12 Gray, R. (2011) "Occupy Wall Street debuts the new Spokes Council." *The Village Voice.* Available at: <http: //blogs.villagevoice.com/runninscared/2011/11/occupy_ wall_str_25.php>.

13 Occupier Meghann Sheridan wrote "The process is the message" on Occupy Boston's Facebook page, quoted by Hoffman, M. (2011) Protesters debate what demands, if any, to make. *The New York Times.* Available at: <http: //www.nytimes.com/2011/10/17/nyregion/occupy-wall-street-trying-to-settle-on-demands.html>.

14 Cited by Lawson-Remer, T. (2011) #OccupyDemocracy. *Possible Futures: A Project of the Social Science Research Council.* Available at: <http://www.possible-futures. org/2011/12/08/occupydemocracy>.

15 Comment on "Demands Working Group." Available at: <http://occupywallst.org/article/so-called-demands-wor king-group/#comment-175161>.

16 Rapport, M. (2011) Bank Transfer Day: CUNA Says 650,000 have so far. *Credit Union Times.* Available at: <http://www.cutimes.com/2011/11/03/ba nk-transfer-day-cuna-says-650000-have-so-far>.

17 *The New York Times* (2011) Public opinion and the Occupy Movement. Available at: <http://www.nytimes. com/interactive/2011/11/09/us/ows-grid.html>.

18 The Pew Research Center for the People and the Press. (2011) Frustration with congress could hurt Republican incumbents. Available at: <http://www.people-press. org/2011/12/15/frustration-with-congress-could-hurt-re publican-incumbents/>.

19 The Pew Research Center for the People and the Press. (2011) A Political Rhetoric Test: little change in public's response to "Capitalism," "Socialism." Available at: <http://www.people-press.org/files/legacy-pdf/12-28-11%20Words%20release.pdf>.

20 "Ye are the salt of the earth: but if the salt have lost its savor, wherewith shall it be salted? It is thenceforth good for nothing but to be cast out and trodden under the foot of men" (Matthew 5:3–16).

"Salt of the earth: A person or group of people regarded as the finest of their kind" (Collins English Dictionary).

The obvious historical analogy is Gandhi's march to the ocean to collect salt, challenging the British colonial prohibition, and so starting the process to bring down the empire. I acknowledge Terra Lawson-Remer for suggesting the comparison.

REFERENCES

Castells, M. (2003) *The Power of Identity*, 2nd edn. Blackwell, Oxford.

Castells, M. (2009) *Communication Power*. Oxford University Press, Oxford.

Costanza-Chock, S. (2012) Preliminary Findings: Occupy Research Demographic and Political Participation Survey 2012. *Occupy Research*. <http://www.occupyresearch.net/2012/03/23/preliminary-findings-occupy-research-demographic-and-political-participation-survey/>.

Graham-Felsen, S. (2011) Is Occupy Wall Street the Tumblr Revolution? *GOOD: Technology*. Available at: <http://www.good.is/post/is-occupy-wall-street-the-tumblr-revolution>.

Klein, E. (2011) Who are the 99 percent? *Wonkblog, The Washington Post*. Available at: <http://www.washingtonpost.com/blogs/ezra-klein/post/who-are-the-99-percent/2011/08/25/gIQAt87jKL_blog.html>.

Lakoff, G. (2011) How Occupy Wall Street's moral vision can beat the disastrous conservative world view. *AlterNet*. Available at: <http://www.alternet.org/teaparty/152800/

lakoff%3A_how_occupy_wall_street%27s_moral_vision_
can_beat_the_disastrous_conservative_worldview>.

Lawson-Remer, T. (2011) #OccupyDemocracy. *Possible
Futures: A Project of the Social Science Research Council.*
Available at: <http://www.possible-futures.org/2011/12/
08/occupydemocracy>.

Rosen, R. (2011) The 99 Percent Tumblr: self-service history. *The Atlantic.* Available at: <http://www.theatlantic.
com/technology/archive/2011/10/the-99-percent-tumblr-
self-service-history/246385/>.

Tarrow, S. (2011) Why Occupy Wall Street is not the Tea
Party of the Left. *Foreign Affairs, Snapshot.* Available at:
<http://www.foreignaffairs.com/articles/136401/sidney-
tarrow/why-occupy-wall-street-is-not-the-tea-party-of-the
-left>.

SELECTED OTHER SOURCES USED IN THIS CHAPTER

On the origins and development of the Occupy Wall Street movement

Beeston, L. (2011) The ballerina and the bull. *The Link.*
Available at: <http://thelinknewspaper.ca/article/1951>.

Chafkin, M. (2012) Revolution Number 99: An oral history
of Occupy Wall Street. *Vanity Fair.* Available at: <http://
www.vanityfair.com/politics/2012/02/occupy-wall-street-
201202>.

Eifling, S. (2011) AdBusters' Kalle Lasn talks about Occupy
Wall Street. *The Tyee.* Available at: <http://thetyee.ca/
News/2011/10/07/Kalle-Lasn-Occupy-Wall-Street/>.

Elliott, J. (2011) The origins of Occupy Wall Street explained.
Salon. Available at: <http://www.salon.com/2011/10/04/
adbusters_occupy_wall_st/>.

Kaste, M. (2011) Exploring Occupy Wall Street's "AdBuster" origin. *NPR Morning Edition*. Available at: <http://www.npr.org/2011/10/20/141526467/exploring-occupy-wall-streets-adbuster-origins>.

Kennedy, M. (2011) Global solidarity and the Occupy Movement. *Possible Futures*. Available at: <http://www.possible-futures.org/2011/12/05/global-solidarity-occupy-movement/>.

Kroll, A. (2011) How Occupy Wall Street really got started. *Mother Jones*. Available at: <http://motherjones.com/politics/2011/10/occupy-wall-street-international-origins>.

Schwartz. M. (2011) Pre-occupied: the origins and future of Occupy Wall Street. *The New Yorker*. Available at: <http://www.newyorker.com/reporting/2011/11/28/111128fa_fact_schwartz>.

Sledge, M. (2011) Reawakening the radical imagination: the origins of Occupy Wall Street. *The Huffington Post*. Available at: <http://www.huffingtonpost.com/2011/11/10/occupy-wall-street-origins_n_1083977.html>.

Weigel, D. and Hepler, L. (2011) A timeline of the movement, from February to today. *Slate*. Available at: <http://www.slate.com/articles/news_and_politics/politics/features/2011/occupy_wall_street/what_is_ows_a_complete_timeline.html>.

On daily life of camps

Ashraf, N. (2011) Brown Power at #OccupyWallStreet. *Killing New York*. Available at: <http://killingnewyork.tumblr.com/post/10839600460/brownpower>.

Carney, J. (2011) Occupy Wall Street: What life is like for protesters. *NetNet, CNBC*. Available at: <http://www.cnbc.com/id/44874685/Occupy_Wall_Street_What_Life_Is_Like_for_Protesters>.

Donovan, J. (2011) Who are the people in your neighborhood, #OccupyLA? *Occupy the Social.* Available at: <http://www.occupythesocial.com/post/12316820038/who-are-the-people-in-your-neighborhood-occupyla>.

Kleinfield, N. and Buckley, C. (2011) Wall Street occupiers, protesting till whenever. *New York Times.* Available at: <http://www.nytimes.com/2011/10/01/nyregion/wall-street-occupiers-protesting-till-whenever.html?pagewanted=all>.

Packer, G. (2011) All the angry people. *New Yorker.* Available at: <http://www.newyorker.com/reporting/2011/12/05/111205fa_fact_packer>.

Scradie, J. (2011) Why tents (still) matter for the Occupy Movement. *Common Dreams.* Available at: <http://www.commondreams.org/view/2011/11/24-1>.

Stoller, M. (2011) #OccupyWallStreet is a church of dissent, not a protest. *Naked Capitalism.* Available at: <http://www.nakedcapitalism.com/2011/09/matt-stoller-occupywallstreet-is-a-church-of-dissent-not-a-protest.html>.

"The State of the Occupation." (2012) *Fire Dog Lake.* Available at: <http://firedoglake.com/state-of-the-occupation>.

Tool. (2011) A day in the life of Occupy Wall Street. *Daily Kos.* Available at: <http://www.dailykos.com/story/2011/10/23/1029380/-A-Day-In-A-Life-At-Occupy-Wallstreet>.

On communication networks in the movement

Captain, S. (2011) Inside Occupy Wall Street's (kinda) secret media HQ. *Threat Level, Wired.* Available at: <http://www.wired.com/threatlevel/2011/11/inside-ows-media-hq/?pid=195&pageid=32957>.

Donovan, J. (2012) Conference calling across the Occupy

rhizome. *The Occupied Wall Street Journal.* Available at: <http://occupiedmedia.us/2012/02/conference-calling-acr oss-the-occupy-rhizome/>.

Gladstone, B. (2011) Occupy Wall Street after Zuccotti Park. *On the Media.* Available at: <http://www.onthe media.org/2011/nov/18/ows-communications/>.

Global Revolution. (2012) Available at: <http://www.live stream.com/globalrevolution>.

Kessler, S. (2011) How Occupy Wall Street is building its own Internet. *Mashable.* Available at: <http://mashable. com/2011/11/14/how-occupy-wall-street-is-building-its-own-internet-video/>.

Martin, A. (2011) Occupy Wall Street is building its own social network. *Atlantic Wire.* Available at: <http://www. theatlanticwire.com/national/2011/10/occupy-wall-street-building-its-own-social-network/43637/>.

Occupy Streams. (2012) Available at <http://occupystreams. com>.

Polletta, F. (2011) Maybe you're better off not holding hands and singing We Shall Overcome. *Mobilizing Ideas.* Available at: <http://mobilizingideas.wordpress. com/2011/11/21/maybe-youre-better-off-not-holding-ha nds-and-singing-we-shall-overcome/>.

Porzucki, N. (2011) The informal media team behind Occupy Wall Street. *All Things Considered.* Available at: <http://www.npr.org/2011/10/19/141510541/the-inform al-media-team-behind-occupy-wall-street>.

Santo, A. (2011) Occupy Wall Street's media team. *Columbia Journalism Review.* Available at: <http://www.cjr.org/the_ news_frontier/occupy_wall_streets_media_team.php>.

Shlinkert, S. (2011) The technology propelling Occupy Wall Street. *Daily Beast.* Available at: <http://www. thedailybeast.com/articles/2011/10/06/occupy-wall-street-protests-tech-gurus-televise-the-demonstrations.html>.

Stetler, B. (2011) Occupy Wall Street puts protests in the spotlight. *New York Times*. Available at: <http://www.nytimes.com/2011/11/21/business/media/occupy-wall-street-puts-the-coverage-in-the-spotlight.html>.

Trope, A. and Swartz, L. (2011) A visual primer of the occupation, month one and counting. *Civic Paths*. Available at: <http://civicpaths.uscannenberg.org/2011/10/the-visual-culture-of-the-occupation-month-one-and-counting/>.

Ungerleider, N. (2011) How virtual private networks keep Occupy Wall Street networks up and protesting. Available at: <http://www.fastcompany.com/1792974/why-occupy-wall-street-uses-vpns>.

Wagstaff, K. (2012) Occupy the Internet: Protests give rise to DIY data networks. *Techland, Time*. Available at: <http://techland.time.com/2012/03/28/occupy-the-internet-protests-give-rise-to-diy-networks/>.

Weinstein, A. (2011) "We are the 99%" creators revealed. *Mother Jones*. Available at: <http://motherjones.com/politics/2011/10/we-are-the-99-percent-creators>.

On organization and decision-making in the camps

Graeber, D. (2011a) Enacting the impossible (on consensus decision making). *Occupy Wall Street*. Available at: <http://occupywallst.org/article/enacting-the-impossible/>.

Graeber, D. (2011b) Occupy Wall Street's anarchist roots. *Al Jazeera*. Available at: <http://www.aljazeera.com/indepth/opinion/2011/11/2011112872835904508.html>.

Grusin, R. (2011) Premediation and the virtual occupation of Wall Street. *Theory and Event*, Vol. 114, No. 4.

Hepler, L. and Weigel, D. (2011) Twinkling, "mic check," and Zuccotti Park: a guide to protest terminology. *Slate*. Available at: <http://www.slate.com/articles/

news_and_politics/politics/features/2011/occupy_wall_stre
et/what_is_ows_a_glossary_of_the_protest_movement_.
html>.

Kim, R. (2011) We are all human microphones now. *The Nation*. Available at: <http://www.thenation.com/blog/163767/we-are-all-human-microphones-now>.

Klein, A. (2011) Jazz hands and waggling fingers: How Occupy Wall Street makes decisions. *New York Magazine*. Available at: <http://nymag.com/daily/intel/2011/10/occupy_wall_street_hand_gestur.html>.

Loofbourow, L. (2011) The livestream ended: How I got off my computer and into the streets at Occupy Oakland. *The Awl*. Available at: <http://www.theawl.com/2011/10/the-livestream-ended-how-i-got-off-my-computer-and-into-the-streets-at-occupy-oakland>.

Schneider, N. (2011) Wall Street occupiers inch toward a demand – by living it. *Waging Nonviolence*. Available at: <http://wagingnonviolence.org/2011/09/wall-street-occup iers-inch-toward-a-demandby-living-it/>.

Vargas-Cooper, N. (2011) The night Occupy LA tore itself in two. *The Awl*. Available at: <http://www.theawl. com/2011/10/the-night-occupy-los-angeles-tore-itself-in-two>.

Wood, D. and Goodale, G. (2011) Does "Occupy Wall Street" have leaders? Does it need any? *Christian Science Monitor*. Available at: <http://www.csmonitor.com/USA/Politics/2011/1010/Does-Occupy-Wall-Street-have-leade rs-Does-it-need-any>.

W.W. (2011) Leaderless, consensus-based participatory democracy and its discontents. *Economist*. Available at: <http://www.economist.com/blogs/democracyinamerica/2 011/10/occupy-wall-street-3>.

Zick, T. (2012) Occupy Wall Street and democratic protest. *Al Jazeera*. Available at: <http://www.aljaz

eera.com/indepth/opinion/2012/03/20123185220379942.
html>.

On violence and non-violence

Calhoun, C. (2011) Evicting the public. *Possible Futures.*
Available at: <http://www.ssrc.org/calhoun/2011/11/18/
evicting-the-public-why-has-occupying-public-spaces-bro
ught-such-heavy-handed-repression>.

Elliott, J. (2011) Occupy Wall Street's struggle for
non-violence. *Salon.* Available at: <http://www.salon.
com/2011/10/17/occupy_wall_streets_struggle_for_non_
violence>.

Goodale, G. (2012) Occupy Wall Street non-violence: Is
Oakland the exception or the future? *The Christian Science
Monitor.* Available at: <http://www.csmonitor.com/USA/
Politics/2012/0131/Occupy-Wall-St.-nonviolence-Is-Oak
land-the-exception-or-the-future-video>.

Gordillo, G. (2011) The human chain as a non-violent
weapon. *Space and Politics.* Available at: <http://spaceandpol
itics.blogspot.com/2011/11/weapon-of-occupy-movemen
t_23.html>.

Graeber, D. (2012) Concerning the Violent Peace-Police:
an open letter to Chris Hedges. *n+1.* Available at:
<http://nplusonemag.com/concerning-the-violent-peace-
police>.

Haberman, C. (2011) *A new generation of dissenters.* City
Room, *New York Times.* Available at: <http://cityroom.ny
times.com/2011/10/10/a-new-generation-of-dissenters>.

Hedges, C. (2012) The cancer in Occupy. *Truth Dig.*
Available at: <http://www.truthdig.com/report/item/the_
cancer_of_occupy_20120206/>.

"Occupy LA protesters are evicted – in pictures." (2011)
The Guardian. <http://www.guardian.co.uk/world/gallery

/2011/nov/30/occupy-la-protesters-are-evicted-in-pictu
res>.

Schneider, N. (2011) What "diversity of tactics" really means
for Occupy Wall Street. *Waging Nonviolence*. Available at:
<http://wagingnonviolence.org/2011/10/what-diversity-of
-tactics-really-means-for-occupy-wall-street/>.

On campaigns and actions in the movement

Doll, J. (2011) Kristen Christian, who created "Bank Transfer
Day," the November 5 bank boycott, tells us why. *The
Village Voice*. Available at: <http://blogs.villagevoice.com/
runninscared/2011/10/kristen_christian_bank_boycott_ba
nk_transfer_day_occupy_wall_street.php>.

Gabbat, A. (2011) Occupy aims to shut down West Coast
ports – as it happened. *The Guardian*. Available at: <http://
www.guardian.co.uk/world/blog/2011/dec/12/occupy-west
-coast-ports-shut-down>.

Goodale, G. (2011) Bank Transfer Day: How much impact
did it have? *Christian Science Monitor*. Available at: <http://
www.csmonitor.com/USA/Politics/2011/1107/Bank-Tran
sfer-Day-How-much-impact-did-it-have>.

Hamilton, W., Reckard, S. and Willon, P. (2011) Occupy
Movement moves into neighborhoods. *Los Angeles Times*.
Available   at: <http://articles.latimes.com/2011/dec/06/
business/la-fi-occupy-home-20111206>.

"Occupy Wall Street goes home." (2011) *Occupy Wall Street*.
Available at: <http://occupywallst.org/article/occupy-wall-
street-goes-home/>.

Riquier, A., Gopal, P. and Brandt, N. (2011) Occupy
Movement targets home evictions in US Day of Action.
Bloomberg. Available at: <http://www.bloomberg.com/
news/2011-12-06/occupy-protest-movement-targets-hom
e-evictions-in-u-s-day-of-action-.html>.

Swartz, L. (2010) Ghoulish ATMs, It's a Wonderful Bank, and Bloody Valentines: Personal finance as civic communication. *Civic Paths*. Available at: <http://civicpaths. uscannenberg.org/2010/11/ghoulish-atms-its-a-wonderf ul-bank-and-bloody-valentines-personal-finance-as-civic-communication/>.

On relationships between the movement and politics

Bowers, C. (2011) Politicians start to take sides on Occupy Wall Street. *Daily Kos*. Available at: <http://www.dailykos. com/story/2011/10/05/1023087/-Politicians-start-to-take-sides-on-Occupy-Wall-Street>.

Dovi, C. (2011) Can Occupy and the Tea Party team up? *Salon*. Available at: <http://www.salon.com/2011/12/07/ can_occupy_and_the_tea_party_team_up/>.

Francis, D. (2011) The politics and economics of Occupy Wall Street. *US News*. Available at: <http://money.usnews.com/ money/business-economy/articles/2011/12/12/the-econo mics-of-occupy-wall-street>.

Gautney, H. (2011) Why Occupy Wall Street wants nothing to do with our politicians. *Washington Post*. Available at: <http://www.washingtonpost.com/national/ on-leadership/why-occupy-wall-street-wants-nothing-to-do-with-our-politicians/2011/10/21/gIQAc2wT3L_story. html>.

Klein, R. (2011) Democrats seek to own "Occupy Wall Street." *ABC News*. Available at: <http://abcnews.go.com/Politics/ democrats-seek-occupy-wall-street-movement/story?id=1 4701337>.

Lawler, K. (2011) Fear of a slacker revolution. *Possible Futures*. Available at: <http://www.possible-futures.org/ 2011/12/01/fear-slacker-revolution-occupy-wall-street-cu ltural-politics-class-struggle/>.

Lessig, L. (2011) #OccupyWallSt, then #OccupyKSt, then #OccupyMainSt. *Huffington Post*. Available at: <http://www.huffingtonpost.com/lawrence-lessig/occupywallst-then-occupyk_b_995547.html>.

Marcuse, P. (2011) Perspective on Occupy: occupiers, sympathizers, and antagonists. *Peter Marcuse's Blog*. Available at: <http://pmarcuse.wordpress.com/2011/12/31/perspective-on-occuppy-occupiers-sympathizers-and-antagonists/>.

Neal, M. (2012) Politicians react to the Occupy Wall Street Movement. *Huffington Post*. Available at: <http://www.huffingtonpost.com/2011/10/17/occupy-wall-street-politician-reactions_n_1014273.html>.

"Occupy Wall Street protesters fed up with both parties." (2011) *AP/Huffington Post*. Available at: <http://www.huffingtonpost.com/2011/10/06/occupy-wall-street-protesters_n_999289.html>.

Pierce, C. (2011) We must give Occupy a politics worthy of its courage. *Politics Blog, Esquire*. Available at: <http://www.esquire.com/blogs/politics/occupy-class-warfare-6592653>.

Wolf, N. (2011) How to Occupy the moral and political high ground. *The Guardian*. Available at: <http://www.guardian.co.uk/commentisfree/2011/nov/06/naomi-wolf-occupy-movement>.

On public opinion and the movement

Bartels, L. (2012) Occupy's impact beyond the beltway. *Bill Moyers*. Available at: <http://billmoyers.com/2012/01/18/has-the-occupy-movement-altered-public-opinion/>.

"Bay Areas news group poll finds 94% support for Occupy Oakland." (2012) *Occupy Oakland*. Available at: <http://occupyoakland.org/2012/02/bay-area-news-group-poll-finds-94-support-occupy/>.

Montopoli, B. (2011) Occupy Wall Street: More popular than you think. *CBS News*. Available at: <http://www. cbsnews.com/8301-503544_162-20120052-503544.html? tag=mncol;lst;1>.

Reich, R. (2011) Occupy Wall Street has transformed public opinion. *Salon*. Available at: <http://www.salon. com/2011/10/31/how_ows_has_transformed_public_opin ion/>.

Sargeant, G. (2011) Will Occupy Wall Street alienate the middle of the country? It hasn't yet. *Washington Post*. Available at: <http://www.washingtonpost.com/blogs/ plum-line/post/will-occupy-wall-street-alienate-the-midd le-of-the-country-it-hasn't yet/2011/10/24/gIQAZ1zJDM _blog.html>.

General sources

Blodget, H. (2011) CHARTS: Here's what the Occupy Wall Street protesters are so angry about. *Business Insider*. Available at: <http://www.businessinsider.com/what-wall-street-protesters-are-so-angry-about-2011-10?op=1>.

"By the Numbers." (2011) *Demos*. Available at: <http:// archive.demos.org/inequality/numbers.cfm>.

Gilson, D. (2011) Charts: Who are the 1%? *Mother Jones*. Available at: <http://motherjones.com/mojo/2011/10/ one-percent-income-inequality-OWS>.

Gosztola, K. (2011-2012) The dissenter. *Fire Dog Lake*. Available at: <http://dissenter.firedoglake.com/>.

InterOccupy: Connecting Occupations. Available at: <http://int eroccupy.org/>.

Kilkenny, A. (2011) Occupy Wall Street: Searching for hope in America. *The Nation*. Available at: <http://www. thenation.com/blog/163462/occupywallstreet-searching-hope-america>.

Mitchell, G. (2011-2012) The Occupy USA blog. *The Nation*. Available at: <http://www.thenation.com/blogs/greg-mitchell>.

New York City General Assembly. Available at: <http://www.nycga.net/>.

Occupied Wall Street Journal. Available at: <http://occupied-media.us/>.

Occupy! N+1. Available at: <http://nplusonemag.com/occupy/>.

Occupy Together. Available at: <http://www.occupytogether.org/>.

Rushkoff, D. (2011) Think Occupy Wall Street is a phase? You don't get it. *CNN*. Available at: <http://www.cnn.com/2011/10/05/opinion/rushkoff-occupy-wall-street/index.html>.

Samuelson, T. (2011) Meet the occupants. *New York Magazine*. Available at: <http://nymag.com/news/intelligencer/topic/occupy-wall-street-2011-10/>.

Sassen, S. (2011) The global street comes to Wall Street. *Possible Futures*. Available at: <http://www.possible-futures.org/2011/11/22/the-global-street-comes-to-wall-street/>.

Schneider, N. (2011) Occupy Wall Street: FAQs. *The Nation*. Available at: <http://www.thenation.com/article/163719/occupy-wall-street-faq>.

Sifry, M. (2011) #OccupyWallstreet: There's something happening here, Mr. Jones. *Tech President*. Available at: <http://techpresident.com/blog-entry/occupywallstreet-theres-something-happening-here-mr-jones>.

Tidal: Occupy Theory, Occupy Strategy. Available at <http://www.occupytheory.org>.

Waging Nonviolence. <http://wagingnonviolence.org>.

Weigel, D. (2011) A complete guide to the anti-corporate protests taking place around the nation. *Slate*. Available at: <http://www.slate.com/articles/news_and_politics/pol

itics/features/2011/occupy_wall_street/what_is_ows_a_gu
ide_to_the_anti_corporate_protests.html>.

Wolff, R. (2011) Occupy Wall Street ends capitalism's alibi. *The Guardian.* Available at: <http://www.guardian.co.uk/
commentisfree/cifamerica/2011/oct/04/occupy-wall-street
-new-york>.

CHANGING THE WORLD IN
THE NETWORK SOCIETY

We have brought down the wall of fear
U brought down the wall of our house
We'll rebuild our homes
But u will never build that wall of fear
                    Tweet from @souriastrong (Rawia Alhoussaini)

Throughout history, social movements have been, and continue to be, the levers of social change.[1] They usually stem from a crisis of living conditions that makes everyday life unbearable for most people. They are prompted by a deep distrust of the political institutions managing society. The combination of a degradation of the material conditions of life and of a crisis of legitimacy of the rulers in charge with the conduct of public affairs induces people to take matters into their own hands, engaging in collective action outside the prescribed institutional channels, to defend their demands and, eventually, to change the rulers, and even the rules shaping their lives. Yet, this is risky behavior, because the maintenance of social order and the stability of political institutions express power relationships that are enforced, if necessary, by intimidation and, in the last resort, by the use of force. Thus, in the historical experience, and in the observation of the movements analyzed in this book, social movements are most often triggered by emotions derived from some meaningful event that help the protesters to overcome fear and challenge the powers that be in spite of the danger inherent to their action. Indeed, social change involves an action, individual and/or collective that, at its root, is motivated emotionally, as is all human behavior, according to recent research in social neuroscience (Damasio 2009). In the context of the six basic emotions that have been identified by neuro-psychologists (fear, disgust, surprise, sadness, happiness, anger; Ekman 1973), the theory of affective intelligence in political communication (Neuman et al. 2007) argues that the trigger is anger, and the repressor is fear. Anger increases with the perception of an unjust action and with the identification of the agent responsible for the action. Fear triggers anxiety, which is associated with avoidance of danger. Fear is overcome by sharing and identifying with others in a process of communicative action. Then anger takes over: it leads to risk-taking behavior. When the process of communicative action induces collective action and change is enacted, the most potent positive emotion prevails: enthusiasm, which powers purposive social mobilization. Enthusiastic networked individuals, having overcome fear, are transformed into a conscious, collective actor. Thus social change results from communicative action that involves connection between networks of neural networks from human brains stimulated by signals from a communication environment through communication networks. The technology and morphology of these communication networks shape the process of mobilization, and thus of social change, both as a process and as an outcome. In recent years, large scale communication has experienced a deep technological and organizational transformation, with the rise of what I have called mass self-communication, based on horizontal networks of interactive, multidirectional communication on the Internet and, even more so, in wireless communication networks, the now prevalent platform of communication everywhere (Castells 2009; Castells et al. 2006; Hussain and Howard 2012; Shirky 2008). This is the new context, at the core of the network society as a new social structure, in which the social movements of the twenty-first century are being formed.

The movements studied in this book, and similar social movements that have sprung up around the world, did originate from a structural economic crisis and from a deepening crisis of legitimacy (see Appendix to this chapter). The financial crisis that shook up the foundations of global informational capitalism from 2008 onwards called into question prosperity in Europe and in the United States; threatened governments, countries and major corporations with financial collapse; and led to a substantial shrinking of the welfare state on which social stability had been predicated for decades (Castells et al. 2012; Engelen et al. 2011). The global food crisis impacted the livelihood of most people in the Arab countries as the price of basic staples, and particularly of bread, reached unaffordable levels for a population that spends most of its meager income on food. Rampant social inequality everywhere became intolerable in the eyes of many suffering the crisis without hope and without trust. The cauldron of social and political indignation reached boiling point. Yet, social movements do not arise just from poverty or political despair. They require an emotional mobilization triggered by outrage against blatant injustice, and by hope of a possible change as a result of examples of successful uprisings in other parts of the world, each revolt inspiring the next one by networking images and messages in the Internet. Moreover, in spite of the sharp differences between the contexts in which these movements arose, there are certain common features that constitute a common pattern: the shape of the social movements of the Internet Age.

NETWORKED SOCIAL MOVEMENTS: AN EMERGING PATTERN?

The social movements studied in this book, as well as others taking place around the world in recent years,[2] present a number of common characteristics.

They are networked in multiple forms. The use of Internet and mobile communication networks is essential, but the networking form is multimodal. It includes social networks online and offline, as well as pre-existing social networks, and networks formed during the actions of the movement. Networks are within the movement, with other movements around the world, with the Internet blogosphere, with the media and with society at large. Networking technologies are meaningful because they provide the platform for this continuing, expansive networking practice that evolves with the changing shape of the movement. Although movements are usually rooted in urban space through occupations and street demonstrations, their ongoing existence takes place in the free space of the Internet. Because they are a network of networks, they can afford not to have an identifiable centre, and yet ensure coordination functions, as well as deliberation, by interaction between multiple nodes. Thus, they do not need a formal leadership, command and control centre, or a vertical organization to distribute information or instructions. This decentered structure maximizes chances of participation in the movement, given that these are open-ended networks without defined boundaries, always reconfiguring themselves according to the level of involvement of the population at large. It also reduces the vulnerability of the movement to the threat of repression, since there are few specific targets to repress, except for the occupied sites, and the network can reform itself as long as there are enough participants in the movement, loosely connected by their common goals and shared values. Networking as the movement's way of life protects the movement both against its adversaries and against its own internal dangers of bureaucratization and manipulation.

While these movements usually start on the Internet social networks, *they become a movement by occupying the urban space*, be it the standing occupation of public squares or the persistence of street demonstrations. The space of the movement is always made of an interaction between the space of flows on the Internet and wireless communication networks, and the space of places of the occupied sites and of symbolic buildings targeted by protest actions. This hybrid of cyberspace and urban space constitutes a third space that I call the space of autonomy. This is because autonomy can only be insured by the capacity to organize in the free space of communication networks, but at the same time can only be exercised as a transformative force by challenging the disciplinary institutional order by reclaiming the space of the city for its citizens. Autonomy without defiance becomes withdrawal. Defiance without a permanent basis for autonomy in the space of flows is tantamount to discontinuous activism. *The space of autonomy is the new spatial form of networked social movements.*

Movements are local and global at the same time. They start in specific contexts, for their own reasons, build their own networks, and construct their public space by occupying urban space and connecting to the Internet networks. But they are also global, because they are connected throughout the world, they learn from other experiences, and in fact they are often inspired by these experiences to engage in their own mobilization. Furthermore, they keep an ongoing, global debate on the Internet, and sometimes they call for joint, global demonstrations in a network of local spaces in simultaneous time. They express an acute consciousness of the intertwining of issues and problems for humanity at large, and they clearly display a cosmopolitan culture, while being rooted in their specific identity. They prefigure to some extent the supersession of the current split between local communal identity and global individual networking.

Like many other social movements in history, they have generated their own form of time: *timeless time*, a transhistorical form of time, by combining two different types of experience. On the one hand, in the occupied settlements, they live day by day, not knowing when the eviction will come, organizing their living as if this could be the alternative society of their dreams, limitless in their time horizon, and free of the chronological constraints of their previous, disciplined daily lives. On the other hand, in their debates and in their projects they refer to an unlimited horizon of possibilities of new forms of life and community emerging from the practice of the movement. They live in the moment in terms of their experience, and they project their time in the future of history-making in terms of their anticipation. In between these two temporal practices, they refuse the subservient clock time imposed by the chronometers of their existence. Since human time only exists in human practice, this dual timeless time is no less real than the measured time of the assembly line worker or the around the clock time of the financial executive. It is an emerging, alternative time, made of a hybrid between the now and the long now.

In terms of their genesis, these movements are largely

spontaneous in their origin, usually triggered by a spark of indignation either related to a specific event or to a peak of disgust with the actions of the rulers. In all cases they are originated by a call to action from the space of flows that aims to create an instant community of insurgent practice in the space of places. The source of the call is less relevant than the impact of the message on the multiple, unspecified receivers, whose emotions connect with the content and form of the message. The power of images is paramount. YouTube has been probably one of the most potent mobilizing tools in the early stages of the movement. Particularly meaningful are images of violent repression by police or thugs.

Movements are viral, following the logic of the Internet networks. This is not only because of the viral character of the diffusion of messages themselves, particularly of mobilizing images, but because of the demonstration effect of movements springing up everywhere. We have observed virality from one country to another, from one city to another, from one institution to another. Seeing and listening to protests somewhere else, even in distant contexts and different cultures, inspires mobilization because it triggers *hope* of the possibility of change.

The transition from outrage to hope is accomplished by deliberation in the space of autonomy. Decision-making usually happens in assemblies and committees designated in the assemblies. Indeed, these are usually *leaderless movements*. Not because of the lack of would-be leaders, but because of the deep, spontaneous distrust of most participants in the movement towards any form of power delegation. This essential feature of the observed movements results directly from one of the causes of the movements: rejection of political representatives by the represented, after feeling betrayed and manipulated in their experience of politics as usual. There are multiple instances in which some of the participants are more active or more influential than others, just by committing themselves full-time to the movement. But these activists are only accepted in their role as long as they do not make major decisions by themselves. Thus, in spite of obvious tensions in the daily practice of the movement, the widely accepted, implicit rule is the self-government of the movement by the people in the movement. This is at the same time an organizational procedure and a political goal: it is setting the foundations of a future real democracy by practicing it in the movement.

Horizontal, multimodal networks, both on the Internet and in the urban space, create *togetherness*. This is a key issue for the movement because it is through togetherness that people overcome fear and discover hope. Togetherness is not community because community implies a set of common values, and this is a work in progress in the movement, since most people come to the movement with their own motivations and goals, setting out to discover potential commonality in the practice of the movement. Thus, community is a goal to achieve, but togetherness is a starting point and the source of empowerment: *"Juntas podemos"* ("Together we can"). *The horizontality of networks supports cooperation and solidarity while undermining the need for formal leadership.* Thus, what appears to be an ineffective form of deliberation and decision-making is in fact the foundation needed to generate trust, without which no common action could be undertaken against the backdrop of a political culture characterized by competition and cynicism. The movement builds its own antidotes against the pervasiveness of the social values that they wish to counter. This is the constant principle emerging from the debates in all movements: not only does the goal not justify the means; the means, in fact, embody the goals of transformation.

These are *highly self-reflective movements*. They constantly interrogate themselves as movements, and as individuals, about who they are, what they want, what they want to achieve, which kind of democracy and society they wish for, and how to avoid the traps and pitfalls of so many movements that have failed by reproducing in themselves the mechanisms of the system they want to change, particularly in terms of political delegation of autonomy and sovereignty. This self-reflexivity is manifested in the process of assembly deliberations, but also in multiple forums on the Internet, in a myriad of blogs and group discussions on the social networks. One of the key themes in debate is the question of violence, which the movements, everywhere, encounter in their practice. In principle, *they are non-violent movements*, usually engaging, at their origin, in peaceful, civil disobedience. But they are bound to engage in occupation of public space and in disruptive tactics to put pressure on political authorities and business organizations, since they do not recognize the feasibility of fair participation in the institutional channels. Thus, repression, at different levels of violence depending on the institutional context and the intensity of the challenge by the movement, is a recurrent experience throughout the process of collective action. Since the goal of all movements is to speak out on behalf of society at large, it is critical to sustain their legitimacy by juxtaposing their peaceful character with the violence of the system. Indeed, in every instance, images of police violence have increased the sympathy for the movement among citizens, and have reactivated the movement itself. On the other hand, it is difficult, individually and collectively, to refrain from the basic instinct of self-defence. This was particularly important in the case of the Arab uprisings when, faced with repeated massacres by using utmost military violence, some democratic movements ultimately became contenders in bloody civil wars. The situation is obviously different in liberal democracies, but the arbitrariness and impunity of police violence in many cases opens the way for the action of small, determined groups ready to confront the system with violence in order to expose its violent character. Violence provides spectacular, selective footage for the media, and plays into the hands of those politicians and opinion leaders whose aim is to suppress as swiftly as possible the criticism embodied in the movement. The thorny question of violence is not just a matter of tactics. It is the defining question in the life and death of the movements, since they only stand a chance of enacting social change if their practice and discourse generates consensus in society at large (the 99%) (Lawrence and Karim 2007).

These movements are rarely programmatic movements, except when they focus on a clear, single issue: down with the dictatorial regime. They do have multiple demands: most of the time, all possible demands from citizens avid about deciding the conditions of their own lives. But because demands are multiple and motivations unlimited, they cannot formalize any organization or leadership because their consensus, their togetherness, depends on ad hoc deliberation and protest, not on fulfilling a program built around specific goals: this is both their strength (wide open appeal), and their weakness (how can anything be achieved when the goals to be achieved are undefined?). Accordingly, they cannot focus on one task or project. On the other hand they cannot be channeled into a political action that is narrowly instrumental. Therefore, they can hardly be co-opted by political parties (which are universally distrusted), although political parties may profit from the change of mind provoked by the movement in the public opinion. Thus, they are social movements, *aimed at changing the values of society*, and they can also be public opinion movements, with electoral consequences. They aim to transform the state but not to seize the state. They express feelings and stir debate but do not create parties or support governments, although they may become a target of choice for political marketing. However, *they are very political in a fundamental sense*. Particularly, when they propose and practice direct, deliberative democracy based on networked democracy. They project a new utopia of networked democracy based on local communities and virtual communities in interaction. But utopias are not mere fantasy. Most modern political ideologies at the roots of political systems (liberalism, socialism, communism) originated from utopias. Because utopias become material force by incarnating in people's minds, by inspiring their dreams, by guiding their actions and inducing their reactions. What these networked social movements are proposing in their practice is a new utopia at the heart of the culture of the network society: the utopia of the autonomy of the subject vis-à-vis the institutions of society. Indeed, when societies fail in managing their structural crises by the existing institutions, change can only take place out of the system by a transformation of power relations that starts in people's minds and develops in the form of the networks built by the projects of new actors constituting themselves as the subjects of the new history in the making. And the Internet that, like all technologies, embodies material culture, is a privileged platform for the social construction of autonomy.

INTERNET AND THE CULTURE OF AUTONOMY

The role of the Internet and wireless communication in the current networked social movements is crucial, as documented in this book. But their understanding has been obscured by a meaningless discussion in the media and in the academic circles denying that communication technologies are at the roots of social movements. This is obvious. Neither the Internet, nor any other technology for that matter, can be a source of social causation. Social movements arise from the contradictions and conflicts of specific societies, and they express people's revolts and projects resulting from their multidimensional experience. Yet, at the same time, it is essential to emphasize the critical role of communication in the formation and practice of social movements, now and in history.[3] Because people can only challenge domination by connecting with each other, by sharing outrage, by feeling togetherness, and by constructing alternative projects for themselves and for society at large. Their connectivity depends on interactive networks of communication. And the fundamental form of large scale, horizontal communication in our society is based on the Internet and wireless networks. Furthermore, it is through these digital communication networks that the movements live and act, certainly in interaction with face-to-face communication and with the occupation of urban space. But digital communication networks are an indispensable component in the practice and organization of these movements as they exist. The networked social movements of our time are largely based on the Internet, a necessary though not sufficient component of their collective action. The digital social networks based on the Internet and on wireless platforms are decisive tools for mobilizing, for organizing, for deliberating, for coordinating and for deciding. Yet, the role of the Internet goes beyond instrumentality: it creates the conditions for a form of shared practice that allows a leaderless movement to survive, deliberate, coordinate and expand. It protects the movement against the repression of their liberated physical spaces by maintaining communication among the people within the movement and with society at large in the long march of social change that is required to overcome institutionalized domination (Juris 2008).

Furthermore, there is a deeper, fundamental connection

between the Internet and networked social movements: *they share a specific culture, the culture of autonomy, the fundamental cultural matrix of contemporary societies.* Social movements, while emerging from the suffering of people, are distinct from protest movements. They are essentially cultural movements, movements that connect the demands of today with the projects for tomorrow. And the movements we are observing embody the fundamental project of transforming people into subjects of their own lives by affirming their autonomy vis-à-vis the institutions of society. This is why, while still demanding remedial measures to the current miseries of a large segment of the population, the movements as collective actors do not trust the current institutions, and engage in the uncertain path of creating new forms of conviviality by searching for a new social contract.

In the background of this process of social change is the cultural transformation of our societies. I have tried to document in other writings that the critical features in this cultural transformation refer to the emergence of a new set of values defined as individuation and autonomy, rising from the social movements of the 1970s, and permeating throughout society in the following decades with increasing intensity (Castells 2009: 116–36). Individuation is the cultural trend that emphasizes the projects of the individual as the paramount principle orientating her/his behavior (Giddens 1991; Beck 1992). Individuation is not individualism, because the project of the individual may be geared towards collective action and shared ideals, such as preserving the environment or creating community, while individualism makes the well-being of the individual the ultimate goal of his/her individuated project. The concept of autonomy is broader, as it can refer both to individual or collective actors. Autonomy refers to the capacity of a social actor to become a subject by defining its action around projects constructed independently of the institutions of society, according to the values and interests of the social actor. The transition from individuation to autonomy is operated through networking, which allows individual actors to build their autonomy with likeminded people in the networks of their choice. I contend that the Internet provides the organizational communication platform to translate the culture of freedom into the practice of autonomy. This is because the technology of the Internet embodies the culture of freedom, as shown in the historical record of its development (Castells 2001). It was deliberately designed by scientists and hackers as a decentered, computer communication network able to withstand control from any command center. It emerged from the culture of freedom prevailing in the university campuses in the 1970s (Markoff 2006). It was based on open source protocols from its inception, the TCP/IP protocols developed by Vint Cerf and Robert Kahn. It became user friendly on a large scale thanks to the World Wide Web, another open source program created by Tim Berners-Lee.

In continuity with this emphasis on autonomy building, the deepest social transformation of the Internet came in the first decade of the twenty-first century, from the shift from individual and corporate interaction on the Internet (the use of email, for instance), to the autonomous construction of social networks controlled and guided by their users. It came from improvements in broadband, and in social software and from the rise of a wide range of distribution systems feeding the Internet networks. Furthermore, wireless communication connects devices, data, people, organizations, everything, with the cloud emerging as the repository of widespread social networking, as a web of communication laid over everything and everybody. Thus, the most important activity on the Internet nowadays goes through social networking sites (SNS), and SNS have become platforms for all kinds of activities, not just for personal friendships or chatting but for marketing, e-commerce, education, cultural creativity, media and entertainment distribution, health applications, and, yes, socio-political activism. SNS are living spaces connecting all dimensions of people's lives (Naughton 2012). This is a significant trend for society at large. It transforms culture by inducing the culture of sharing. SNS users transcend time and space, yet they produce content, set up links and connect practices. There is now a constantly networked world in every dimension of human experience. People in their networks co-evolve in permanent, multiple interactions. But they choose the terms of their co-evolution. SNS are constructed by users themselves building both on specific criteria of grouping and on broader friendship networks, tailored by people, on the basis of platforms provided by the merchants of free communication, with different levels of profiling and privacy. The key to the success of an SNS is not anonymity, but on the contrary, self-presentation of a real person connecting to real persons. People build networks to be with others, and to be with others they want to be with, on the basis of criteria that include those people who they already know or those they would like to know (Castells 2010). So, it is a self-constructed network society based on perpetual connectivity. But this is not a purely virtual society. There is a close connection between virtual networks and networks in life at large. The real world in our time is a hybrid world, not a virtual world or a segregated world that would separate online from offline interaction (Wellman and Rainie 2012). And it is in this world that networked social movements came to life in a natural transition for many individuals, from sharing their sociability to sharing their outrage, their hope and their struggle.

Thus, the culture of freedom at the societal level, and the culture of individuation and autonomy at the level of social actors, induced at the same time the Internet networks and the networked social movements. Indeed, there is a synergistic effect between these two developments. Let me illustrate this analysis with the results of the survey research I conducted in 2002–7 with Tubella and others on a representative sample of the population of Catalonia (Castells and Tubella et al. 2005; 2007). We defined empirically in the population at large six statistically independent projects of autonomy: personal, professional, entrepreneurial, communicative, bodily and socio-political. We found that the more people were autonomous in each one of the six dimensions of autonomy, the more frequently and intensely they would use the Internet. And, over a span of time, the more they would use the Internet, the more their degree of autonomy would enhance. There is indeed a virtuous circle between the technologies of freedom and the struggle to free the minds from the frames of domination.

These findings are in cognitive coherence with a 2010 study in Britain, conducted by sociologist Michael Willmott on the basis of the global data obtained from the World Values Survey of the University of Michigan. He analyzed 35,000 individual answers between 2005 and 2007. The study showed that Internet use empowers people by increasing their feelings of security, personal freedom and influence: all feelings that have a positive effect on personal well-being. The effect is particularly positive for people with lower income and less qualifications, for people in the developing world, and for women.[4] Empowerment, autonomy and enhanced sociability appear closely connected to the practice of frequent networking on the Internet.

Networked social movements, as all social movements in history, bear the mark of their society. They are largely made of individuals living at ease with digital technologies in the hybrid world of real virtuality. Their values, goals and organizational style directly refer to the culture of autonomy that characterizes the young generations of a young century. They could not exist without the Internet. But their significance is much deeper. They are suited for their role as agents of change in the network society, in sharp contrast with the obsolete political institutions inherited from a historically superseded social structure.

NETWORKED SOCIAL MOVEMENTS AND REFORM POLITICS: AN IMPOSSIBLE LOVE?

The consensus seems to be that, at the end of the day, the dreams of social change will have to be watered down, and channeled through the political institutions, either by reform or revolution. Even in the latter case, the revolutionary ideals will be interpreted (betrayed?) by the new powers in place and their new constitutional order. This creates a major dilemma, both analytical and practical, when assessing the political productivity of movements that, in most cases, do not trust existing political institutions, and refuse to believe in the feasibility of their participation in the predetermined channels of political representation. It is true that the paradigmatic experience of Iceland shows the possibility of a new departure both in the institutions of governance and in the organization of the economy without a traumatic process of change. Yet, in most of the movements studied, and in similar movements around the world, the critical passage from hope to implementation of change depends on the permeability of political institutions to the demands of the movement, and on the willingness of the movement to engage in a process of negotiation. When both conditions are met in positive terms, a number of demands may be satisfied and political reform may happen, with different degrees of change. It did happen in the case of Israel (Nahon

2012). However, since the fundamental challenge from these movements concerns the denial of legitimacy of the political class, and the denunciation of their subservience to the financial elites, there is little room for a true acceptance of these values by most governments. Indeed, a comprehensive review of empirical studies on the political consequences of social movements, mainly focusing on the United States, shows that, on the one hand, the biggest social movements in the past have been politically influential in several ways, particularly in contributing to set policy agendas. On the other hand, "for a movement to be influential, state actors need to see it as potentially facilitating or disrupting their own goals – augmenting or cementing new electoral coalitions, gaining in public opinion, increasing the support for the missions of governmental bureaus" (Amenta et al. 2010: 298).

In other words, influence of social movements on politics and policies is largely dependent upon their potential contribution to the pre-set agendas of political actors. This is squarely at odds with the main critique of the networked social movements I studied, which concerns the lack of representativeness of the political class, as elections are conditioned by the power of money and media, and constrained by biased electoral laws designed by the political class for its own benefit. Yet, the usual answer to the protest movements from political elites is to refer to the will of the people as expressed in the previous election, and to the opportunity of changing politics according to the results of the next election. This is precisely what is objected to by most movements, in agreement with a substantial proportion of citizens everywhere in the world, as shown in the Appendix. Movements do not object to the principle of representative democracy, but denounce the practice of such democracy as it is today, and do not recognize its legitimacy. Under such conditions, there is little chance of a positive direct interaction between movements and the political class to push for political reform, that is a reform of the institutions of governance that would broaden the channels of political participation, and limit the influence of lobbies and pressure groups in the political system, the fundamental claims of most social movements. The most positive influence of the movement on politics may happen indirectly through the assumption by some political parties or leaders of some of the themes and demands of the movement, particularly when they reach popularity among large sectors of citizens. This is for instance the case in the United States, where the reference to the social cleavage between the 99% and the 1% has come to symbolize the extent of inequality. Yet, cautious leaders, such as Obama, while claiming to represent the aspirations expressed in the movement, stop short of endorsing its activism out of fear of being seen as condoning radical practices.

Since the road to policy changes goes through political change, and political change is shaped by the interests of the politicians in charge, the influence of the movement on policy is usually limited, at least in the short term, in the absence of a major crisis that requires the overhaul of the entire system, as happened in Iceland. Nevertheless, there is a much deeper connection between social movements and political reform that could activate social change: it takes place in the minds of the people. The actual goal of these movements is to raise awareness among citizens at large, to empower them through their participation in the movement and in a wide deliberation about their lives and their country, and to trust their ability to make their own decisions in relation to the political class. The influence of the movement in the population at large proceeds through the most unsuspected avenues.[5] If the cultural and social influence of the movement expands, particularly in the younger, more active generations, astute politicians will address their values and concerns, seeking electoral gain. They will do so within the limits of their own allegiance to their bank rollers. But the more the movement is able to convey its messages over the communication networks, the more citizen consciousness rises, and the more the public sphere of communication becomes a contested terrain, and the lesser will be the politicians' capacity to integrate demands and claims with mere cosmetic adjustments. The ultimate battle for social change is decided in the minds of the people, and in this sense networked social movements have made major progress at the international level. As shown in the Appendix to this chapter, in an international poll of 23 countries conducted in November 2011, with the exception of Japan, more people were favorable than unfavorable toward Occupy and similar movements in their context, and the majority of citizens agreed with their criticism of governments, politicians and financial institutions. This is particularly remarkable when referring to movements that place themselves outside the institutional system and engage in civil disobedience. True, when polled about the movement's tactics in the United States, only a minority supported the movement, but even in this regard the fact that about 25–30 percent approved of the disruptive actions of the movement indicates a groundswell of support to the challengers of the institutions that have lost the trust of citizens. The uncertainty of an uncharted process of political change seems to be the main barrier to overcome for movements that have already exposed the illegitimacy of the current powers that be. Nevertheless, love between social activism and political reformism does not appear to be impossible: it is simply hidden from the public view while citizens waver in their minds between desire and resignation.

NOTES

1 My theoretical perspective on the analysis of social movements builds on Alain Touraine's theory, as presented in Touraine (1978). The most complete formulation of my own analytical perspective was published in Castells (1983), and applied in Castells (1983; 2003). See also Johnston (2011), Snow et al. (2004), Tilly (2004), Staggenborg (2008), Chesters and Welsh (2000), Diani and McAdam (2003), Hardt and Negri (2004).

2 In 2008–12 there were a number of powerful, networked social movements, beyond the cases presented in this book, that sprung up around the world, with different emphases, origins and orientations, particularly in Iran, Greece, Portugal, Italy, Israel, Chile and Russia. Symbolic occupations of public space that never reached the level of a full-fledged social movement took place in most European countries, and in some Latin American countries. See Shirky (2008), Scafuro (2011), Mason (2012), Cardoso and Jacobetti (2012).

3 On the role of communication in the development of social movements, both historically and in contemporary societies, see, besides my own work (2003; 2009), Thompson (2000), Downing (2000), Couldry and Curran (2003), Oberschall (1996), Neveu (1996), Curran (2011), Juris (2008), Cardoso and Jacobetti (2012).

4 Report by the BCS Institute, a UK-chartered institute on IT, in a study carried out by Trajectory Partnership, a UK-based think tank, as reported at: <www.time.com/time/health/article/0,8599,1989244,00.html>.

5 For instance, according to a post on March 23, 2012, by Kristen Gwynne from AlterNet:

Sex strike is being utilized as a form of activism against the banks. According to RT News, high-class escorts in Madrid, Spain are protesting the banking sector by refusing to sell bankers their highly sought-after commodity: Sex.

RT reports: The largest trade association for luxury escorts in the Spanish capital has gone on a general and indefinite strike on sexual services for bankers until they go back to providing credits to Spanish families, small- and medium-size enterprises and companies.

It all started with one of the ladies who forced one of her clients to grant a line credit and a loan simply by halting her sexual services until he "fulfills his responsibility to society." The trade association's spokeswoman praised their success by stressing how the government and the Bank of Spain have previously failed to adjust the credit flow.

"We are the only ones with a real ability to pressure the sector," she stated. "We have been on strike for three days now and we don't think they can withstand much more."

The woman quoted above says bankers are desperate for sex services, and have become so pitiful they are unsuccessfully pretending to have other careers, and have even asked the government for help.

The Minister of Economy and Competitiveness Luis de Guindos reportedly told the Mexican website SDPnoticias.com, which broke the story, that the escort industry's lack of regulations makes government intervention difficult.

"In fact, there has not even been a formal communication of the strike – the escorts are making use of their right of admission or denying entry to . . . well, you know. So no one can negotiate," he told SDPnoticias.

com, making it clear that sex is a valuable tool, and refusing it sends a very strong, direct message.

By Kristen Gwynne, AlterNet, posted on March 23, 2012; printed on March 23, 2012. <http://www.alternet. org/newsandviews/866354/sex_strike%21_madrid%5C %27s_escorts_launch_coordinated_attack_against_ban ks%2C_withhold_sex_services_from_desperate_bank ers>

REFERENCES AND SOURCES

Amenta, E., Caren, N., Chiarello, E. and Su, Y. (2010) The political consequences of social movements. *Annual Review of Sociology*, 36: 287–307.

Beck, U. (1992) *The Risk Society*. Polity Press, Cambridge.

Cardoso, G. and Jacobetti, P. (2012) Surfing the crisis: Alternative cultures and social movements in Portugal. In M. Castells, J. Caraca, and G. Cardoso (eds.) *Aftermath: The cultures of the economic crisis*. Oxford University Press, Oxford.

Castells, M. (1983) *The City and the Grassroots. A cross-cultural theory of urban social movements*. University of California Press, Berkeley, CA.

Castells, M. (2001) *The Internet Galaxy*. Oxford University Press, Oxford.

Castells, M. (2003) *The Power of Identity*. Blackwell, Oxford.

Castells, M. (2009) *Communication Power*. Oxford University Press, Oxford.

Castells, M. (2010) Social Networks in the Internet: What Research Knows About It. Lecture delivered at the Symposium: Web Science, a New Frontier, on the Occasion of the 350th Anniversary of the Royal Society, London, September 28.

Castells, M., Caraca, J. and Cardoso, G. (eds.) (2012)

Aftermath: The cultures of the economic crisis. Oxford University Press, Oxford.

Castells, M., Fernandez-Ardevol, M., Qiu, L. and Sey, A. (2006) *Mobile Communication and Society. A global perspective*. MIT Press, Cambridge, MA.

Castells, M., Tubella, I., et al. (2005) The transformation of the social structure of the network society: Social uses of the Internet in Catalonia. In M. Castells (ed.) *The Network Society: A cross-cultural perspective*. Edward Elgar, Malden, MA.

Castells, M., Tubella, I., et al. (2007) *La transicion a la sociedad red*. Ariel, Barcelona.

Chesters, G. and Welsh, I. (2000) *Complexity and Social Movements: Multitudes at the edge of chaos*. Routledge, London.

Couldry, N. and Curran, J. (eds.) (2003) *Contesting Media Power: Alternative media in a networked world*. Rowman and Littlefield, Lanham, MD.

Curran, J. (2011) *Media and Democracy*. Routledge, London.

Damasio, A. (2009) *Self Comes to Mind*. Pantheon Books, New York.

Diani, M. and McAdam, D. (2003) *Social Movements and Networks*. Oxford University Press, Oxford.

Downing, J. (2000) *Radical Media: Rebellious communication and social movements*. Sage Publications, Thousand Oaks, CA.

Ekman, P. (1973) *Darwin and Facial Expression: A century of research in review*. Academic Press, New York.

Engelen, E., et al. (2011) *After the Great Complacence: Financial crisis and the politics of reform*. Oxford University Press, Oxford.

Giddens, A. (1991) *Modernity and Self-Identity: Self and society in the Late Modern Age*. Polity Press, Cambridge.

Hardt, M. and Negri, A. (2004) *Multitude: War and democracy in the age of Empire*. Penguin, New York.

Howard, P. (2012) Digital technologies in the Arab Revolutions. Paper delivered at the meeting of the International Studies Association, San Diego, April 1.

Hussain, M. M. and Howard, P. N. (2012) Democracy's Fourth Wave? Information Technology and the Fuzzy Causes of the Arab Spring. Unpublished paper presented at the meeting of the International Studies Association, San Diego, April 1.

Johnston, H. (2011) *States and Social Movements*. Polity Press, Cambridge.

Juris, J. (2008) *Networked Futures*. Duke University Press, Durham, NC.

Lawrence, B. B. and Karim, A. (eds.) (2007) *On Violence: A reader*. Duke University Press, Durham, NC.

Markoff, J. (2006) *What the Dormouse Said: How the sixties counterculture shaped the personal computer industry*. Penguin, New York.

Mason, P. (2012) *Why It's Kicking Off Everywhere: The new global revolutions*. Verso, London.

Nahon, K. (2012) Network Theory and Networked Social Movements: Israel, 2011. Paper delivered at the meeting of the Annenberg Network on Networks, Los Angeles, April 27.

Naughton, J. (2012) *What You Really Need To Know About The Internet: From Guttenberg to Zuckerberg*. Quercus, London.

Neuman, W. Russell, Marcus, G. E., Crigler, A. N. and MacKuen, M. (eds.) (2007) *The Affect Effect: Dynamics of emotions in political thinking and behavior*. University of Chicago Press, Chicago, IL.

Neveu, E. (1996) *Sociologie des mouvements sociaux*. La Decouverte, Paris.

Oberschall, A. (1996) *Social Movements: Ideologies, interests, and identities*. Transaction Publishers, Piscataway, NJ.

Scafuro, E. (2011) *Autocomunicazione orizzontale di massa: Il potere della rete*, Genova, Universita degli Studi di Genova, Facolta di Scienze della Formazione, Masters Thesis.

Shirky, C. (2008) *Here Comes Everybody: The power of organizing without organization*. Penguin Press, New York.

Snow, D., Soule, S. and Kriesi, H. (eds.) (2004) *The Blackwell Companion to Social Movements*. Wiley-Blackwell, Oxford.

Staggenborg, S. (2008) *Social Movements*. Oxford University Press, Oxford.

Thompson, J. (2000) *Political Scandal: Power and visibility in the media age*. Polity Press, Cambridge.

Tilly, C. (2004) *Social Movements, 1768–2004*. Paradigm Publishers, Boulder, CO.

Touraine, A. (1978) *La voix et le regard: sociologie des mouvements sociaux*. Seuil, Paris.

Wellman, B. and Rainie, L. (2012) *Networked*. MIT Press, Cambridge, MA.

BEYOND OUTRAGE, HOPE:

THE LIFE AND DEATH OF

NETWORKED SOCIAL MOVEMENTS

It is not a crisis, it is that I do not love you any more.

Banner in Occupied Plaza del Sol, Madrid,
May 2011.

The networked social movements, whose experiences you and I have shared in this book, will continue to fight and debate, evolve and eventually fade away in their current states of being, as have all social movements in history. Even in the unlikely case that they transform themselves into a political actor, a party or some new form of agency, they will cease their existence by this very fact. Because the only relevant question to assess the meaning of a social movement is the social and historical productivity of its practice, and the effect on its participants as persons and on the society it tried to transform. In this sense, it is too early to evaluate the ultimate outcome of these movements, although we can already say that regimes have changed, that institutions have been challenged and that the belief in the triumphant global financial capitalism has been shaken, perhaps in irreversible ways, in the minds of most people.

In the last analysis, the legacy of a social movement is made of the cultural change it has produced through its action. Because if we think differently about some critical dimensions of our personal and social lives, the institutions will have to yield at some point. Nothing is immutable, although changes in history do not follow a predetermined path because the supposed sense of history sometimes does not make sense. In this regard, what appears to be the possible legacy of the networked social movements still in the making? Democracy. A new form of democracy. An old aspiration, never fulfilled, of humankind.

In any social movement there are multiple expressions of needs and desires. These are moments of liberation when everybody empties her/his bag of frustrations and opens her/his magic box of dreams. Thus, we can find every possible human projection in the themes and actions of these movements: most notably, the stern critique of a merciless economic system that feeds the computerized Automaton of speculative financial markets with the human flesh of daily suffering. Yet, if there is an overarching theme, a pressing cry, a revolutionary dream, it is the call for new forms of political deliberation, representation and decision-making. This is because effective, democratic governance is a prerequisite for the fulfillment of all demands and projects. Because if citizens do not have the ways and means of their self-government, the best designed policies, the most sophisticated strategies, the more well-wishing programs may be ineffective or perverted in their implementation. The instrument determines the function. Only a democratic polity can ensure an economy that works as if people mattered, and a society at the service of human values and the pursuit of personal happiness. Again and again, networked social movements around the world have called for a new form of democracy, not necessarily identifying its procedures but exploring its principles in the practice of the movement. The movements, and the public opinion at large, coincide in denouncing the mockery of democratic ideals in most of the world (see Appendix). Since this is not just a matter of the subjectivity of political actors, who often are sincere and honest within their own mindframes, something must be wrong with "the system," this obscure entity that nobody has met personally but whose effects are pervasive in everybody's life. And so, from the depth of despair, everywhere, a dream and a project have surged: to reinvent democracy, to find ways for humans to manage collectively their lives according to principles that are largely shared in their minds and usually disregarded in their everyday experience. These networked social movements are new forms of democratic movements, movements that are reconstructing the public sphere in the space of autonomy built around the interaction between local places and Internet networks, movements that are experimenting with assembly-based decision-making and reconstructing trust as a foundation for human interaction. They acknowledge the principles that ushered in the freedom revolutions of the Enlightenment, while pinpointing the continuous betrayal of these principles, starting with the original denial of full citizenship to women, minorities and colonized people. They emphasize the contradiction between a citizen-based democracy and a city for sale to the highest bidder. They assert their right to start all over again. To begin the beginning, after reaching the threshold of self-destruction by our current institutions. Or so they believe the actors of these movements, whose words I have just borrowed. The legacy of networked social movements will have been to raise the possibility of re-learning how to live together. In real democracy.

APPENDICES

APPENDIX TO THE EGYPTIAN

REVOLUTION

Egyptian Revolution Timeline: June 2010–December 2011
Source: Information collected and elaborated by Maytha Alhassen

June 6, 2010
Blogger Khaled Said beaten to death by Egyptian authorities at a cybercafé in Alexandria.
Facebook group, "We are all Khaled Said," started by Dubai-based Egyptian Google Executive Wael Ghonim.

January 1, 2011
Alexandria's Al-Qiddissin Church is bombed during a New Year's Eve mass; 21 people are killed.

January 25, 2011
"Day of Revolt": nationwide organized demonstrations protesting the Mubarak regime (also the National Police Holiday).
First day of the occupation of Tahrir Square.

January 26, 2011
Twitter and Facebook blocked by Egyptian authorities.

January 28, 2011
Internet services and mobile phone carriers (Link Egypt, Vodafone/Raya, Telecom Egypt and Etisalat Misr) ordered to shut down by Egyptian authorities.
First year anniversary of the "Friday of Rage," an important day in the uprising which contributed to the downfall of Mubarak.
Mohammed ElBaradei, opposition leader and former head of the International Atomic Energy Agency (IAEA), travels to Cairo to participate in protests.
Ghonim mysteriously disappears. It is later revealed that he was arrested by security officials.

January 31, 2011
"The March of the Millions": reports of 200,000 to two million protesters in Tahrir.

February 1, 2011
Mubarak makes a televised announcement promising political reforms and vowing not to run in the next presidential elections.

February 2, 2011
"Battle of the Camels": a significant turning point. Pro-Mubarak "thugs" on camels and horseback raid Tahrir Square, attacking protesters. A day-long battle between the two ensued.
Internet services restored.

February 6, 2011
Egyptian Copts hold Sunday Mass in Tahrir Square, protected by a ring of Muslims.

February 7, 2011
Ghonim is released from prison and appears on Dream TV immediately after, giving a deeply emotional interview with the station.

February 10, 2011
Mubarak formally addresses the nation (protesters anticipating his resignation) and announces the increased ceding of powers to

Vice President Omar Suleiman. Demonstrations intensify after this announcement.

February 11, 2011
"Friday of Departure": At 6pm, Vice President Omar Suleiman announces Mubarak's resignation and the transfer of leadership to the Supreme Council of Egyptian Armed Forces (SCAF).

February 12, 2011
Protesters clean up the square, anticipating a new Egypt: one with the future now in their hands.

February 13, 2011
SCAF dissolves the parliament and suspends the Constitution while also reassuring the Egyptian civil society that they would only hold power for six months or until elections are held.

March 19, 2011
The constitutional referendum is held and passed.

March 23, 2011
The Egyptian cabinet orders a law criminalizing protests and strikes. Under the new law, anyone organizing or calling for a protest will be sentenced to jail and/or fined.

April 1, 2011
Thousands protest in "Save the Revolution" day, calling on SCAF for the quicker removal of old regime figures from political positions.

April 8, 2011
In "Friday of Cleansing," tens of thousands of protesters return to Tahrir Square to put pressure on SCAF to follow through with revolution promises (demanding the resignation of remaining regime figures and the removal of Egypt's public prosecutor).

May 24, 2011
Announcement that Mubarak and his two sons, Alaa and Gamal, would be tried for the deaths of anti-government protesters.

May 27, 2011
"The Second Angry Friday" or "Second Day of Rage": nationwide protests organized. The largest since the ousting of Mubarak.

May 28, 2011
Mubarak was fined $34 million dollars for cutting off communication during the revolution. The blockade on Gaza and Egypt's Rafah border eases.

June 28, 2011
Clashes between security forces and protesters at Tahrir Square.

July 1, 2011
Nationwide protests (Suez, Alexandria and Cairo) in the "Friday of Retribution" voice disapproval of SCAF's slow pace of change five months after the revolution.

July 8, 2011
The following Friday, increased participation of protesters, this time in a "Friday of Determination," calling for immediate reforms and faster prosecution of former Mubarak regime officials.

August 3, 2011
The start of the televised trial of Hosni Mubarak, Gamal and Alaa, the former Interior Minister as well as other members of his government.

August 14, 2011
Asmaa Mahfouz arrested for criticizing SCAF in a tweet and for opposing the military trials of civilians. Because of public pressure, she is released after four days.

September 9, 2011
Protesters storm the Israeli embassy. In response, the Israeli ambassador flees Egypt. SCAF restores "a state of emergency."

SCAF raids the offices of Al-Jazeera's Mubashir Misr, which shuts down the operations of the network.

October 9, 2011
"Maspero Massacre": a predominantly Coptic Christian protest march on Egypt's state television building, Maspero. Protesters demand equality and action by SCAF against a series of attacks on churches. The march ends with a confrontation with the military. Estimates of 24–31 people, mostly Christian, are reported to have died from the confrontation.

November 19, 2011
Protesters re-occupy Tahrir Square and SCAF uses tear gas on protesters.

November 20, 2011
Police attempt to raid the square clean, but protesters return, doubled in size. Violent clashes ensue as police beat, shoot and use tear gas on protesters.

November 28, 2011
Parliamentary elections begin in a series of three stages (ending in January). The Muslim Brotherhood's Freedom and Justice Party has a strong showing.

December 14, 2011
Second round of elections held.

December 17, 2011
"The girl in the blue bra" incident. Security officials beat, strip (exposing her blue bra) and drag a woman in Tahrir. The assault is captured on camera and receives international outrage.

December 20, 2011
Large nationwide women's demonstrations in response to the blue bra incident and general disapproval of SCAF.

December 27, 2011

25-year-old Samira Ibrahim, one of seven women subjected to "virginity tests" on March 9, wins case against the military. The practice is decreed as "sexual assault" and rendered illegal in Egyptian prisons.

December 29, 2011

Security forces raid offices of six NGOs.

APPENDIX TO DIGNITY, VIOLENCE, GEOPOLITICS: THE ARAB UPRISINGS

Arab Uprisings Timeline: December 2010–December 2011
Source: Timeline elaborated by Maytha Alhassen on the basis of data collected from *The Guardian* timeline by Garry Blight, Sheila Pulham and Paul Torpey

December 17, 2010
Tunisia: Mohamed Bouazizi sets himself on fire.

January 14, 2011
Tunisia: The fall of Ben Ali.

January 23, 2011
Yemen: New protests against Saleh.

January 25, 2011
Egypt: The first major protest thanks to the events that occurred in Tunisia.

February 2, 2011
Yemen: Saleh announces he will retire in 2013. Mass protests continue.

February 11, 2011
Egypt: Mubarak resigns and cedes power to the Supreme Council of the Armed Forces.

February 14, 2011
Bahrain: First major protests against the regime and first protester killed.

February 17, 2011
Libya: Protests break out against Gaddafi.

February 20, 2011
Libya: Rebels seize Benghazi and other eastern cities. 230 reported dead.
Libya: Thousands of people protest in 12 cities, connected through the Internet.

February 23, 2011
Libya: Rebels seize Misrata.

February 27, 2011
Tunisia: Beji Caid Essebsi becomes new Prime Minister.

March 2, 2011
Libya: A massive flight of one million refugees into Egypt and Tunisia.

March 9, 2011
Tunisia: Dissolution of the Benalist Party RCD.
Yemen: Soldiers attack students at the Sana'a University campus. Dozens injured.
Morocco: King Mohammed VI announces a constitutional reform that will limit his power.

March 14, 2011
Bahrain: Saudi Arabia sends troops to help the Sunni Monarchy.

March 16, 2011
Libya: Gaddafi recovers territory and sets sights on Benghazi.

Bahrain: Protests at Pearl Square in Manama prohibited and disbanded.

March 18, 2011
Bahrain: Pearl Square Monument, a symbol of the protest movement, is destroyed.
Libya: UN Security Council authorizes the use of force to protect civilians.
Syria: Protests erupt in Daraa (south) and the rest of the nation.

March 19, 2011
Libya: NATO initiates aerial campaign and stops Gaddafi's advances.

March 20, 2011
Morocco: Second round of protests.

March 21, 2011
Egypt: Referendum on the timetable to transition.

March 30, 2011
Libya: Moussa Koussa, minister of foreign affairs, is added to list of defectors.
Syria: Assad's speech proclaims a foreign conspiracy.

April 8, 2011
Yemen: Saleh rejects plan from the Gulf Cooperation Council to cede power.

April 13, 2011
Egypt: Mubarak and his sons are arrested for corruption and suppression.

April 19, 2011
Syria: Emergency Law repealed. A law in place since 1963.

April 24, 2011
Bahrain: Four activists sentenced to death.

April 25, 2011
Syria: Tanks on the street.

May 4, 2011
Libya: The International Criminal Court accuses the Gaddafi regime of crimes against humanity.

May 8, 2011
Egypt: Attacks against the Copt minority.

May 9, 2011
Syria: European Union imposes sanctions and an arms embargo.

May 10, 2011
Libya: Rebels break Gaddafi's siege on Misrata.

May 11, 2011
Bahrain: Bahrain National Oil fires 300 employees for participating in protests.

May 12, 2011
Syria: Military assault on the city of Homs.

May 24, 2011
Libya: NATO attacks Gaddafi's headquarters in Tripoli.

May 27, 2011
Tunisia: Help from G8. 20 million dollars given to Tunisia and Egypt.

June 3, 2011
Yemen: Saleh survives attack on his palace in Sanaa. Taken to Saudi Arabia.

June 10, 2011
Syria: Army launches operation in the north after police killings.

June 14, 2011
Tunisia: Elections are delayed from June 24 until October 23.

June 20, 2011
Tunisia: Ben Ali and his wife sentenced to 25 years in prison for corruption.

June 29, 2011
Egypt: Thousands injured in protests following delay in the trial of Mubarak's interior minister.

July 1, 2011
Morocco: Moroccans approve constitutional reform in a referendum.

August 3, 2011
Egypt: Mubarak's trial begins.

August 7, 2011
Yemen: Saleh leaves hospital, but remains in Riyadh.

August 22, 2011
Libya: Rebels take control of Tripoli.

September 7, 2011
Bahrain: More than 100 jailed activists go on hunger strike.

September 23, 2011
Yemen: Saleh returns to Sanaa.

September 25, 2011
Yemen: Saleh announces elections. Hundreds dead during the last four days.

September 26, 2011
Syria: Military operations in Hama.

September 29, 2011
Bahrain: A military court jails 20 medics for tending to protesters.

October 7, 2011
Yemen: Opposition leader Tawakkul Karman wins Nobel Peace Prize.

October 9, 2011
Egypt: 24 dead after Copt protest.

October 20, 2011
Libya: Capture and assassination of Gaddafi in Sirte.

October 23, 2011
Tunisia: The moderate Islamist Ennahda party wins election.
Libya: National Transitional Council announces the liberation of Libya.
Bahrain: Retrial begins for medics after international condemnation.

November 18 and 28, 2011
Egypt: Protests in Tahrir against the military junta.

November 19, 2011
Libya: Seif al-Islam, the last fugitive son of the Gaddafi family, is captured.

November 21, 2011
Bahrain: Government admits to using "excessive force" against protesters. New protests ensue.

November 22, 2011
Syria: Erdogan definitively ends ties with Assad. Compares him to Hitler or Mussolini.

November 23, 2011
Yemen: Saleh agrees to leave office in exchange for immunity.

November 25, 2011
Morocco: Islamist victory in legislative elections.

November 27, 2011
Syria: Arab League Sanctions.

November 28, 2011
Egypt: First round of legislative elections. Islamist party wins 65 percent of votes.

November 30, 2011
Morocco: Mohammed VI appoints Islamist leader Abdelilah Benkirane as prime minister.

December 10, 2011
Tunisia: Provisional constitution.

December 13, 2011
Tunisia: Moncef Marzouki becomes New President.
Syria: UN estimates death toll at 5,000.

December 14, 2011
Egypt: Second round of elections.

APPENDIX TO A RHIZOMATIC

REVOLUTION: *INDIGNADAS*

IN SPAIN

Spanish *Indignadas* Movement Timeline: May 2011–May 2012
Source: Information collected and elaborated by Amalia Cardenas and Joana Conill

May 15, 2011
National demonstration called for by Democracia Real Ya (DRY). The demonstrations that drew the largest numbers were those in Madrid, Barcelona, Murcia, Granada, Seville, Malaga, Alicante and Valencia. It is estimated that demonstrations were followed by some 130,000 people in Spain.

May 16, 2011
Between 150 and 200 people decide to camp in the Puerta del Sol, Madrid after the demonstrations on the night of Sunday, May 15. In the early morning of the 16th, police attempt to evict protesters but fail to do so. Thus, the camps begin.
Following the example of Madrid, about 150 people gather in Plaza Catalunya in Barcelona. In Malaga, Granada, Seville, Bilbao and Zaragoza, camps also begin to take place.

May 17, 2011

Demonstrations in several Spanish cities. Noteworthy are those that took place in the Plaza del Sol in Madrid. A second camp starts in Plaza del Sol. This time the demonstrations are not called for by Democracia Real Ya. At this point, 30 Spanish cities have camps.

May 18, 2011

In Madrid a large tent is raised and a food stand is installed with food donated by merchants. A webcam is also set up. Police order evictions in Valencia, Tenerife, Las Palmas and Granada. Protesters agree to have daily assemblies. The Board of Elections in Madrid announces that the demonstrations in the plazas are prohibited. Protesters spread a large roll of paper as a sign of peaceful protection against the police. Demonstrators in Madrid produce a provisional list of proposals. At this point, there are camps in 52 Spanish cities.

May 19, 2011

The Constitutional Court declares the demonstrations legal. Later in the day, the Central Electoral Board issues a statement declaring the demonstrations to be illegal. Despite these announcements, demonstrations are called for in several cities. By this time, 66 cities in Spain and 15 cities outside of Spain have set up camps.

May 20, 2011

The legal committee of Puerta del Sol in Madrid informs the media that no protests will convene on Saturday, May 21, the national day of reflection. However, protests would convene on Friday, May 20. By the morning of May 20, there are 166 different cities with camps. By the evening, the numbers grow to 357, and by the end of the night, there are 480 people total. On this day, Plaza Catalunya is divided into three zones, symbolically called Tahrir, Iceland and Palestine. During the night, a minute of silence is held in response to the pre-election day of reflection in Barcelona and Madrid.

May 21, 2011
Despite the ban on gathering in the plazas, thousands of people fill the Plaza del Sol and surrounding areas during the day. "Cacerolada" demonstrations are held in Barcelona that evening, drawing 5,000 people.

May 22, 2011
Municipal elections are held in Spain. Acampada Sol decides to continue camping for a minimum of one week. The People's Party (PP), Spain's conservative political party, wins with an overwhelming majority.

May 23, 2011
The Confederation of Specialized Trade in Madrid calls for measures to prevent the decline in sales of local businesses surrounding the camps.

May 24, 2011
Acampada Sol begins to extend assemblies to different neighborhoods around Madrid.

May 25, 2011
In Malaga, the Ministry of Defence decides to change the location of several events planned for Friday May 27, on the occasion of Armed Forces Day.

May 26, 2011
The assembly of the Acampada Sol reaches four points of consensus in response to the insistence for clear demands. The four ideas discussed are electoral reforms, measures against corruption, effective separation of public powers and creation of mechanisms to provide more citizen control.

May 27, 2011
At seven in the morning the city of Barcelona sends 350 Catalan police and 100 local police officers to evict the protesters in Plaza Catalunya. The police cite hygiene reasons for the eviction and claim that the plaza needs to be cleaned before the celebrations of

the final of the Champions league in which FC Barcelona participates. The eviction ends with 121 wounded. The same situation
is repeated in Lleida and Sabadell. After the eviction, about 3,000
people return to Plaza Catalunya. In the main cities of Spain,
demonstrations are held in solidarity for the protesters evicted in
Barcelona. An investigation into what occurred that day in Plaza
Catalunya is started.

May 28, 2011
FCB wins the Champions League. In Plaza Catalunya, protesters
organize human chains to avoid confrontations with FCB fans.
The night ends without any sort of confrontation.
Proposals begin to develop to maintain the momentum in
the face of possible evictions. Acampada Sol is decentralized.
Local assemblies begin to be held in 90 municipalities and 41
districts.

May 29, 2011
Demonstrations are held by 23,000 people in Seville and 7,000
people in Valencia. Participants in Madrid and Barcelona decide
to continue camping indefinitely.

May 30, 2011
Democracia Real Ya announces a worldwide protest to be held
on October 15, 2011.

June 5, 2011
People from various cities in Spain meet in Puerta del Sol in
Madrid to analyze the evolution of the 15-M movement and
to discuss further action. The possibility of a national march
to Puerta del Sol is discussed. The Indignant Popular March is
decided upon. In addition, demonstrations for June 11 and 19 are
decided upon.

June 6, 2011
Demonstrators in Plaza Catalunya decide to stop a permanent
camp and instead maintain activities during the day.

June 7, 2011
Acampada Sol demonstrators decide to stop camping on July 12, 2011. However, a minority group refuses to stop camping.

June 8, 2011
Between 1,500 and 2,000 people in Madrid assemble in front of Congress to protest the Labor Reform law.

June 9, 2011
In Valencia, the National Police use heavy tactics against protesters assembled in front of the Valencia courts. Eighteen people are injured. At night, 2,000 people gather in front of the House of Representatives to show their solidarity with the protesters.
In Salamanca, the police use heavy tactics against the 15-M protesters. Five people are injured.

June 11, 2011
15-M protesters demonstrate in front of city councils throughout Spain.

June 12, 2011
Camping ends in Acampada Sol four weeks after its inception. Some cities decide to follow in the steps of Acampada Sol; others continue camping until the weekend. In Valencia, it is decided to keep the camp indefinitely.

June 14, 2011
More than 2,000 people assemble in front of the Catalan Parliament. They decide to spend the night there in order to block the budget cuts that are to be approved the following day.

June 15, 2011
In Barcelona, 15-M protesters try to block members of Parliament from entering the Parliament building. Some parliamentarians arrive by helicopter. Others, who try to enter through the main gate, are pushed back. Thirty-six protesters are wounded and seven are arrested. Democracia Real Ya sepa-

rates itself from protesters who use violence, and assures that the majority of protesters practice nonviolence.

June 16, 2011
Five hundred people gather in front of the courts to protest against corrupt politicians. The courts were in session trying a case against Francisco Camps, who served as President of the Valencia Government. Camps is implicated in a scandal known as the Gürtel Case.

June 17, 2011
Protests in Santander are held during Santander Bank's shareholder meeting.
The 15-M joins other initiatives such as the Plataforma de Afectados por la Hipoteca (PAH), which is an initiative to help those affected by the subprime mortgage crisis in Spain. 15-M protesters begin to concentrate part of their activities on blocking the evictions. This form of civil disobedience successfully halts evictions.

June 18, 2011
Protests are held throughout Spain against the Euro-Plus Pact, a pact signed in which member states of the European Union made commitments to a list of political reforms aimed at improving the fiscal strength and competitiveness of each country.

June 20, 2011
The Indignant Popular Marches begin. The march is organized into eight different main routes.

June 21, 2011
A group of 15-M participants announce their intention to convene a popular referendum on October 15. The Parliament issues its first response. A motion on the 15-M is issued.

June 22, 2011
Two hundred people congregate in front of the Parliament and call for the release of all the 15-M detainees. People demand

that all charges be dropped. Those present call an assembly and approve a general strike to be held on October 15 against the labor reform law.

June 27, 2011
Democracia Real Ya issues a statement in which they disapprove the proposal to have a referendum on October 15.

June 29–30, 2011
An alternative debate on the state of the nation is held in the Puerta del Sol to create a space for reflection on issues that are affecting citizens. The event is nicknamed the "debate of the people."

June 30, 2011
At day break, the Autonomous Police of Catalunya and the City of Barcelona Police evict those camped in Plaza Catalunya. They are met without resistance. The city estimates damage caused to Plaza Catalunya at 240,000 euros.

July 1, 2011
Demonstrations are held against health cuts in Barcelona.

July 3, 2011
The national police evict camps in Cáceres, Badajoz, Las Palmas, Palma de Mallorca, Castellón and Ciudad Real. All of the evictions are peaceful.

July 8, 2011
A dozen people from Lleida, Huesca and Zaragoza depart from the Cortes of Aragon to Madrid in order to demand a more participatory democracy.

July 11, 2011
In the General Assemblies of Andalucia, 15-M participants agree on a popular initiative to pass a regional law that would call for popular consultations. Participants assert that this would achieve a more direct democracy.

July 13, 2011
More than 4,500 people demonstrate in Terrassa against health care cuts.

July 15, 2011
Five thousand people protest in Málaga against pacts made between the government and union leaders.

July 21, 2011
In Barcelona, 200 people assemble in front of the Hospital del Mar to protest against budgeted health care cuts.

July 23, 2011
The Popular Indignant Marches arrive in Madrid.

July 24, 2011
A demonstration is held in Madrid: protesters chant, "It's not the crisis, it's the system."

July 25, 2011
Indignants from different parts of Spain and from different European cities participate in the first 15-M Social Forum.

July 26, 2011
A group of 15-M participants leave from Madrid and begin marching towards Brussels. They leave with the objective of joining other groups from different European countries with the objective of reaching Brussels by foot one week before October 15. Their aim is to collect proposals and give them to the European Parliament.

July 27, 2011
A few members of the 15-M are able to sneak past police security and enter the Parliament to deliver a list of social problems compiled during the Popular Indignant Marches.

August 2, 2011
At six in the morning, the National Police evict the remaining protesters at Puerta del Sol in Madrid. The police destroy the

information center. A walk around Puerta del Sol is arranged to protest the eviction. The walk turns into a massive protest that floods Atocha Street. Nearby metro stations and nearby streets remain closed for 14 hours.

August 3, 2011
After 24 hours of push and pull between protesters and police, circulation is returned to Puerta del Sol. At eight o'clock a new demonstration around the Plaza del Sol occurs.

August 4, 2011
Police brutality in Madrid.

August 5, 2011
People return to Sol. There is an assembly of more than 3,000 people. Protests in solidarity are held in different Spanish cities.

August 6, 2011
The last protesters detained in connection with the events of August 4 are released.

August 7, 2011
General Assembly held in Sol. Events are arranged to protest Pope Benedict XVI's visit to Madrid.

August 8, 2011
It is reported that the city of Madrid has disabled all access to any website with content related to the 15-M.

August 17, 2011
After more than a week of camping in Malaga, protesters are able to get an Algerian citizen who was detained in the Immigrant Detention Center (CIE) of Malaga released.

August 23, 2011
Two hundred people show up for an emergency protest held against the government's plan to reform the constitution in order to include a limit in the deficit of public accounts.

August 28, 2011
Democracia Real Ya and Juventud Sin Future call for protests against the government's decision.
Demonstrations are held against the express reform of the constitution.

August 30, 2011
"Cacerolada" demonstrations are held in front of Parliament to protest the approval of the constitutional reform.

September 16–17, 2011
International BCN Hub meeting is held with the objective of preparing international protests on October 15, 2011.

October 15, 2011
The 15-M movement participates in the United for Global Change event that counted on the attendance of citizens in more than 950 cities in 85 different countries. In Spain, participants call on people to move from Indignation to Action.

October 16, 2011
A group of indignants decide to occupy the old Hotel Madrid, an abandoned building. It is turned into a social center.

January 2012
Virtual assemblies are held throughout January to prepare for the May 12, 2012 world event.

February 4, 2012
A General Assembly is held in the RENFE station of Plaza Catalunya in Barcelona.

February 11, 2012
Protests are held against the labor reform laws in Spain. Workshops are held to reflect on the 15-M.

February 13, 2012
Protests in front of Greek embassies throughout Spain are called to show solidarity against the austerity measures passed.

February 18, 2012

International Mobilization Day is called in solidarity with Greeks. Virtual meetings on Mumble are held to discuss the preparation of the May 12, 2012 world event.

February 15–25, 2012

The Valencia Spring begins. Students and teachers take to the streets to demonstrate against the deep cuts in education. Valencia's government has a debt of over $27 billion dollars, which, in relation to its size, is the largest debt of Spain's autonomous communities. Heavy police brutality is used against the students, sparking outrage.

February 29, 2012

Student strikes and demonstrations are held in cities through Spain.

May 12, 2012

Worldwide demonstrations are being planned for this day, as of March 2012.

References

AcampadaBcn. (2011) Documents. Available at: <http://acampadabcn.wordpress.com/documents/> [Accessed February 28, 2012].

AcampadaSol. (2011) Actas. Available at: <http://actasmadrid.tomalaplaza.net/> [Accessed February 28, 2012].

Personal sources of Joana Conill.

Wikipedia. (2011) Protestas en España de 2011–2012. Available at: <http://es.wikipedia.org/wiki/15M> [Accessed February 28, 2012].

APPENDIX TO OCCUPY
WALL STREET

Occupy Movement Timeline: February 2011–March 2012
Source: Information collected and elaborated by Lana Swartz and
Amalia Cardenas

February 2, 2011
Vancouver-based Adbusters runs an editorial by Kono Matsu
calling for protests similar to those in the Middle East: "If we
want to spark a popular uprising in the west – like a million man
march on Wall Street – then let's get organized, let's strategize,
let's think things through."

June 9, 2011
Adbusters registers the domain name occupywallstreet.org.

July 13, 2011
Adbusters publishes a blog post coining the hashtag #occupywall-
street and calls for a September 17 protest, where "20,000 people
flood into lower Manhattan, set up tents, kitchens, peaceful barricades, and occupy Wall Street for a few months," demanding
"democracy not corporatocracy" and asserting that from their

"one simple demand, a presidential commission to separate money from politics," they would "start setting the agenda for a new America."

July 24, 2011

Spanish *indignadas* discuss their support for the Occupy Wall Street movement in the Retiro Park in Madrid: "Leave Madrid on the 25th of July, reaching Vitoria on the 9th of August and Paris on the 17th of September to support the Wall Street initiative."

July 26, 2011

The Occupy Wall Street website is launched and there is extensive use of Twitter and Facebook to promote the September 17 demonstration.

August 2, 2011

With the debt-ceiling deadline of midnight on August 2 drawing near, "New Yorkers Against Budget Cuts" along with "Bloombergville" and a group planning #occupywallstreet join in a demonstration and hold a General Assembly at the Charging Bull sculpture, which stands in Bowling Green Park in Lower Manhattan. Bloombergville was a two-week-long encampment in the Financial District of New York City near Wall Street that was protesting austerity cuts proposed by Mayor Bloomberg. The Bloombergville initiative takes the name from the Hoovervilles of the 1930s. In addition, Bloombergville was inspired by the Walkerville encampments of February and March of 2011 in Madison, Wisconsin, where thousands of protesters flooded the Wisconsin Capitol and slept in the building to protest Governor Scott Walker's attempt to strip public employees of their collective bargaining rights. Inspiration was also drawn from the Coumoville protests that happened in New York against Governor Andrew Coumo, who had not done enough to strengthen rent regulations. Finally, organizers of Bloombergville drew inspiration from struggles taking place all over the world: Madrid, the Middle East, Greece and the UK.

August 16, 2011

The Acampada Sol's working group on Economics pledges their support to the Occupy Wall Street initiative and calls for a protest outside of the Madrid Stock Exchange. The call is spread through the #TOMALABOLSA hashtag and the "Toma la Bolsa #17S" Facebook Group. Adbusters posts a call on their blog for other countries to also occupy financial districts around the world on September 17.

August 23, 2011

The "hacktivist" group Anonymous pledges to stand with the Occupy Wall Street movement on September 17 and creates a 57 second video calling for peaceful demonstrations and demands of freedom: "The abuse and corruption of corporations, banks and governments ends here."

September 9, 2011

Supporters of the Occupy Wall Street movement start posting photos and moving personal accounts of job loss and helplessness on the "We are the 99 Percent" Tumblr page. The blog is a helpful way to attach human faces and emotion to the movement, highlighting some of the issues that people would like to address.

September 17, 2011

An estimated 1,000–5,000 people, much less than the 20,000 AdBusters had called for, gather in downtown Manhattan and walk up and down Wall Street before settling into Zuccotti Park, two blocks north. Some arrests are made for loitering.

September 20, 2011

As media attention grows, New York City police arrest protesters using a law dating back to an 1845 statute banning masked gatherings. The law was written in 1845 when lawmakers tried to suppress uprisings from tenant farmers who disguised themselves as Native Americans dressed in calico gowns and leather masks to attack law enforcement officers.

September 21, 2011

Keith Olbermann of the news outlet *Current TV* is the first major journalist to cover the protests. Olbermann criticizes the media blackout and states that after five days of protests, North American coverage of the Occupy Wall Street movement was limited to a small mention in a minor Manhattan newspaper and a column in the *Toronto Star*.

September 22, 2011

A rally protesting the killing of Troy Davis, who was executed by lethal injection for a crime many believe he did not commit, snowballs into a massive impromptu march into Wall Street. The "Day of Outrage" protesters are met with cheers by the Wall Street protesters. Four people are arrested.

September 23, 2011

Chicago protesters occupy Federal Reserve Bank.

September 24, 2011

At least 80 arrests are made by the NYPD after protesters begin marching uptown, forcing the closure of several streets. Protesters claim that police used excessive force, in particular when they pepper-sprayed five protesters in the face. A video of 25-year-old Chelsea Elliott, being pepper sprayed in the face by Deputy Inspector Anthony Bologna would later circulate the Internet, sparking indignation.

September 25, 2011

YouTube discloses that Anonymous has uploaded a video threatening the NYPD: "If we hear of brutality in the next 36 hours then we will take you down from the internet as you have taken the protesters' voices from the airwaves." They urge the NYPD to "learn about what happened to the police force in Egypt when they disregarded human rights. Their end was the people's beginnings."

September 26, 2011

Anonymous releases personal information about Anthony Bologna, the police officer who pepper-sprayed Chelsea Elliott.

The group releases phone numbers, addresses, names of relatives and other personal data.

September 27, 2011
An OWS afternoon march is held at a rally of postal workers protesting the five-day delivery week. NYC Councilman Charles Barron visits Zuccotti Park, addressing those gathered with public support for OWS. Cornel West speaks to a crowd of 2,000 gathered at the park and opens the daily General Assembly.

September 28, 2011
More than 700 Continental and United Airlines pilots join Occupy Wall Street demonstrations. The Transport Workers Union of America votes to support Occupy Wall Street. Police Commissioner Kelly publicly states that the NYPD cannot bar protesters from Zuccotti Park since it is a privately owned public park and plaza that is required to stay open 24 hours a day.

September 29, 2011
TWU Local-100 uses Twitter to urge members to take part in a "massive march and rally" on October 5. Protesters in San Francisco attempt to occupy Citibank and Chase, and attempt to enter a Charles Schwab financial institution.

September 30, 2011
More than 1,000 demonstrators, including representatives from labor unions, march to the NYPD headquarters in protest of heavy-handed police response the previous week. Occupation begins in Boston.

October 1, 2011
A reported 5,000 people march towards the Brooklyn Bridge, while hundreds march onto its pedestrian area and car lanes, taking over part of the bridge. Traffic into Brooklyn is stopped by police for two hours. There are over 700 arrests, including that of a *New York Times* reporter. Videos of the arrests proliferate online. Occupations begin in California, Maine, Kansas and all over the United States.

October 3, 2011

"Corporate zombie" dress-up marches are held in cities across the United States.

October 5, 2011

Joined by labor unions including the AFL-CIO, demonstrations swell to the largest yet. It is estimated that the crowd consists of more than 10,000 people. Demonstrators marched from Foley Square to Zuccotti Park.

October 6, 2011

Occupations begin in cities including San Francisco, Tampa, Houston, Austin, Dallas, Philadelphia, New Orleans, Cleveland, Las Vegas, Jersey City, Hartford and Salt Lake City. Obama comments: "I think it expresses the frustrations the American people feel, that we had the biggest financial crisis since the Great Depression, huge collateral damage all throughout the country . . . and yet you're still seeing some of the same folks who acted irresponsibly trying to fight efforts to crack down on the abusive practices that got us into this in the first place."

October 8, 2011

Occupy DC begins. Protesters are pepper-sprayed in Washington DC as they attempt to enter the National Air and Space Museum in protest of the use of unmanned military drones. Arrests reported in Seattle and Redding, CA.

October 10, 2011

Mayor Bloomberg states, "The bottom line is, people want to express themselves, and as long as they obey the laws, we'll allow them to." One hundred and forty protesters from the Occupy Boston movement are arrested after they ignore warnings to move from a downtown greenway near where they have been camped for more than a week.

October 11, 2011

Occupy Wall Street Millionaires march through New York's

Upper East Side, home of many of New York's wealthy political and corporate figures.

October 13, 2011
Mayor Bloomberg announces that Brookfield Properties, the owner of Zuccotti Park, wants the park vacated so that it can be cleaned. Protesters are told that they would be permitted to reoccupy the space once the park had been cleaned. Many protesters worry about the motives behind the cleaning, citing similar tactics used to clear out the 15-M protesters in Spain.

October 14, 2011
Brookfield Properties postpones the cleaning of Zuccotti Park and states that they can work out an agreement with protesters to ensure sanitary conditions are kept and that the park remains safe for the public as well as those inhabiting the park. Protesters form groups to ensure that the park is kept in good condition. Occupy Denver is evicted and 21 are arrested.

October 15, 2011
Day of action and marches. Occupations or protests are reported in 951 cities in 82 countries. 175 are arrested at Occupy Chicago. Cornel West is arrested on the steps of the Supreme Court in Washington DC. United States Marine Corps Sergeant Shamar Thomas defends the Occupy Wall Street protesters against police officers. The video of the sergeant in a moment of indignation has since gone viral with over two million views. A group begins #OccupyMarines in solidarity and pledges organization, direction, supply logistics and leadership.

October 16, 2011
The White House issues a statement saying that Obama is "working for the interests of the 99%."

October 17, 2011
At its one month anniversary, Occupy Wall Street reportedly has received cumulative $300,000 in monetary donations. The money is deposited at the Amalgamated Bank, the only 100 percent union

owned bank in the United States. Adbusters proposes a October 29 "#RobinHood Global March" and a candidate for the group's unifying demand: "On October 29, on the eve of the G20 Leaders Summit in France, let's the people of the world rise up and demand that our G20 leaders immediately impose a 1 percent #ROBINHOOD tax on all financial transactions and currency trades."

October 17 and 20, 2011
Two NPR-affiliated freelance journalists are fired for Occupy involvement.

October 21, 2011
Arrests at Occupy Tampa and Occupy Orlando.

October 23, 2011
Arrests at Occupy Chicago, Occupy Philadelphia and Occupy Cincinnati. Occupations reported in Hong Kong, Tel Aviv and Iran.

October 24, 2011
New York District Attorney's Office offers deferred adjudication to 340 of 750 disorderly conduct charges against protesters. MTV announces reality show episode: "True Life: I'm Occupying Wall Street" to air November 5.

October 25, 2011
Oakland Police aggressively use non-lethal rounds to disperse peaceful protesters from Occupy Oakland. Their actions seriously injured an Iraq war veteran, Scott Olsen, leaving him hospitalized with a fractured skull. Occupy Oakland called for a general strike to be held on November 2. The actions taken by Oakland police are the most violent used against the Occupy Wall Street protesters so far. Egyptian activists release a statement in solidarity with occupiers.

October 26, 2011
Hundreds of Occupy Wall Street protesters march near Union Square in support of Olsen and Occupy Oakland.

October 29, 2011
Arrests made at Occupy Denver.

October 30, 2011
Protesters are arrested at Occupy Portland for failing to leave a park when it closed at midnight. Thirty-eight are arrested at Occupy Austin after they refuse to put away food tables at 10pm.

November 2, 2011
Occupy Oakland city-wide general strike held in response to Olsen injury. First general strike in 65 years. The demonstrations are able to shut down operations at the Port of Oakland, the nation's fifth busiest port. Protests are mostly peaceful, but some banks are vandalized by people wearing black scarves to cover their faces. Many OWS participants don't approve of the tactics. A man is arrested for sexual assault and rape at the NYC OWS encampment.

November 3, 2011
Firing tear gas and flash bang grenades, riot police clash with Occupy Oakland protesters who had built a bonfire in the street and refused to leave. Over a hundred protesters are arrested, including a second Iraq veteran who was seriously injured.

November 4, 2011
"Occupy Koch Brothers" protest at a conservative summit in DC.

November 5, 2011
Guy Fawkes Day and Bank Transfer Day. Demonstrators protest outside major banks and financial institutions. In the preceding month, over 600,000 people closed their bank accounts and opened accounts with local credit unions.

November 7, 2011
Two protesters are married at the Occupy Philadelphia camp.

November 9, 2011
Day of Action for Public Education is led by Occupy Cal, a movement of UC students formed to raise awareness of tuition

fee increases and budget cuts. The first General Assembly is held and several tents are set up. Police shut down the tents and beat several peaceful protesters.

November 10, 2011
Occupy protesters interrupt a speech by Bachmann. The event was one of several Mic Check actions where protesters take the opportunity to address government and voice grievances. A man reported to be living at Occupy Oakland is found shot and killed near the camp.

November 11, 2011
Occupy Burlington Vermont is evicted after an occupier commits suicide in his tent.

November 12, 2011
Man found dead at Salt Lake City encampment. Sixteen arrested after refusing to clear.

November 13, 2011
Occupy Portland is evicted after an overnight stand-off.

November 14, 2011
Occupy Oakland is evicted. Twenty protesters are arrested. Oakland Mayor Jean Quan cites the eviction as a response to the "tremendous strain" the camp had put on the city's resources. The mayor's legal advisor resigns in protest of the eviction.

November 15, 2011
Occupy Wall Street: At about 1am, NYPD begins to clear Zuccotti Park. Health and safety concerns are cited by the city. Press, including CBS press helicopters, are prevented from covering the eviction. City Councilman Ydanis Rodriguez is arrested during the eviction, along with 70 other protesters. 5,554 books at The People's Library are confiscated. A judge rules that although the protesters do not have a First Amendment right to camp out in the park, they are allowed to return to Zuccotti sans tents and tarps. Impromptu General Assemblies and meet-ups

have started in different locations. Occupy DC stages a sit-in at the DC offices of Brookfield Properties, which owns New York City's Zuccotti Park. Occupy UC Davis holds a rally on campus, which was attended by approximately 2,000 people. Later, about 400 individuals occupied the Administration building and held a General Assembly in the space. Occupy Seattle rallies and marches downtown; police clash with protesters, use pepper spray and arrest six.

November 16, 2011
Protesters regroup after eviction to organize a Global Day of Action. Despite the wave of evictions, planning for the Global Day of Action moves forward. Actions to block entry points to the stock exchange and the subway, and to take over Foley Square and the Brooklyn Bridge are called for. Arrests take place in Portland, Berkeley, San Francisco (95 protesters are arrested that night), St. Louis and Los Angeles.

November 17, 2011
Global Day of Action to mark the second month of the movement. Occupy Wall Street sees crowds of more than 30,000 marching in the streets of New York City. Crowds are assembled in and around Zuccotti Park, Union Square, Foley Square, the Brooklyn Bridge and other locations throughout the city. In Occupy Boston, a judge issues a restraining order preventing police from evicting protesters. At Occupy Cal, students at UC Berkeley maintain their re-established encampment. Occupy Dallas is evicted and 18 arrests are made. Students continue their occupation of the administration building and protesters erect tents on the campus quad at Occupy Davis and Occupy UC Davis. In Los Angeles, at least 30 are arrested as protesters occupy the Bank of America plaza. Occupy Milwaukee protesters shut down the North Avenue Bridge. Police in Portland use pepper spray on protesters, and at least 25 are arrested on the Steel Bridge. Occupy Seattle protesters march on University Bridge, blocking traffic. A permit is issued allowing Occupy Spokane to camp.

Approximately 1,000 Occupy St. Louis protesters march from the Kiener Plaza Occupy site to Martin Luther King Bridge, where 14 are arrested for blocking an on-ramp, and later in the afternoon a group temporarily occupies the old Municipal Courts Building adjacent to city hall and unveils large banners proclaiming "Occupy Everything."

November 18, 2011
Retired former Philadelphia police Captain Ray Lewis arrested for disorderly conduct, violating local laws and refusing to move on. Police stage a 2am raid at Occupy Cal. Campus police raid the Occupy Davis encampment in the morning, pepper-spraying multiple students.

November 19, 2011
Newt Gingrich, former Speaker of the House, suggests OWS protesters "Go get a job, right after you take a bath." Campus police at the University of California Davis pepper-spray protesters who are peacefully obstructing a public walkway. Footage of the incident quickly goes viral online, prompting the school's chancellor to place the offending officers on leave and order an investigation.

November 20, 2011
Occupy Mayor Bloomberg's Mansion: A 24-hour drum circle in front of Mayor Bloomberg's home on East 79th Street is planned. Protesters are blocked at each corner by a line of police and metal barricades. Around 300 people bang iron skillets and pots while the drum circle continues.

November 22, 2011
President Obama is briefly interrupted by Occupy Wall Street protesters, who use the Mic Check technique to send a message to the president. Protesters later handed the president a note which read, "Mr. President: Over 4,000 peaceful protesters have been arrested. While bankers continue to destroy the American economy. You must stop the assault on our 1st amendment

rights. Your silence sends a message that police brutality is acceptable. Banks got bailed out. We got sold out."

November 30, 2011

Two days after the eviction notice had been given, police officers clear out the Occupy Los Angeles camp, arresting more than 200 people.

December 1, 2011

Violence at the Occupy San Francisco protests erupts when police officers set up barricades around the encampment. One police officer receives a small injury. Following the altercation, the Occupy San Francisco protesters are offered to move from their waterfront camp to another site.

December 6, 2011

National kick-off for a new aim of the occupy movement: Occupy Homes, which involves the occupation of vacant bank-owned homes for those in need.

December 9, 2011

Occupy Boston camp is evicted in an early morning raid. Forty-six people are arrested. Some protesters claim that police badges were not visible, and that members of the media were kept at a distance from the camp as arrests were being made. The city's clean-up crew uses leaf blowers, moves garbage into dump trucks, and utilizes power washing methods to clean up the camp.

December 10, 2011

It is reported, according to government and police sources, that undercover police officers had infiltrated the Occupy Los Angeles camp a month prior to verify claims of organized stockpiling of human waste and weapons to resist eviction.

December 12, 2011

Coordinated attempt to shut down ports throughout the US west coast causes some disruption to several port terminals, but falls short of the complete blockage protesters intended. Some clashes between protesters and police result. Reaction of labor unions is divided.

December 14, 2011

Newt Gingrich is interrupted by a group of Occupy protesters at the University of Iowa.

December 16, 2011

To advocate for voting rights for DC, US Congressman Keith Ellison, a Democrat from Minnesota, goes on a 24-hour hunger strike in solidarity with four Occupy DC protesters who have also been on a hunger strike since December 8.

December 17, 2011

On the three-month anniversary of the OWS protests, protesters attempt to "re-occupy" Zuccotti Park, damaging a fence. Nearby Duarte Square is occupied by thousands, accompanied by a march through Manhattan. Fifty protesters are arrested.

December 18, 2011

Occupy members march in solidarity with immigrant and economic refugees to celebrate the International Day of Migrants.

January 1, 2012

New York police arrest 68 people who attempt to move back into Zuccotti Park.

January 2, 2012

Occupy protesters interrupt Mitt Romney's speech in Des Moines.

January 3, 2012

Flashmob action was organized in Grand Central Station to protest the National Defence Authorization Act signed by President Obama. Three people were arrested for disorderly conduct.

January 10, 2012

Barricades around Zuccotti Park are removed by NYPD enforcing new rules set by the owner that protesters are not allowed to lay down or sleep in the park. Hundreds re-enter.

January 15, 2012
The Occupy movement joins in worldwide candlelight vigil for unity held in honor of Rev. Martin Luther King Jr.

January 17, 2012
The four month anniversary of the OWS movement. An estimated 2,000 protesters gather on the West Lawn of the Capitol Building for an event called Occupy Congress. Several arrests are made. Activities involve meeting with representatives, occupying the steps of the three congressional office buildings, and teach-ins. A march that evening goes first to the steps of the Supreme Court, where police are unprepared for the large number of protesters who illegally run to the top of the steps and then to the White House.

January 20, 2012
Occupy Wall Street holds a national day of action against the Citizens United decision in hope of amending the US Supreme Court decision.

January 25, 2012
Recalling the 1968 Chicago protests, Adbusters, the magazine that had been credited with launching the Occupy movement, publishes an ad calling for 50,000 protesters to occupy the G8 summit scheduled for May 2012.

January 28, 2012
Individuals affiliated with Occupy Oakland break into City Hall and steal and burn an American flag from the City Council chamber. Faced with projectiles, the police deploy tear gas and arrest 300 protesters. The authorities note the increased violence of the protests and suggest it was caused by a small faction of protesters.

February 4, 2012
Occupy K Street in Washington DC evicted. Occupy protesters march against police brutality in the Bronx.

February 11, 2012

The "Occupy CPAC" demonstration is held in conjunction with AFL-CIO, SEIU, National Nurses United, Metro Labor Council and OurDC outside the Conservative Political Action Conference in Washington DC. Occupy San Francisco holds a march against police repression.

February 14, 2012

"Occupy AT&T" in Atlanta protests lay-offs by the company. In honor of Valentine's Day, "Break up with Your Bank" encourages people to move their money to credit unions and community banks.

February 16, 2012

Occupy Homes actions in Los Angeles, Denver and Queens halt foreclosure auctions.

February 17, 2012

Occupy groups in cities all over the United States participate in International Day of Action in solidarity with Greek demonstrators fighting against austerity measures.

February 18, 2012

Occupy Chicago protesters, along with parents, teachers and students, occupy Brian Piccolo Specialty School, a public school facing closure due to budget cuts.

February 19, 2012

Events part of National Occupy Day of Action in Support of Prisoners' Rights are held outside San Quentin State Prison in California and in cities across the United States, including Austin, Baltimore, Boston, Chicago, Columbus, Denver, Durham, Fresno, New York, Philadelphia, Portland, San Francisco and Washington DC.

February 27, 2012

Global Day of Action for Occupy Food Supply in protest of industrialized agriculture. Seed exchange held outside New York

Stock Exchange, and community garden events held in other cities.

February 29, 2012
To take advantage of the extra day, Leap Day is promoted as a day of action. A reported 80 #F29 actions are held around the world. Occupiers attempt to retake Zuccotti Park with some arrests.

March 1, 2012
Day of Action for Education events held in New York City, Chicago, Washington DC, Los Angeles, Boston, Miami and Philadelphia.

March 8, 2012
Occupiers in conjunction with Code Pink, a women-initiated grassroots peace and social justice movement working to end US-funded wars and occupations, hold demonstrations to celebrate International Women's Day.

March 17, 2012
To celebrate the six month anniversary of the occupation of Wall Street, occupiers converge on New York City for actions including the attempted reoccupation of Zuccotti Park. Hundreds are arrested in what appears to demonstrators to be an increased degree of police aggression. @OccupyWallStNYC tweets, "In our first 6 months we changed the national conversation. In the next 6 months we will change the world."

Public opinion toward the occupy movement in the United States

Source: Information collected and elaborated by Lana Swartz

Familiarity

How familiar are you with the protests going on in New York City and other locations around the country referred to as Occupy Wall Street?

Very familiar	17%
Somewhat familiar	33%
Not very familiar/Heard of it, but know nothing about it	32%
Never heard of it	17%
Don't know/Refused	1%

October 6–10, 2011/Source: Ipsos/Reuters Poll

How much have you heard or read about the protests and rallies being held in New York City and in other cities, called Occupy Wall Street?

A lot	34%
Some	36%
Not much	14%
Not at all	15%
Don't know/No answer	1%

October 19–24, 2011/Source: CBS/New York Times Poll

General public opinion

Do you consider yourself to be a supporter of the Occupy Wall Street movement, an opponent, or neither?

	October 2011	*November 2011*
Supporter	26%	24%
Opponent	19%	19%
Neither	52%	53%
No opinion	4%	3%

Source: Gallup

	November 2011	*December 2011*	*January 2012*
Rate your feelings toward the Occupy Wall Street Movement			
Very positive/Somewhat positive	32%	27%	28%
Neutral	20%	19%	21%
Negative/Somewhat negative	35%	44%	39%
Don't know/Not sure	13%	10%	12%

Do you consider yourself a supporter of the Occupy Wall Street Movement?			
Yes	28%	25%	23%
No	63%	67%	64%
Not sure/Depends	9%	8%	13%

Source: NBC News/Wall Street Journal Poll

Is your opinion of the Occupy Wall Street movement favorable, not favorable, undecided, or haven't you heard enough about the Occupy Wall Street movement yet to have an opinion?

	October 2011	*January 2012*
Favorable	25%	21%
Unfavorable	20%	28%
Undecided	17%	23%
Haven't heard enough	36%	27%
Refused	2%	1%

Source: CBS/New York Times Poll

Goals and views

Do you approve or disapprove of the goals of the Occupy Wall Street movement, or don't you know enough to say?

	October 2011	*November 2011*
Approve	22%	25%
Disapprove	15%	16%
Don't know/No answer	63%	60%

Source: Gallup

From what you have heard or read, would you say you generally agree or disagree with the views of the Occupy Wall Street movement?

Agree	43%
Disagree	27%
Don't know/No answer	30%

October 2011/Source: CBS/New York Times Poll

To what extent, if at all, do you personally identify with the ideals of the Occupy Wall Street or the We Are The 99% movement?

Identify strongly/Identify	28%
Identify a little	23%
Do not identify	42%
Don't know/Not sure	6%

October 2011/Source: Reuters/Ipsos Public Affairs Poll

Do you think that the Occupy Wall Street movement is anti-capitalist or not?

Yes, it is	37%
No, it isn't	46%
Don't know	17%

October 2011/Source: Fox News Poll

Movement tactics

Do you approve or disapprove of the way Occupy Wall Street protests are being conducted?

	October 2011	*November 2011*
Approve	25%	20%
Disapprove	20%	31%
Don't know	55%	49%

Source: Gallup

Attitude toward political impact

Do you feel that the Occupy Wall Street movement has been a good thing or a bad thing for the American political system, or has it not made much difference either way?

Good thing	25%
Bad thing	16%
Not much difference	49%
Not sure/Some of both	10%

Source: NBC News/Wall Street Journal Poll

Which group do you think will have more influence over who wins the election for president in 2012?

The Tea Party	50%
Occupy Wall Street	33%
Neither/Unsure	16%

Which group comes closer to your views?

The Tea Party	40%
Occupy Wall Street	40%
Neither/Unsure	19%

November 2011/Source: McClatchy/Marist College Institute for Public Opinion

Public opinion by demographic features

Support for aspects of Occupy Wall Street by party identification

	Democrat	*Independent*	*Republican*
Position toward movement*			
Supporter	38%	24%	9%
Opponent	10%	17%	35%
Neither	48%	57%	54%
Goals of the movement			
Approve	40%	23%	13%
Disapprove	6%	12%	34%
No opinion	54%	65%	54%

Way protests being conducted

Approve	28%	20%	11%
Disapprove	20%	26%	55%
No opinion	52%	55%	35%

* "Don't know" omitted

November, 2011/Source: Gallup

Attitude toward Occupy Wall Street movement

	Support	Oppose	Neither/ Don't know
Party identification			
Conservative Republican	14%	68%	18%
Moderate/Liberal Republican	38%	43%	19%
Independent	46%	34%	20%
Conservative/Moderate Democrat	55%	25%	20%
Liberal Democrat	72%	17%	11%
Age			
18–29	49%	27%	24%
30–49	45%	32%	23%
50–64	45%	38%	17%
65+	33%	37%	28%
Education level			
College graduate and more	48%	40%	12%
Some college	50%	33%	17%
High school or less	39%	33%	28%
Family income			
$75,000 or more	45%	43%	43%
$30,000–$74,999	48%	37%	18%
Less than $30,000	43%	30%	27%

December 2011/Source: Pew Research Center

Attitude toward related issues

State of the economy

All in all, thinking about where the United States is today, do
you feel we are experiencing the kind of tough times the country
faces from time to time, or is this the start of a longer-term
decline where the US is no longer the leading country in the
world?

Experiencing a tough time	40%
Start of longer-term decline	54%
A little of both	4%
Neither/Not sure	2%

Thinking about the country's economic recession, do you think
that the worst is behind us or the worst is ahead of us?

Worst is behind us	49%
Worst is ahead of us	44%
Somewhere in between	2%
Not sure	5%

November 2011/Source: NBC/Washington Post Poll

Which of the following has been the most disappointing event
of the past year (2011) for you personally?

The wealthiest one percent getting richer and the middle class declining	31%
The lack of economic recovery	29%
The failure of Congress to reach a compromise on the budget deficit	27%
The continuation of war in Afghanistan	6%
Scandals like Penn State and Syracuse	3%
Other/None/Not sure	4%

December 2011/Source: NBC News/Wall Street Journal Poll

How would you rate the condition of the national economy
these days? Is it very good, fairly good, fairly bad, or very bad?

Very good	1%
Fairly good	20%
Fairly bad	47%
Very bad	32%

January 2012/Source: CBS/New York Times Poll

Economic inequality

Do you think that the US economic system is fair or unfair to
you, personally?

Fair	54%
Unfair	44%
No opinion	2%

October 2011/Source: Gallup

Do you feel that the distribution of money and wealth in this
country is fair, or do you feel that the money and wealth in
this country should be more evenly distributed among more
people?

Fair	26%
Should be more evenly distributed	66%
Don't know/No answer	8%

October 2011/Source: CBS/New York Times Poll

The current economic structure of the country is out of balance
and favors a very small proportion of the rich over the rest
of the country. America needs to reduce the power of major
banks and corporations and demand greater accountability and
transparency. The government should not provide financial aid
to corporations and should not provide tax breaks to the rich.

Strongly agree	60%
Mildly agree	16%
Feel neutral	9%
Mildly disagree	6%
Strongly disagree	6%
Agree with some parts and disagree with others/Not sure	3%

November 2011/Source: NBC/Washington Post Poll

Public perception of conflict between rich and poor

% who say there are "strong" or "very strong" conflicts between the rich and the poor

	2009	2011
All	47	66
Race		
White	43	65
Black	66	74
Hispanic	55	61
Age		
18–34	54	71
35–49	48	64
50–64	45	67
65+	36	55
Income		
Less than $20k	47	64
$20k–40k	46	66
$40k–75k	47	71
$75k or more	49	67
Education		
College graduate	48	66
Some college	50	70
High school or less	44	64
	2009	2011
Party identification		
Republican	38	55
Democrat	55	73
Independent	45	68
Ideology		
Conservative	40	55
Moderate	50	68
Liberal	55	79

Source: Pew Research Center, 2011

Blame for financial crisis

If you had to choose, who do you blame more for the economic
problems facing the United States – financial institutions on
Wall Street or the federal government in Washington?

Financial institutions	30%
Federal government	64%
No opinion	5%

Thinking about the economic problems currently facing
the United States, how much do you blame . . . the federal
government in Washington for these – a great deal, a moderate
amount, not much, or not at all?

A great deal	56%
A fair amount	31%
Not much	9%
Not at all	2%
No opinion	2%

Thinking about the economic problems currently facing
the United States, how much do you blame . . . the financial
institutions on Wall Street for these – a great deal, a moderate
amount, not much, or not at all?

A great deal	45%
A fair amount	33%
Not much	13%
Not at all	6%
No opinion	3%

October 2011/Source: Gallup

Who is most to blame for current economic problems – Wall
Street bankers, George W. Bush, or Barack Obama?

Wall Street bankers	36%
George W. Bush	34%
Barack Obama	21%
Not sure	9%

When it comes to improving the oversight of Wall Street
and the banks has the Obama administration lived up to your
expectations or has it fallen short?

Lived up to expectations	18%
Fallen short	74%
Some of both/Not sure	8%

When it comes to the effect of President Obama's policies in
improving economic conditions, would you say his policies have
helped or hurt economic conditions, or have they not made
much of a difference one way or the other?

Helped	22%
Hurt	30%
Not much of a difference	47%
Not sure	1%

November 2011/Source: NBC/Washington Post Poll

What do you think was the primary cause of the financial crisis
that began in 2007?

Businesses taking too many risks	7%
Consumers taking too many risks	5%
Too little regulation of big Wall Street banks	19%
Banks giving mortgages to people who could not afford them	42%
Banks offering mortgages with unclear and predatory terms and conditions	13%
Economic factors beyond anyone's control	4%
Don't know/Refused	11%

January 2012/Source: AARP Consumer Financial Protection
Survey/Sample: Adults age 50+

Economic policy

Now thinking about the wealthiest one percent of Americans,
what percentage of their income do you think they should pay to
the federal government in income taxes each year?

Pay in taxes

0–10%	21%
11–20%	14%

21–30%	18%
31–40%	11%
More than 40%	7%
No opinion	28%

October 2011/Source: Gallup

Generally speaking, do you think there should be more
government oversight of financial companies, such as Wall
Street banks, mortgage lenders, payday lenders, and credit card
companies, less oversight of these companies or about the same
amount of oversight?

More oversight	46%
About the same amount of oversight	20%
Less oversight	25%
Don't know/Refused	9%

How important is it to you that people be protected from
predatory lending practices, such as excessive fees and penalties,
on products ranging from mortgages to credit cards?

Very important	86%
Somewhat important	9%
Somewhat unimportant	1%
Very unimportant	1%
Don't know/Refused	3%

How important is it to you that financial salespeople who engage
in deceptive marketing be held accountable?

Very important	94%
Somewhat important	4%
Somewhat unimportant	>.5%
Very unimportant	1%
Don't know/Refused	3%

January 2012/Source: AARP Consumer Financial Protection
Survey/Sample: Adults age 50+

Public opinion in selected countries toward Occupy and similar movements

Source: Figures elaborated by Lana Swartz on the basis of data collected from the sources cited for each graph.

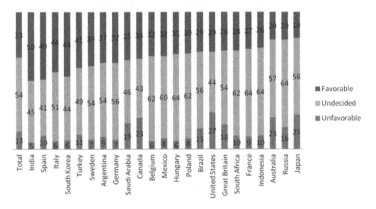

Figure A1: Attitude toward "Occupy Wall Street" protests

Question: How favorable or unfavorable are you toward the "Occupy Wall Street" protests, as far as you understand them? *Source*: Ipsos Global Advisor poll conducted on behalf of Reuters News. November 2011.

Attitudes of citizens toward governments, political and financial institutions in the United States, the European Union, and the world at large

Source: Figures elaborated by Lana Swartz on the basis of data collected from the sources cited for each graph.

European Union

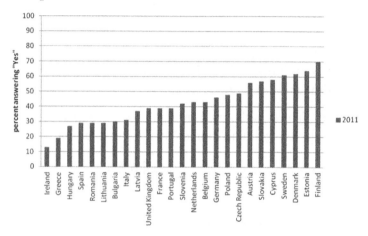

Figure A2: Confidence in European financial institutions

Question: In this country, do you have confidence in each of the following or not? Financial institutions and banks.
Source: Gallup. June 2011.

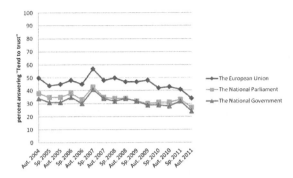

Figure A3: Trust in European political institutions

Question: I would like to ask you a question about how much trust you have in certain institutions. For each of the following institutions, please tell me if you tend to trust it or tend not to trust it: the European Union, the National Parliament and the National Government. *Source*: Eurobarometer

United States

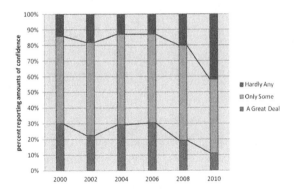

Figure A4: Confidence in US banks and financial institutions

Question: I am going to name some institutions in this country. As far as the people running these institutions are concerned, would you say you have a great deal of confidence, only some confidence, or hardly any confidence at all in them? Banks and financial institutions? *Source*: General Social Survey, National Opinion Research Center, University of Chicago.

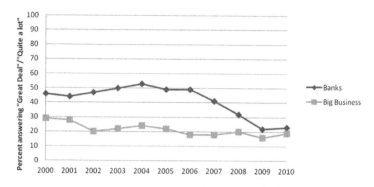

Figure A5: Confidence in US financial institutions

Question: Now I am going to read you a list of institutions
in American society. Please tell me how much confidence you,
yourself, have in each one – a great deal, quite a lot, some, or very
little? Banks; big business. *Source*: Gallup

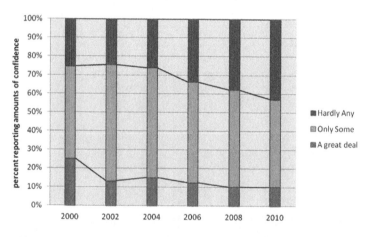

Figure A6: Confidence in executive branch of US federal government

Question: I am going to name some institutions in this country. As
far as the people running these institutions are concerned, would
you say you have a great deal of confidence, only some confidence,
or hardly any confidence at all in them? The Executive Branch of
the Federal Government. *Source*: General Social Survey, Conducted
by National Opinion Research Center, University of Chicago.

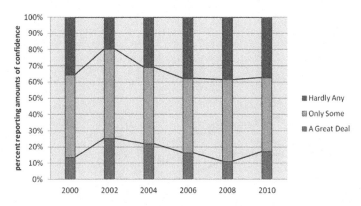

Figure A7: Confidence in US Congress

Question: I am going to name some institutions in this country. As far as the people running these institutions are concerned, would you say you have a great deal of confidence, only some confidence, or hardly any confidence at all in them? Congress. *Source*: General Social Survey, National Opinion Research Center, University of Chicago.

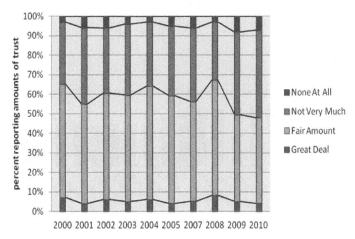

Figure A8: Trust in US politicians

Question: How much trust and confidence do you have in general in men and women in political life in this country who either hold or are running for public office – a great deal, a fair amount, not very much, or none at all? *Source*: Gallup

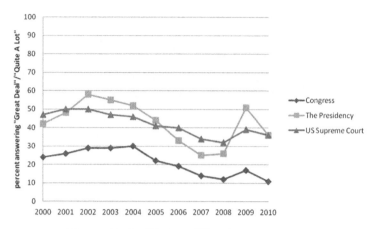

Figure A9: Confidence in US political institutions

Question: Now I am going to read you a list of institutions in American society. Please tell me how much confidence you, yourself, have in each one – a great deal, quite a lot, some, or very little? The United States Supreme Court, Congress, The Presidency. *Source*: Gallup

World at large

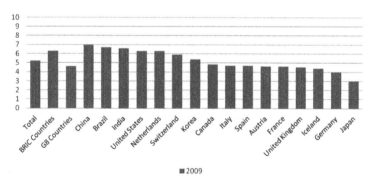

Figure A10: Trust in government to manage the financial crisis

Question: On a scale of 1 to 10 (where 1 means you don't trust at all and 10 means you trust completely), what is your level of trust in your government to manage the financial crisis? *Source*: ICM

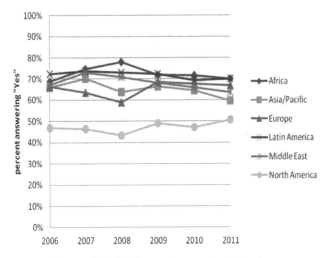

Figure A11: Widespread corruption in business

Question: Is corruption widespread within businesses located in this country, or not? *Source*: Gallup World View

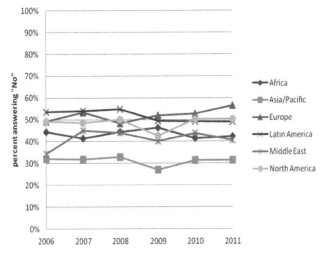

Figure A12: Confidence in national government

Question: In this country, do you have confidence in each of the following, or not? How about national government? *Source*: Gallup World Voice

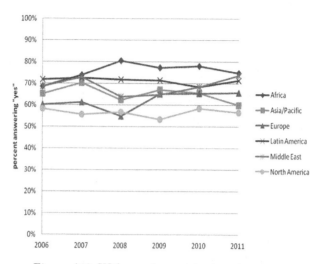

Figure A13: Widespread corruption in government

Question: Is corruption widespread throughout the government in this country, or not? *Source*: Gallup World Voice

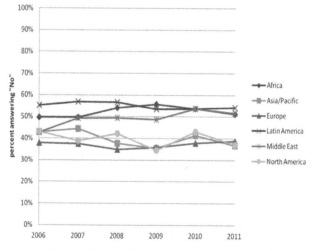

Figure A14: Confidence in honesty of elections

Question: In this country, do you have confidence in each of the following, or not? How about honesty of elections? *Source*: Gallup World View